The Mask We Wear

Unorthodox Memoirs of Love, Pain, and Power

MoneyBazs

Published by Kinetic Digital Publishers

www.kineticdigitalpublishers.com

For permissions, inquiries, or other correspondence, please visit our website.

ebook ISBN: 979-8-90235-991-3
Paperback ISBN: 979-8-90235-989-0
Hardcover: 979-8-90235-990-6
LCCN: 2026910133

TABLE OF CONTENTS

1

A Lost Son's Journey to Love

Born into a world where silence spoke louder than words, I was the youngest child in a home that rarely felt like one. I searched for love in the shadows of absent figures. My mother lived in another state, and my father, like so many in my community, was a ghost in my life.

At 18, when life was already a maze of wrong turns and broken promises, my father unexpectedly appeared. For three weeks, we shared a fragile connection, one that felt more like a question than an answer. Then, as quickly as he came, he was gone, leaving me with a heart full of grief and a mind full of questions.

Why did he visit? Was it closure for a man seeking peace, or a final gift of presence for a son who had spent his life longing for it?

The Visit That Changed Everything

I was the youngest child in a house filled with empty rooms. The kind of silence that lingered wasn't peaceful; it was heavy, like a reminder of all the things that weren't there. My mother lived miles away in another state, and my father was the kind of absent that felt like a wound that never stopped aching.

Growing up, I searched for love in all the wrong places—crowds that felt like family until they didn't, relationships that promised connection but only deepened the void. I carried anger like armor, protecting myself from the world that had betrayed me. Resentment became a constant companion, whispering bitter truths about those who were supposed to stay but never did.

Then, at 18, my father came back. Out of nowhere, the man who had been a ghost in my life appeared on my doorstep. For three weeks, we shared moments that were both healing and haunting. He told stories, laughed, and for the first time, tried to be the man he should have been all along.

But just as quickly as he returned, he was gone. Three weeks after our reunion, my father passed away, leaving behind a flood of emotions that couldn't be contained.

At first, the anger roared louder than ever. Why now? Why come back just to leave me again? It felt like betrayal, like the universe was playing some cruel joke. But as the days turned into weeks, something shifted. Beneath the anger was a flicker of something else—something softer.

It wasn't closure, not yet. But it was a start. For the first time, I allowed myself to feel the grief, not just the rage. I realized my father's visit wasn't about answers or apologies—it was about presence, however fleeting. It was a gift wrapped in pain, a chance to see a side of my father I'd never known.

The journey to healing wasn't easy. There were days when the resentment still burned, when the questions felt like they'd never be answered. But there were also moments of clarity, where I could see my father's visit for what it was: an attempt, however imperfect, to connect.

And in those moments, I began to find the strength to forgive—not just my father, but myself. For the choices I made while searching for love, for the anger I carried, for the walls I built to survive.

This wasn't the end of my story; it was the beginning. A beginning born out of pain, but one that carried the promise of healing, of breaking cycles, of finding the unconditional love I'd always been searching for—first within myself, and one day, in others.

The Cost of Silence

At 19, I was already carrying more than most people could imagine. But when my son came into my life, he was my light, my reason to keep going. I poured everything I had into him, trying to be the parent I never had. I thought I was doing enough. I thought love alone could protect him. Then my mother showed up.

The woman who gave me life but never stayed to raise me. She came to visit, out of the blue, and for a moment, I let myself believe it was about me. But it wasn't—it was about her grandson. She noticed something I didn't—or maybe something I didn't want to see. A slight change in his skin tone, she said. Her voice was firm, but to me, it felt intrusive, almost accusatory. She insisted I take him to the doctor. And I did, if only to prove her wrong. The doctors said he was fine. Healthy. Thriving. "95%," they said.

But my mother wasn't convinced. She told me they were wrong, that something wasn't right. I brushed her off. How could I trust her? She hadn't been there for me. She didn't know me or my son. What could she possibly know about being a parent? Her absence in my life loomed large in that moment. The hurt, the betrayal, the resentment—it all clouded my judgment. I let my pride and my pain drown out her voice. I told myself she was wrong. Three months later, I lost my son. Deformed intestines.

A condition that went unnoticed, untreated. Something that could have been caught, maybe even fixed, if I had just listened. The guilt hit me like a tidal wave, pulling me under with no mercy. I couldn't breathe, couldn't think, couldn't forgive myself. Every "what if" tore at my soul. What if I had listened? What if I had put my son's life above my own anger? What if I hadn't been so stupid? I hated myself. I hated her. I hated the doctors.

But most of all, I hated the silence between us—the years of distance and hurt that made it impossible for me to trust her when it mattered most. I replayed that moment in my mind over and over, trying to rewrite the ending, trying to find a version of the story where my son lived. But no matter how many times I went back, the result was always the same. I was lost. Completely and utterly lost. In the months that followed, I didn't know how to move forward. The grief was unbearable, the guilt suffocating. I blamed myself for everything—for not listening, for letting my past dictate my present, for failing the one person who needed me most. But somewhere in the darkness, a small voice began to whisper. It wasn't forgiveness, not yet.

It was something else—an understanding, maybe. A realization that my pain and my mistakes didn't have to define me forever. I started to see my mother differently, too. Not as the woman who abandoned me, but as a flawed human being who was trying, in her own way, to show up when it mattered. It didn't erase the past. It didn't bring my son back. But it gave me a reason to keep going.

I began to search for ways to honor my son's memory, to turn my pain into purpose. It wasn't easy, and it wasn't quick. But step by step, I started to find my way out of the darkness. And in doing so, I learned that healing isn't about forgetting—it's about learning to carry the weight of your pain without letting it crush you.

Stolen Too Soon

At 21, I thought I had seen enough loss to last a lifetime. But nothing prepared me for the call that shattered my world. My mother—flawed, distant, but still my mother—was gone. Murdered.

Shot six times by a man who couldn't take "no" for an answer. A piece of shit who thought his ego was worth more than her life. He was already married, already living a lie, and when my mother refused to be his side piece, he took her life like it was his to take.

Six bullets. Six echoes of rage, selfishness, and cowardice.

She had just started to find her footing, trying to be more present in my life and make up for lost time. And just like that, she was gone. Not because of an accident, not because of illness, but because of a man who couldn't handle rejection.

The rage that followed was like nothing I'd ever felt before. It wasn't just anger—it was a fire that consumed me, that left no room for anything else.

I wanted justice. I wanted revenge. I wanted him to suffer the way we were suffering.

But he never did.

The bastard died before he could even see the inside of a prison cell. A heart attack, they said. Just like that, he was gone, taking with him any chance of accountability, any hope of justice.

It was a slap in the face, a cruel reminder that life doesn't always work the way it should. He got to escape the consequences of his actions while we were left to pick up the pieces of a shattered life.

I hated him. I hated the system that let him slip away. But most of all, I hated how powerless I felt.

Losing my mother didn't just break my heart—it broke something deeper. It reopened every wound I thought I had buried. Her absence in my childhood, the strained relationship we were only beginning to mend, the chance to say everything I never got to say—it was all gone.

And yet, beneath the anger, beneath the grief, there was a small, stubborn part of me that refused to let her story end with him.

She was more than what he did to her. She was a woman who fought to reclaim her life, who refused to settle for less than she deserved, even when it cost her everything.

I started to tell her story—not just to keep her memory alive, but to remind myself that her strength was still a part of me. That even in her absence, she could guide me, teach me, and inspire me.

But the path to healing wasn't easy. The anger didn't just disappear. There were days when it felt like it would consume me, when the weight of everything I'd lost was too much to bear.

Still, I kept going. For her. For myself. For the life she didn't get to live.

Turning Pain Into Purpose

For a long time, my pain felt like a prison. Losing my mother the way I did left me angry at the world and, at times, angry at myself. I questioned everything—how life could be so unfair, how someone so selfish could take her away, and why justice never came.

But slowly, I realized I couldn't let that anger define me. I couldn't let the man who took her life take mine, too—not physically, but emotionally, spiritually. I had to find a way to honor her memory, to turn the pain she endured into something meaningful.

The first step was acknowledging the depth of my grief and anger. For years, I tried to bury it, thinking that if I ignored it, it would go away. But grief doesn't work like that. It demands to be felt, to be faced.

I started going to therapy—a step I resisted for a long time. Sitting across from a stranger and unpacking my pain felt uncomfortable at first, but it became a lifeline. My therapist helped me see that my anger Lo wasn't just about my mother's death. It was about a lifetime of loss, of feeling abandoned, of carrying burdens that no one should have to bear alone.

Through therapy, I began to understand that healing wasn't about forgetting or moving on—it was about learning to live with the pain, to carry it in a way that didn't crush me.

I also found healing in action. Volunteering at domestic violence shelters became more than just a way to give back—it became a way to reclaim my power. Sharing my mother's story and listening to the stories of other survivors and their families reminded me that I wasn't alone. It gave me a sense of purpose, a reason to keep going.

I started organizing events to raise awareness about domestic violence, speaking at schools, churches, and community centers. I wanted people to understand the signs, to know that help was out there, and to realize that no one deserves to endure what my mother went through.

At the same time, I began to focus on breaking the cycles of pain and trauma in my own life. I looked at the relationships I had, the patterns I was repeating, and asked myself what kind of legacy I wanted to leave. I didn't want my story—or my mother's—to be one of anger and regret. I wanted it to be one of resilience, of growth, of love.

Writing became another outlet for my healing. I started journaling, not just about my pain, but about my hopes, my dreams, and the lessons I was learning along the way. Eventually, I turned those journals into a book—a tribute to my mother and a guide for others navigating their own grief and trauma.

Healing didn't happen overnight. There were still days when the weight of everything I'd lost felt unbearable. But there were also moments of joy, of connection, of peace. I learned to celebrate the small victories, to find beauty in the brokenness, and to forgive—not for the man who took my mother's life, but for myself.

Through it all, I held onto one truth: my mother's strength lived on in me. Her courage, her resilience, her love—they were all a part of me, shaping the person I was becoming.

And though the pain of losing her would never completely fade, I found comfort in knowing that her legacy was one of strength, and that through my actions, her story would continue to inspire others.

Lost in the Game

From 21 to 45, I lived in a world that mirrored the chaos inside me. The streets became my refuge, my battleground, and my cage all at once. Selling drugs and running with the wrong crowd felt like the only way to survive, the only way to numb the pain that never seemed to leave.

The losses I'd endured—my son, my mother, my father—had left me hollow. I didn't trust anyone, not even myself. The streets taught me that trust was a liability, that the only person you could rely on was you. But the irony was, I wasn't even sure I could trust myself anymore.

Fake friends surrounded me, smiling in my face while plotting behind my back. They'd snitch, steal, and sabotage without a second thought. The game wasn't about loyalty; it was about survival, and survival meant staying one step ahead of everyone else.

We'd shoot together, hustle together, and then watch each other fall apart. Some ended up dead, others locked up, and some turned into the very thing we all despised—informants, betrayers. I thought I was different, thought I could outsmart the system, but deep down, I knew the game didn't love anybody.

I used the money, the power, and the chaos to mask the emptiness inside me. But no matter how high I climbed, the pain was always there, waiting for me in the quiet moments.

By the time I hit 42, the streets caught up with me. I found myself facing prison—not for snitching, but for refusing to. I stayed silent, even when it cost me my freedom, because the one thing I couldn't stomach was becoming what I hated.

Prison wasn't just a punishment; it was a reckoning. It forced me to sit with myself, to confront the choices I'd made and the pain I'd been running from for decades.

Inside those walls, I saw the same cycle of betrayal and violence I'd lived on the outside. But I also saw glimpses of something else—moments of clarity, of humanity, of possibility.

I started to ask myself questions I'd been avoiding my whole life:

Why did I let my pain control me? Why did I trust a world that had only ever betrayed me? And most importantly, was it too late to change?

The answers didn't come all at once. They came in fragments, in quiet moments of reflection, in conversations with people who'd lived through similar struggles.

Prison didn't break me—it forced me to rebuild myself. It made me see that the anger and distrust that had fueled me for so long were also the things keeping me trapped.

When I walked out of those gates, I knew I couldn't go back to the life I'd been living. I didn't know exactly where I was headed, but I knew I had to find a way to turn my pain into something meaningful.

The losses I'd endured, the mistakes I'd made, the years I'd spent lost in the game—they didn't define me. They were a part of my story, but they weren't the end of it.

Taking Back My Time

Prison was supposed to break me, but I refused to let it. Instead, I turned it into my battlefield, a place where I fought to reclaim the time and life that had been stolen from me—not just by the system, but by my own choices.

Every resource that place offered, I grabbed with both hands. I didn't care if it was a GED program, a trade class, or a self-help group—I took it all. Out in the real world, those services would've cost me money I didn't have. In there, they were free, and I wasn't about to let them go to waste.

I learned how to weld, how to write, how to speak in a way that commanded respect without violence. I read every book I could get my hands on—books about history, psychology, business, and redemption. Each one gave me a piece of the puzzle I'd been missing, a glimpse of the man I could become if I just stayed focused.

But it wasn't just about skills and knowledge. It was about mindset. I started to see prison for what it really was—a place designed to strip you of your humanity, to make you feel like you're nothing. I refused to let it win.

I used every second of that time to rebuild myself from the ground up. I reflected on the choices that led me there, the pain I'd buried, the anger that had consumed me for so long. And in those moments of reflection, I realized something: I didn't want to just survive anymore. I wanted to live.

I wanted to be free—not just from the walls and bars, but from the chains of my past.

By the time I walked out of those gates, I wasn't the same person who had walked in. Prison didn't change me—it gave me the space to change myself. It taught me the value of freedom, of family, of time.

I started to appreciate the little things I had taken for granted—watching the sunrise, hearing the laughter of my loved ones, feeling the wind on my face. Things that seemed so small before now felt like gifts.

Freedom wasn't just about being on the outside. It was about breaking free from the anger, the pain, and the cycles of bad decisions that had defined so much of my life.

Family became my anchor. I realized how much I had missed, how many moments I had let slip away because my own hurt had consumed me too. I vowed to make up for lost time, to show the people I loved that I was ready to be present, to be better.

And while the world outside wasn't easy—it never is—I faced it with a new determination. I wasn't just surviving anymore. I was living and determined to win.

The Real MVP

At 31, the world lost a light that could never be replaced. My grandmother—my rock, my teacher, my everything—lost her battle with colon cancer. It wasn't just her life that ended that day; it felt like a part of me died with her.

She wasn't just my grandmother. She was the woman who taught me how to be a man when no one else was there. She showed me how to love, even in the face of unimaginable pain. In a world full of hate, she was my safe haven, the one person who made me believe in kindness, grace, and resilience.

Her life wasn't easy. She endured verbal and physical abuse from a proud but broken Black man—a man beaten down by the weight of racism and systemic oppression in the 1940s and 1950s. His pain, like so many Black men of his time, turned inward and lashed out at the people closest to him.

But even through her suffering, she never let bitterness define her. She didn't let the hate she endured poison her heart. Instead, she chose love. She chose understanding. She decided to break the cycle, to be a source of light in a world that often seemed so dark.

She never treated me poorly because of the things she went through. If anything, her struggles made her more compassionate, more patient, more determined to teach me the values of love and forgiveness. She taught me that strength wasn't about how hard you hit—it was about how much you could endure without losing your humanity.

She was elegance, grace, and beauty personified. A true queen in every sense of the word. She carried herself with a dignity that demanded respect, even in a world that tried to deny her worth.

And yet, she was also real. She didn't sugarcoat life. She taught me about the harsh realities of the world, about the racism, violence, and struggles that came with being Black in America. But she also taught me that those things didn't have to define me. That I could rise above them, just as she had.

When she passed, I felt like I was truly alone for the first time. The one person who had always been there, who had always believed in me, was gone. And in a world full of hate and betrayal, her absence felt unbearable.

But even in my grief, I held onto her lessons. I remembered her strength, her resilience, her unwavering love. I remembered the way she fought for her family, the way she carried herself with pride and dignity, the way she loved me unconditionally.

She was the real MVP of my life. The one who showed me what it meant to be human, to be kind, to be strong.

Her death was a loss I'll never fully recover from, but her legacy lives on in me. In the way I love, in the way I fight for what's right, in the way I strive to be better every day.

She may be gone, but she's still with me—guiding me, inspiring me, reminding me that even in the face of adversity, love and grace can prevail.

A Heart Shattered, A Legacy Carried

When my grandmother passed, it felt like the last thread holding me together had snapped. She wasn't just my grandmother—she was my compass, my protector, the only person who had ever truly seen me. Losing her wasn't just losing a loved one; it was losing the foundation of everything I understood about love and resilience.

I remember sitting in the hospital room, watching her take her last breaths, feeling completely powerless. She had always been the strongest person I knew, surviving things that would have broken anyone else. And yet, there she was, fragile and fading, slipping away from me.

I wanted to scream, to bargain with God, to do anything to keep her here. But deep down, I knew she had fought long enough. She had carried so much for so many years—her own pain, her family's pain, my pain. Maybe it was time for her to rest.

But that didn't make it any easier.

In the days after her death, the world felt colder, emptier. I'd find myself reaching for the phone to call her, only to remember she wasn't there. I'd hear her voice in my head, her laugh, her advice, and then the crushing realization would hit me all over again: she was gone.

For a while, I was angry—not just at the cancer that took her, but at life itself. How could someone who had given so much, who had endured so much, be taken away like this? Why her? Why now?

And then there was the guilt. I thought about all the times I could've spent more time with her, listened more closely, told her how much she meant to me. I thought about the moments I let my own pain and distractions keep me from fully appreciating her.

But even in my grief, her voice stayed with me.

She had always told me that life wasn't about the things you couldn't control—it was about how you responded to them. "You can't stop the storm," she'd say, "but you can learn to dance in the rain."

Her life was proof of that. She had faced unimaginable pain—abuse, loss, racism—but she never let it make her bitter. Instead, she used it to make her stronger, kinder, more determined to show love in a world that often gave her none.

And so, even in my heartbreak, I tried to honor her.

I started by carrying on her legacy in small ways. I treated people with kindness, even when they didn't deserve it, because that's what she would've done. I found myself speaking up for those who couldn't speak for themselves, because she had taught me the value of courage.

I also began to confront the pain I'd been carrying for so long. The losses, the betrayals, the anger—it was all still there, but instead of running from it, I faced it head-on. I realized that the best way to honor her was to heal, to break the cycles of pain and trauma that had defined so much of my life.

Her death also made me reevaluate what truly mattered. The streets, the money, the power—they all felt so empty compared to the love she had shown me. I wanted to live a life that would make her proud, a life that reflected the values she had instilled in me.

It wasn't easy. Grief doesn't have a timeline, and there were days when the weight of her absence felt unbearable. But in those moments, I'd close my eyes and remember her smile, her laugh, the way she'd call me "baby" no matter how grown I thought I was.

And I'd remember her words: "Love is stronger than hate, baby. Always has been, always will be."

She was right.

Her love didn't die with her—it lived on in me, in the way I carried myself, in the way I treated others, in the way I refused to let the pain of the past define my future.

She was, and always will be, the real MVP of my life.

The Crossroads

Eight months out of prison, I was finally starting to see a glimmer of light in my life. College classes, rebuilding relationships, trying to find a purpose—it wasn't easy, but I was making progress. And then, in an instant, it all came crashing down.

My firstborn, my son, my flesh and blood, was gone. Not just gone—taken in the most violent, heart-wrenching way imaginable.

He laid himself down on an exit ramp, and three cars ran over him. Three. His body—my baby—was left unrecognizable. No arms. No legs. No neck. Just broken pieces of the child I had once held in my arms, the child I had dreamed would have a better life than I did.

And to make it even more unbearable, it happened on the exact same day his brother had died 27 years earlier. The universe didn't just take my sons—it mocked me with the timing, as if to say, You'll never escape this pain.

I felt the anger rise in me like a fire. That old, familiar rage—the one that had carried me through so many losses before—was back with a vengeance. Fuck the world, I thought. Fuck everything.

I wanted to numb the pain, to escape it, to forget it. A blunt, a drink, a violation of probation—it all seemed so easy, so tempting. Prison didn't scare me anymore. Nothing did.

But then, in the midst of my despair, I thought about my son.

He was gone, but his memory wasn't. His life, his struggles, his joys—they were still with me, etched into my soul. And I knew, deep down, that he wouldn't want me to throw it all away.

He wouldn't want me to go back to prison, to let the system take me again. He wouldn't want me to drown myself in anger and pain, to let the grief consume me like it had so many times before.

He'd want me to keep going.

So I sat there, torn between two paths: one that led back to the darkness I knew so well, and one that led to an uncertain but hopeful future.

I thought about the college classes I'd started taking, the dreams I'd begun to build for myself. I thought about the people who still loved me, who were still rooting for me, even when I couldn't see it.

And most of all, I thought about my son.

I realized that living vicariously through his memory didn't mean staying stuck in the pain of his loss. It meant honoring his life by living mine to the fullest. It meant taking every opportunity I had to grow, to heal, to make something of myself—not just for me, but for him.

So I made my decision.

I put the blunt down. I stayed out of trouble. I went back to class.

It wasn't easy. The pain didn't go away overnight. Some days, it felt like it never would. But I kept going, one step at a time, because I knew that was what my son would have wanted.

And every time I felt like giving up, I reminded myself of the promise I'd made: to turn my pain into purpose, to honor his memory by building a life he'd be proud of.

A War Within

The rage came first. It always did.

When I got the call about my son, it wasn't just grief that hit me—it was fire. Hot, unrelenting, and all-consuming. My mind raced with questions I couldn't answer. Why? Why him? Why now? Why the same damn day as his brother? It felt like the universe had chosen me as its personal punching bag, and I was ready to punch back.

I wanted to destroy something. Someone. Anything. I wanted to scream at the world for its cruelty, to lash out at anyone who dared cross my path. The pain was too much, and the anger was the only thing that made me feel alive.

But the anger wasn't new—it had been my shadow for years. It had been there when I lost my first son, when my mother was murdered, and when my grandmother passed. It was the demon I knew best, the one that whispered in my ear, "Burn it all down. Forget the world before it forgets you."

And for a moment, I almost listened.

I sat there, staring at the blunt in my hand, thinking about how easy it would be to let it all go. To numb the pain, to violate my probation, to give the world the middle finger and go back to the chaos I knew so well. Prison didn't scare me. Nothing did—not anymore.

But then, something stopped me.

It wasn't peace. It wasn't hope. It wasn't even love. It was the memory of my sons—their faces, their laughter, their dreams.

I thought about how much they had suffered, how much they had fought to find their place in a world that seemed hell-bent on breaking them. And I realized that if I gave in to the rage, if I let it consume me, I'd be betraying them.

But the war inside me wasn't over.

Grief and anger don't just disappear because you want them to. They claw at you, pulling you back into the darkness when you least expect it. Some nights, I'd wake up drenched in sweat, my mind replaying the details of my son's death like a broken record.

I'd see his body on that exit ramp, mangled and broken, and the rage would come flooding back. Who could do this to him? Why didn't someone stop it? And then the guilt would follow, whispering, You could've saved him. You should've been there.

It was a cycle I couldn't escape—anger, guilt, despair, repeat.

But even in the midst of it all, I knew I couldn't let the demons win.

I started fighting back, one battle at a time.

Some days, that meant forcing myself to go to class when all I wanted to do was stay in bed. Other days, it meant talking to someone about the pain I'd buried for so long—pain I thought I'd never be able to share.

And then there were the moments when the rage felt too big to contain, when I wanted to smash something just to feel the release. In those moments, I'd close my eyes and think about my sons. I'd think about their laughter, their dreams, their love.

I'd remind myself that they deserved better than a father who gave up.

So I channeled the anger. I used it to fuel my determination, to push me forward when the weight of the world felt unbearable. I told myself that every step I took—every class I attended, every assignment I completed—was a step toward honoring their memory.

The war inside me isn't over. It might never be. But I'm still here, still fighting, still choosing to live.

Because as much as the rage wants to consume me, as much as the pain tries to pull me under, I know one thing for certain: I owe it to my sons to keep going. To turn my pain into purpose. To show the world that even in the face of unimaginable loss, I can rise.

Faith Over Fear

At 51, I thought I'd seen it all. Life had thrown more at me than most could imagine—loss, heartbreak, prison, and pain that left scars far deeper than the physical ones. But nothing prepared me for the day I walked into the hospital for what I thought was a routine check-up, only to leave with all five of my toes amputated and a heart attack that nearly claimed my life.

Diabetes had finally caught up with me. Years of neglecting my health, burying my pain in bad habits, and ignoring the signs had led me here. The doctors didn't mince words: "You're lucky to be alive," they said. But their next words hit me even harder.

"We might have to remove your leg."

The room spun. I could barely process what they were saying. I thought about everything I'd already lost—my sons, my mother, my grandmother, my freedom. Was I about to lose my leg too?

For a moment, the anger came rushing back. I wanted to scream at God, to ask Him why He kept testing me like this. But then, something inside me shifted.

I remembered the lessons my grandmother had taught me about faith, about resilience, about trusting in a higher power even when the odds seemed impossible. I remembered her telling me, "God's plan is bigger than anything you can imagine, baby. You just have to believe."

So I made a decision.

When the doctor came back with her grim prognosis, I looked her in the eye and said, "God told me something different."

She raised an eyebrow, skeptical. "The tests don't lie," she said. "The damage is severe. If we don't act, you could lose more than just your leg."

But I wasn't backing down. "God said if I eat right, do the work, and take care of myself, I'll be walking and driving by next year," I told her.

She sighed, clearly thinking I was in denial. "The machines are telling us otherwise," she said gently.

I shook my head. "God's plan is greater than your machines."

And from that moment on, I committed myself to proving her—and the odds—wrong.

It wasn't easy. The road to recovery was brutal. Learning to walk again without toes felt impossible at first. The pain was constant, and there were days when I wanted to give up. But every time I felt myself slipping, I remembered my promise to God—and to myself.

I changed everything. My diet, my habits, my mindset. I started eating the way I should've been all along, cutting out the junk that had wreaked havoc on my body. I went to therapy to deal with the emotional wounds I'd been carrying for decades, because I knew healing wasn't just physical—it was mental and spiritual too.

And slowly, I started to see progress.

The first time I stood up without assistance, I cried. Not because of the pain, but because I could feel God's promise coming to life. The first time I took a step, I felt like I was reclaiming a part of myself that I thought was gone forever.

By the end of the year, I was walking. By the grace of God, I was driving.

When I went back to the doctor for a follow-up, she couldn't believe it. "I don't know how you did it," she admitted.

"I didn't," I told her. "God did. I just did the work."

This journey taught me that healing isn't just about medicine or machines—it's about faith, determination, and the willingness to fight for your life, even when the odds are stacked against you.

At 51, I could've given up. I could've let the pain, the loss, and the fear consume me. But instead, I chose to believe in something greater. I chose to fight.

And in doing so, I proved that no matter how broken you feel, no matter how impossible the road ahead seems, there's always a way forward—if you're willing to do the work.

Faith in the Face of the Streets

For years, I lived by the code of the streets—a code built on survival, power, and distrust. Love and faith weren't part of the game. In the streets, you learned fast that weakness would get you killed, and God was only someone you called on when the cops had you in cuffs or when you were staring down 25 to life.

I'd seen too much, done too much, and lost too much to believe in the kind of love and forgiveness the church preached about. God? God was for the ones who had time to pray—not for people like me, who had to hustle to eat, to live, to stay alive.

But the thing about the streets is, they're a dead end. No matter how high you climb, no matter how much you make, it always comes crashing down. And when it does, you're left with nothing but regrets and a long list of people you can't trust.

When I went to prison, I saw the same cycle play out over and over again. The same guys who'd laughed at the idea of God on the outside suddenly found Him on the inside. Myself included.

But let's be real—most of us didn't turn to God because we believed. We turned to Him because we were scared. Scared of the time we were facing, scared of the demons we couldn't escape, scared of the silence that came when the cell door slammed shut.

I was no different. At first, my prayers were selfish. "God, get me out of here." "God, protect me." "God, don't let me die in this place." I wasn't looking for a relationship with Him—I was looking for a way out.

But something shifted during my time behind bars.

It wasn't an overnight transformation. It wasn't some dramatic moment where I saw the light and fell to my knees. It was slow, almost imperceptible, like a seed being planted in soil that hadn't seen rain in years.

I started reading the Bible—not because I wanted to, but because it was one of the few things in my cell that didn't remind me of the streets. At first, the words felt foreign, like they were written for someone else. But the more I read, the more I started to see myself in the stories.

I saw myself in the prodigal son, who squandered everything before finally coming home. I saw myself in David, who was flawed and broken but still chosen by God. I saw myself in Paul, who went from persecuting believers to becoming one of the most powerful voices for Christ.

And slowly, I started to believe that maybe—just maybe—God hadn't given up on me.

But believing in God and living for Him are two very different things.

When I got out of prison, I was faced with a choice: go back to the streets and the life I knew so well, or try to build something new. The streets were calling—they always are. The money, the power, the respect—it's hard to walk away from.

But then I thought about everything I'd been through: the losses, the pain, the lessons I'd learned the hard way. I thought about my sons, my grandmother, and the promise I'd made to myself to honor their memories by living a life they'd be proud of.

And I realized that going back to the streets wasn't just a betrayal of them—it was a betrayal of God, who had carried me through it all.

So I made a decision.

I walked away from the streets.

It wasn't easy. The streets don't let you go without a fight. There were people who doubted me, who mocked me, who said I'd be back. And there were moments when I almost proved them right.

But every time I felt myself slipping, I turned to God.

I prayed like my life depended on it—because it did. I surrounded myself with people who lifted me up instead of pulling me down. I poured myself into my education, my health, and my faith.

And slowly but surely, I started to see the fruits of my labor.

The streets taught me how to survive, but God taught me how to live.

I'm not perfect, and I never will be. There are still days when the anger, the pain, and the temptation creep in. But I've learned that resilience isn't about never falling—it's about getting back up, every single time.

God didn't just save me from the streets. He saved me from myself. And for that, I'll keep fighting, keep growing, and keep believing.

Because if I can overcome the streets, the prison, and the demons that once controlled me, I can overcome anything.

2

When the Door Slammed So Did Her Childhood

The door slammed, hard, right in Lily's face, and with it, her entire world shattered. The wood might as well have been a hammer, driving a nail into everything she thought she knew about people, about friendship, and about trust. It wasn't just a door slamming shut. It was Anna's father that piece of shit cracker, Jim letting her know, once and for all, what the world truly thought of her.

Lily stood there, frozen, her breath caught in her throat, her heart pounding so loud in her chest she thought it might break through her ribcage. She didn't cry, not yet, because the anger hadn't allowed it. She was too stunned to even feel the full weight of the insult, but deep down, something cracked. It was the first time she'd felt the world slice into her so brutally. And it wasn't just Jim; it was Anna too that cowardly little bitch hiding behind her father's shadow, too scared to stand up for the one friend who had given a damn about her.

Eight years old, and already, Lily was learning what the world was really about. She thought back to the summer days she and Anna had spent running through the fields, stealing fruit from the trees, and laughing as if the world wasn't divided by hate. In those moments, they were just two little girls, playing in the sun, not knowing or maybe not caring that their skin color separated them in ways that would soon come crashing down. But now, standing there in front of Anna's house, that door shutting like a punch to her gut, all of that was gone. Erased.

Anna's father had told her she didn't belong, that she wasn't welcome, and the way he'd spat the word "n****r" still rang in her ears. He was marking her, branding her with the filth of his hate. It wasn't the first time she'd heard the word. Hell, it wasn't even the first time someone had made her feel less than, but this time, it was personal. It wasn't some stranger in a grocery store or a teacher giving her the side-eye in class. This time, it was the father of the girl she'd thought was her friend.

The heat of her anger started to build, her fists clenched tight by her sides as she turned and ran. She ran home, her feet pounding against the pavement, her chest heaving with every step. When she reached the front porch, her mother met her at the door, worry etched in her face.

"What happened, baby?"

Lily could barely get the words out, her voice a hoarse whisper. "They said I'm not allowed to play with Anna anymore."

Her mother's face hardened, showing a sadness Lily hadn't seen before. She didn't say anything; she just pulled her into a hug. In that moment, Lily wanted to cry. She wanted to break down and let the tears come, but she couldn't. The anger was too strong.

Later that night, when her father got home, it was like lighting a fuse. Robert was a proud man who had taught Lily from day one that she was worth more than what this racist world tried to make her feel. When Lily told him what had happened, the fire in his eyes told her this was about to become something much bigger.

He stormed out of the house, his face set in a grim line, and Lily knew where he was headed: straight to Jim's house, straight to the man who'd dared to slam a door in his daughter's face and call her a name meant to break her.

Lily ran to the window and watched her father march down the street. Her heart pounded with a strange mixture of fear and pride. She knew her father wasn't one to back down for anything. He'd faced worse, but this time, it was his little girl they were messing with. And that was a line you didn't cross.

When Robert reached Jim's front door, he didn't knock. He banged on it, hard enough to shake the frame. Jim opened the door, his face contorting into a sneer when he saw Robert standing there, fists clenched, muscles taut, rage pouring off him in waves.

"You got a problem, n****r?" Jim spat the words like venom.

Robert didn't hesitate. He lunged forward, his fist connecting with Jim's jaw before the words were even fully out. They tumbled to the ground in a fury of fists and rage, years of pent-up frustration, humiliation, and oppression exploding into violence.

Lily's heart was racing. She watched, terrified but exhilarated, as her father fought. He fought for her. He fought for their family. He fought for every Black person in that godforsaken town who had ever been told they didn't belong.

But the police arrived quickly. They always did when a Black man was involved. They were on Robert in seconds, pulling him off Jim, slapping the cuffs on him like they'd been waiting for this moment. Jim lay on the ground, blood dripping from his busted lip, smirking as if he'd won. The cops were on his side. And maybe they were.

That night, Robert was taken away in a squad car. Lily watched from the porch, her mother's arms around her, both of them knowing this was far from over. Her father wasn't the type to back down, and they knew what that meant in a town like theirs. Being Black in the 1960s wasn't just about surviving; it was about standing your ground, even when the deck was stacked against you.

Jail Time and Hard Lessons

Robert spent the next six months behind bars, but he wasn't broken. He wasn't the type to let jail time make him feel small. If anything, it hardened him, making him more determined than ever to teach his daughter what it meant to be Black in America what it meant to be strong in the face of a world that hated you simply because of the color of your skin.

Lily visited him every Sunday, sitting on the other side of the glass, holding the cold phone receiver to her ear, listening to her father's voice as he told her stories. Not the kind that made you feel good, but the kind that made you tough. The kind that reminded you the world wasn't fair, that life wasn't fair, but that didn't mean you had to roll over and take it.

"You listen to me, Lily," Robert would say, his voice steady but fierce. "These people? These white folks out here who think they're better than us? They ain't shit. You hear me? They ain't got nothing but their hate, and they're scared. Scared that we'll rise up, scared that we'll take what's ours. Don't you ever let them make you feel small."

Lily nodded, absorbing every word. Her father was the only person who ever made her feel like she could take on the world, like she was invincible, even when the odds were stacked against her.

But the reality of being a Black girl in the South was never far from her mind. Every day at school, she was reminded of her difference. The white kids kept their distance, and the teachers barely gave her the time of day. But she didn't care. Fuck them, she thought. She wasn't there for their approval. She was there to prove to herself and to her father that she was better than them smarter, stronger, more determined than any of those weak-ass white boys who thought they owned the world.

By the time her father got out of jail, Lily had already begun to change. She was harder, tougher, more determined than ever to make something of herself. And she wasn't going to let anyone stand in her way.

The Rise of a Ghetto Soldier

Lily's teenage years were a battlefield. The 1970s were full of revolution and rage, and she soaked it all up like a sponge. The Black Panthers, the

Civil Rights Movement, the riots in the streets it was all fuel for the fire burning inside her. She was done being the little Black girl who had to take shit from anyone. She was ready to fight back.

But fighting back didn't always mean throwing punches. Lily had learned from her father that the real power came from knowledge from being smarter than the white folks who thought they could run the show. So she hit the books hard. She studied like her life depended on it, because in a way, it did. If she wanted to escape her town, the poverty, and the hate, she needed to be more than just tough. She needed to be brilliant.

She graduated from high school with honors, her valedictorian speech a giant middle finger to every racist piece of shit who had ever doubted her. When it was time for college, she set her sights high: The University of Texas. A school full of white faces and white privilege, but she didn't give a damn. She was going to take up space where they didn't want her.

The day she walked onto that campus, she felt their eyes on her the weight of their judgment, their curiosity, their fear. But she walked with her head held high, her father's words echoing in her ears: *These white folks ain't shit. They ain't got nothing but their hate.*

College was a battleground in its own right. The University of Texas, full of rich white boys with their daddy's money, their frat parties, and their casual racism, was a far cry from the world Lily had come from. But she wasn't intimidated not by the sprawling campus, not by the looks she got walking to class, and sure as hell not by the weak-ass white boys who thought they ran the place. If anything, their bullshit only fueled her more. Every smirk, every racist joke muttered under their breath, every professor who pretended she wasn't there it all made her hungrier. She wasn't just there to survive; she was there to conquer.

Lily wasn't about to sit in the back of the classroom like the rest of the Black students. Fuck that. She was always front and center, her hand raised, her voice loud. She answered every question, challenged every professor, and called out any white kid who tried to undermine her. Her intelligence was her weapon, and she wielded it like a sword, cutting through the bullshit they tried to throw at her.

She studied harder than anyone. While the white kids partied, she stayed in the library until they turned the lights off, pouring over textbooks, taking notes, making sure she understood every detail better than the rest of them. In Lily's world, she didn't get to be mediocre. She didn't get to be average. She had to be exceptional. These white kids could scrape by, barely doing the work, and still walk out with a degree and a cushy job waiting for them. Not her. She had to be better than all of them, and she knew it.

But it wasn't just the academic pressures that tested her. It was the social landscape. UT was a sea of white faces, and the campus wasn't shy about letting her know she didn't belong. Parties were segregated, not by official policy, but by unspoken rule. The Black students kept to themselves; the white kids had their frats and sororities; and there was an invisible line no one was supposed to cross. But fuck that, Lily crossed it anyway. She wasn't going to let them scare her into silence or keep her boxed into their expectations.

It wasn't long before the white boys started noticing her. Some were curious, fascinated by her confidence and her fire. They weren't used to a Black girl like her someone who didn't give a fuck about their power or their privilege. She wasn't the kind of girl who would bow her head or play nice to make them comfortable. And that pissed them off.

More than once, she had to deal with some entitled white prick trying to talk down to her, treating her like she was less than, like she was something to conquer. They tried to fuck with her in their own little ways: inviting her to parties just to see if she'd come, trying to get her drunk, or pulling that fake "woke" bullshit where they pretended to be down with Black culture to get close. She saw through it all. She saw the racism wrapped in curiosity, the fetishization, the manipulation, and the power plays.

One night, some white boy Brad, or Chad, or some other basic frat name had the nerve to hit on her at a party, slurring his words and trying to pull her closer. He was drunk off his ass, his breath reeking of cheap beer and entitlement.

"You're pretty hot for a Black girl," he said, as if it were a fucking compliment.

Lily's blood boiled. She'd heard enough of that shit to last a lifetime. Without even thinking, she shoved him so hard he stumbled back, his beer spilling all over his polo shirt.

"Fuck you, and fuck your racist ass," she spat, her voice cutting through the music.

The whole party froze. Every white face turned toward her, shocked that she'd dared to call him out. But Lily didn't care. She stood there, her chin up, daring anyone to say something, daring anyone to challenge her. But no one did. They all just stood there, silent, afraid of her fire.

She walked out of that party with her head held high, not giving a damn what they thought of her. She wasn't there to make friends. She wasn't there to fit into their bullshit social structures. She was there to win.

Into the Lion's Den: The Military

After graduating with honors fuck anyone who thought she couldn't do it Lily didn't stop there. She had bigger plans, and those plans involved walking right into one of the whitest, most patriarchal institutions in America: the military.

Lily had always been a fighter, but now she was going to do it on a bigger scale. She wasn't just fighting for herself anymore. She was fighting for her people, for the ones who couldn't. She knew that being a Black woman in the military was going to be hell. She knew the racism, the sexism, the constant microaggressions, and outright disrespect she'd face. But she didn't care. She'd been preparing for this her whole life.

The first day she walked onto base, she could feel the eyes on her. She was one of the few Black women there, and it didn't take long for the whispers to start. The men didn't know what to do with her. They'd never seen anyone like her a woman who commanded attention the moment she walked into a room. She wasn't some weak, scared little girl who would be grateful just to be there. She was a fucking force of nature, and they knew it.

Lily didn't have time for their bullshit. The white men who tried to fuck with her, who tried to throw their rank around to intimidate her, didn't stand a chance. She saw right through their insecurities, their fragile egos. They tried to belittle her, tried to break her spirit with their racist jokes, their sexist comments, and their constant attempts to undermine her authority. But every time they tried, she came back stronger.

One time, during a training exercise, some white guy, Sergeant Fucking Daniels, tried to test her, tried to make her look bad in front of the rest of the unit. He thought he was slick, thought he could embarrass her. But Lily wasn't having it.

"Looks like you're struggling there, Johnson," he said, his voice dripping with condescension as she maneuvered through the obstacle course. "Maybe this isn't the place for a woman like you."

Lily stopped, her eyes locking onto his. The rest of the unit watched, waiting to see how she'd respond. But Lily wasn't about to let some weak-ass white man take her down.

"Maybe you should focus on your own shit, Daniels, instead of worrying about what I'm doing," she shot back, her voice cold and sharp. "Last I checked, I'm outranking your ass."

The unit erupted in laughter, and Daniels' face flushed red with embarrassment. He didn't say another word for the rest of the day. Lily had put him in his place, and he knew it.

But it wasn't just the men who tested her. The system itself was stacked against her. She had to work twice as hard, prove herself over and over again, just to be seen as half as competent as the white men around her. But she did it, day in and day out. She showed up early, stayed late, and made sure no one could ever say she didn't earn her place.

Rising Through the Ranks

Lily's rise through the military wasn't easy. It was a constant battle, fighting against the deeply ingrained racism and sexism that ran through the institution like poison. But she never backed down. Her father's lessons, his strength, and his fire carried her through the toughest moments.

She became known as the soldier who didn't take shit from anyone. She wasn't there to make friends, and she wasn't there to placate fragile white men who couldn't handle a Black woman in charge. She was there to lead. And lead she did.

Every mission, every exercise, every time she was tested, she rose to the occasion. Eventually, even the white men who had doubted her had to admit it: Lily was a leader. She commanded respect, not because she demanded it, but because she earned it. The men under her command might not have liked her, but they followed her. They had to. She was smarter, tougher, and more determined than any of them, and they knew it.

The higher she climbed in the ranks, the more power she wielded. And with that power came the opportunity to change things. She didn't just want to succeed for herself. She wanted to make space for other Black women, other soldiers of color who had been sidelined and disrespected by the same system that had tried to keep her down.

The Legacy of a Ghetto Soldier

By the time Lily became a high-ranking officer, she had seen it all the racism, the sexism, the dirty looks, the attempts to take her down. It was all just noise to her now. She had built herself into something stronger than any of them could ever understand. She had become a force, a ghetto soldier, a woman who didn't just survive in a white man's world. She fucking dominated it.

But Lily never forgot where she came from. She never forgot that little girl standing in front of Anna's house, the door slamming in her face. That moment had changed everything; it had taught her that the world wasn't fair, that people weren't always kind, and that the fight for respect, for dignity, was everything.

Lily carried the lessons of her past like weapons in an arsenal, ready to be drawn at a moment's notice. She knew the world had been rigged against her from day one. To be Black and a woman in America, especially in the 1960s and '70s, meant two strikes against you before you even opened your mouth. The whole damn system was designed to keep her quiet, small, and subservient. But that wasn't who Lily was. That wasn't who her father raised her to be.

To be a strong Black woman in a racist world wasn't just a choice. It was survival. Lily knew that every day she walked out of her house, she was stepping onto a battlefield. The bullets weren't always literal, but they were there, aimed at her dignity, her intelligence, her very existence. The sneers, the disrespect, the systemic roadblocks they were all part of the same war. If she didn't come prepared, if she wasn't tough enough to handle it, the world would chew her up and spit her out like she was nothing. But that wasn't going to happen to Lily. She had too much fire in her for that.

She thought back to her father, Robert, locked in that jail cell for six long months, his pride never breaking. He had taught her that strength didn't always come from fists. It came from knowing your worth when everyone else was trying to make you doubt it. It came from standing tall even when you were surrounded by people who wanted to see you fall. And most of all, it came from refusing to let the hate of others define who you were. That was the lesson Lily carried with her into every space she entered. It wasn't about fitting in or gaining acceptance; it was about forcing the world to reckon with her existence.

When Lily looked around in the military, at the rows of white men saluting her as she moved up in rank, she saw the contempt in their eyes. They weren't used to a Black woman telling them what to do, weren't used to someone like her making decisions that they had to follow. But that was their problem, not hers. She didn't need their approval, and she sure as hell didn't need their respect to do her job. She was there to lead, and she was damn good at it.

In those early years, every command she gave felt like a revolution in itself. When she told those white soldiers to fall in line, to carry out her orders without question, she knew she was breaking more than just military ranks. She was breaking centuries of racial and gender expectations. Every time they obeyed, it wasn't just a victory for her; it was a victory for every Black woman who had ever been told to stay quiet, to stay in her place. Lily's place, she decided, was at the top, and anyone who had a problem with that could choke on their own ignorance.

The Price of Strength

But being a strong Black woman in that world wasn't without its price. Lily knew that her strength scared people. It intimidated them. It made them uncomfortable. In a society built on white supremacy and patriarchal bullshit, a woman like Lily was seen as a threat. She was too loud, too bold, too defiant. She didn't fit into the boxes they wanted to shove her into, and that made her dangerous.

For a long time, Lily didn't care. She didn't care if people thought she was "too much," or that she was stepping out of line. She had lines of her own, drawn by her experience and her determination to never be less than what she knew she was capable of. But over time, she started to see how that strength isolated her, how it made it harder for people to truly see her. Her father had always told her: "The world won't see you for who you really are, baby. They'll see what they're afraid of. You have to be strong enough to bear that."

And Lily was. But it didn't mean it didn't hurt sometimes.

The higher she rose in the military, the more the isolation set in. Sure, her command was respected, mostly because it had to be, but outside of the uniform, it was another story. The men she commanded didn't want to have a drink with her after hours. They didn't invite her to their barbecues or their family gatherings. She wasn't one of them, and she never would be. And honestly, she didn't want to be. But there were moments, late at night, when she'd sit alone in her quarters, the weight of it all pressing down on her, that she wished the world could be different that she could exist without always having to prove something.

But she had long since learned that being a Black woman meant always being on your guard. It meant being stronger, faster, and sharper than everyone around you just to survive. If it meant being alone sometimes, then so be it. She wasn't here to make friends. She was here to win, to lead, and to change the damn game. If the price of that was isolation, then she'd pay it a thousand times over.

Civil Rights, Revolution, and the Fight for Dignity

While Lily was navigating the treacherous waters of military life, the world outside was on fire. The Civil Rights Movement had exploded into the 1970s with a fury that had been building for centuries. Black people were no longer content to ask for equality. They were demanding it, taking it by force if necessary. The Black Panthers patrolled the streets with guns slung over their shoulders, ready to protect their communities from police violence. The streets were alive with protests, marches, and a defiant energy that Lily could feel all the way from her military base.

She wasn't on the frontlines of those protests, but she felt the weight of them in her bones. Every time she saw footage of Black men and women standing up to the cops, their fists raised high in defiance, she felt a surge of pride. This was her people, her community, and she was part of that fight, even if her battlefield looked different.

Lily's struggle in the military was a reflection of the larger fight for equality happening outside. She was breaking down doors in the same way that Black people across the country were breaking down barriers in schools, in the workplace, and in the streets. And just like them, she was met with resistance at every turn.

There were moments in her career when the racism was so thick, so blatant, that it felt like she was drowning in it. Promotions that should have been hers were handed to less-qualified white men. Her suggestions were ignored in meetings, only to be brought up by someone else later and treated as brilliant ideas. And there were always whispers always some fucking whispers about how she'd gotten where she was because of "diversity quotas" or because the military was trying to look good by promoting a Black woman. But Lily didn't let that shit touch her. She had clawed her way up from the bottom, and she'd earned every stripe on her uniform. She was here to stay.

But Lily didn't let that shit touch her. She knew the truth. She had clawed her way up from the bottom, and she'd earned every stripe on her uniform. No one could take that from her. Let them whisper. Let them choke on their jealousy. She was here to stay, and they were just going to have to deal with it.

Commanding Respect

By the time Lily reached the rank of Captain, she had built a reputation that preceded her. She was the kind of leader who didn't take shit from anyone, and her soldiers, both Black and white, knew it. They followed her not out of fear, but out of respect. She wasn't just tough; she was smart, strategic, and always three steps ahead. Her troops knew that when Lily Johnson gave an order, it wasn't just to flex her power. It was because she knew exactly what needed to be done to win.

But commanding respect in the military wasn't the same as commanding equality. Lily knew that while she had earned the respect of the men under her command, that didn't mean they saw her as their equal. Even the ones who looked up to her still held onto their deeply ingrained beliefs about race and gender. It was the quiet racism, the kind that slithered underneath their words, that showed up in the jokes they made when they thought she wasn't listening, or in the way they hesitated just a little too long before calling her "ma'am."

One night, after a long day of training exercises, Lily overheard two white soldiers talking in the mess hall. They were drunk, laughing too loud, their voices carrying across the room.

"I don't know how a woman like her got to be in charge," one of them slurred. "I mean, she's good, but come on, she's Black. You really think she got here without someone pulling some strings?"

His buddy snorted. "Yeah, but she scares the shit out of me, man. She's not like the others. She doesn't take shit from anyone."

"Still doesn't mean she's better than us."

Lily felt the familiar burn of anger in her chest, but she didn't react. She'd heard it all before. This was just more of the same a reminder that no matter how far she climbed, no matter how much she proved herself, she would always be seen as less in their eyes. But fuck them. Their opinions didn't mean shit to her. She wasn't fighting for their approval. She was fighting for herself, for her father, for her community, and for every Black woman who had ever been told she wasn't good enough.

The more success Lily found, the bigger her next move became.

From Military to Real Estate: Taking on the White Man's World, Again

By the time Lily retired from the military, she had already shattered enough ceilings to fill a damn landfill. She had led, commanded, and earned the respect of men who, deep down, didn't want to admit they feared her. Feared her brilliance, feared her strength, feared her Blackness. But she wasn't done yet. Hell, life was just getting started.

At 60, Lily Johnson was still that same ghetto soldier her father had raised, that same fire burning inside her. But now, with the discipline of a military career behind her and decades of fighting against the system under her belt, she had her sights set on a new battlefield: real estate.

It was the same game, just with different players. Now, instead of navigating the toxic waters of white male dominance in the military, she was about to dive headfirst into the old boys' club of property development and real estate. And let's be real the world of real estate, especially in Texas, was run by the same kind of white, entitled men who thought they owned everything, including the rules of the game.

But Lily wasn't new to this. These white men weren't shit to her. They could own the buildings, the banks, the companies, but they couldn't own her. And with her sharp mind, iron will, and unrelenting work ethic, she was going to carve out her own space. Not just for her, but for every Black woman who had been told she didn't belong in these spaces, for every sister fighting to survive in this white man's world.

Building Her Empire

Lily didn't just dabble in real estate. She came in guns blazing. She knew from the start that this industry was about power, about owning something that couldn't be taken from you. And for a Black woman in America, there was no greater power than owning land, owning buildings, owning a piece of the very country that had tried to break her since birth.

She started small, flipping a few houses and learning the ropes of the game. But it didn't take long for Lily to see the bigger picture. She wasn't content just flipping homes in middle-class neighborhoods. She wanted to reshape communities, lift up those who had been left behind, and create wealth for people like her people who had been locked out of the American Dream for far too long.

The real estate game wasn't easy, but Lily was no stranger to hard shit. The same white men who had dismissed her in the military were the ones who now tried to shut her out of business deals, tried to undercut her, and tried to play games. They didn't know who they were dealing with.

There was this one asshole. Let's call him Bill, because of course his name was fucking Bill. He was an old-school, good-ol'-boy real estate developer who had been running shit in the city for decades. He didn't think twice about stepping on people to get what he wanted, and he sure as hell didn't think twice about treating Lily like she was some rookie who didn't know what she was doing.

At one property auction, she had her eye on a building that could be the centerpiece of her next project: a low-income housing development that would provide affordable units for Black families, something the community desperately needed. Bill tried to outbid her, smug as hell, like he was doing her a favor by even acknowledging her presence.

But Lily wasn't backing down. Not to Bill, and not to anyone else.

When Bill tried to make his move, pushing the price higher and higher, thinking he could squeeze her out, Lily doubled down. She didn't just meet his bid; she went higher, making it clear that this property was hers, no matter how much money he threw around. She had already lined up the financing, already built her network, and already calculated every possible outcome.

When the final bid was called, it wasn't Bill's name that was announced. It was Lily's. She owned the property now. Bill looked at her, red-faced, with that same contempt she'd seen in the military. The same contempt she'd seen her whole life.

"Why don't you stick to flipping houses, Johnson?" he muttered as they crossed paths after the auction. "You're out of your league."

Lily didn't miss a beat. She stared him dead in the eye, her voice calm and steady. "I don't play in leagues, Bill. I make my own."

And that's exactly what she did. Over the next decade, Lily built an empire of her own. She didn't just develop properties; she developed people, lifting up those who had been left out of the housing market, providing opportunities for Black women and families to own their own homes, and to build their own wealth. She became known not just as a real estate mogul, but as an advocate for her community, a woman who used her power and influence to create real, lasting change.

Advocating for Black Women in a White Man's World

But for Lily, it wasn't enough to just succeed on her own. She knew there were too many Black women out there who were still struggling, still trying to find their footing in a world that wasn't built for them. And Lily wasn't about to let them fight that battle alone.

By the time she was 60, she had become a mentor, a teacher, and a fierce advocate for other Black women trying to navigate the cutthroat world of business, real estate, and finance. She hosted workshops, gave speeches, and met with young Black women one-on-one, teaching them the same lessons her father had taught her: don't take shit from anyone, know your worth, and fight like hell for what's yours.

Lily didn't sugarcoat shit. She didn't have time for the kind of feel-good bullshit that people tried to sell to young professionals. She told them the truth: this world was going to try to break you. These white men were going to look down on you, treat you like you didn't belong, try to fuck with your mind. But that didn't mean you had to accept it.

"You want to make it in this world?" she would tell them. "You gotta be stronger, faster, smarter than everyone around you. Because they're not gonna hand you shit. They'll smile in your face, act like they're your friend, then stab you in the back the minute you turn around. You gotta know who you are, what you're worth, and never let these motherfuckers make you forget it."

She wasn't about to let the next generation of Black women fall into the same traps she had to fight her way out of. She gave them the tools, the knowledge, and the unbreakable spirit they needed to succeed. Because she knew that being a Black woman in America wasn't just about surviving. It was about thriving. And if she had anything to do with it, every Black woman she mentored was going to rise up and take what was theirs, just like she had.

Still Unstoppable at 60

At 60 years old, Lily was still that same force of nature she had been in her youth, just with more wisdom, more experience, and more power. She didn't slow down. She didn't retire. Fuck that. Retirement was for people who didn't have a fight left in them, and Lily's fire wasn't even close to burning out.

She was still out there, making deals, building properties, and mentoring the next generation of Black women. And she was still taking on the white man's world, still fighting against the same systems of oppression that had tried to hold her back for decades.

Her empire had grown. She now owned properties across Texas, and her developments had helped hundreds of Black families get a leg up in a world that was determined to keep them down. But she wasn't finished. She was never finished. There was always more to do, more barriers to break, more spaces to carve out for herself and for her people.

She walked into boardrooms with the same confidence she'd had in the military, commanding respect the minute she stepped into the room. And if any of those old white men thought they could push her around, they were in for a rude awakening. Lily was the kind of woman who could dismantle a man's entire career with one well-placed comment, one perfectly timed move. And she'd done it before, more than once.

At this point, the white men in her industry knew her name, and they knew what she was capable of. She wasn't someone they could dismiss. She was someone they had to reckon with. Because Lily Johnson had earned her place at the table, and no one was going to take it from her.

The Legacy of a Black Queen

Lily's life, from the 1960s to 2024, was a testament to what it meant to be a strong, Black woman in a white man's world. She had fought battles on every front... from the playground as a little girl, to the military as a soldier, to the real estate world as a business mogul. And through it all, she had never let the hate, the racism, or the patriarchy break her.

She was unbreakable. Unstoppable. And she knew that her legacy wasn't just about the buildings she owned or the deals she made. It was about the lives she touched, the women she mentored, the barriers she broke. It was about showing the world that a Black woman could not only survive in this world, but thrive, excel, and dominate.

For every Black woman trying to navigate this racist, sexist, cracker-ass world, Lily's message was clear: Don't let them break you. You're fearless.

3

The Mind Becomes a Motel

He said, "Good morning, beautiful," like he always does. Soft voice. Easy smile. The kind that makes you feel like maybe the world isn't as cruel as your past made it out to be.

And just like that... a tiny, poisonous whisper slipped into my head.

Her Mind (whispering): He's probably copy-pasting that same line to three other women right now.

I didn't say anything back at first. Not to him, not out loud. But my silence was loud enough for me to hear every echo of it. I let my fingers hover over the "good morning" reply, hesitating like my response could either save or sabotage something I wasn't even sure was broken yet.

Because that's the problem with loving after damage. Every kind gesture has to pass through a trauma checkpoint.

He kissed my forehead before leaving for work, like he always does. Took his cologne with him and left his comfort behind.

But by the time the door closed, my brain turned into a crime scene investigation unit.

Internal interrogation begins:

"Why did he look at his phone right after he kissed me?"

"Was that a smile or a smirk?"

"Who is he thinking about when I'm not around?"

"Do I actually trust him... or just crave the idea of him being good?"

I went to wash my face, looked in the mirror, and saw two women:

- The first one: loved, chosen, safe.
- The second one: suspicious, shaking, already halfway through preparing for heartbreak.

Only one of them was real. But in that moment… I couldn't tell which.

My mind is a motel with neon lights flickering: Vacancy

Room 101: Overthinking.

Room 202: Past betrayals biting fresh.

Room 303: His last Instagram like—why *that* girl?

Room 404: Trust not found.

And somewhere down the hall… I still want to believe him.

By noon, he texted: "Miss you already." I stared at it too long, trying to decide if this was loyalty speaking… or guilt.

Her Mind**:** Don't fall for it. Men say that to keep you calm while they wander.

Her Heart (tired): But what if he just… actually misses me?

I typed: "Miss you too."

But what I really meant was:

"Please don't make me look stupid for trusting this."

"Please let this be different."

"Please don't turn into them."

Later that night…

He sat next to me watching TV, laughing at a show I barely heard. I was too busy listening inward. He reached out and ran his thumb across my hand… and I jumped like he had discovered a trigger. He didn't do anything wrong today. But I still spent the whole day fighting a war against scenes I directed and acted out in my imagination.

And lying there next to him, I wondered:

"Do I actually have proof? Or just fear?"

"Is he guilty? Or am I just terrified of being played... again?"

"He wasn't my enemy... but my mind had already built him a prison."

And the worst part is he never even knew he was locked inside.

Triggered Without Evidence

He came home at 6:42 PM.

Two minutes later than usual.

That's all it took for the spiral to start.

He dropped his keys in the bowl, kissed me on the cheek like always. But this time... I didn't lean in. I felt stiff. Suspicious. Studying him like he had invisible lipstick stains I couldn't see yet.

Her Mind: He was laughing in the car before he walked in. Heard it through the door. Who was he on the phone with? People don't laugh like that with just coworkers. Who makes him happy when you're not around?

He kicked off his shoes and started talking about traffic. About some ridiculous driver who cut him off. About nonsense I couldn't process, because my brain was stuck replaying the sound of that laugh from the hallway.

"Who were you talking to?" I asked.

I didn't say it gently. I said it like a detective posing a question they already had the answer to.

He paused. Confused. "My friend Chris. Why?"

A normal answer. But fear doesn't care about logic.

Her Mind: Chris? Or Cristina? Don't be fooled by unisex names.

The silence after his response was heavy. He could feel me pulling away—emotionally, mentally. I watched confusion turn into concern... and concern turn into quiet frustration.

Flashback (Trauma Memory Unleashed)

I was back in my old apartment, watching my ex smile at his phone with dimples that weren't meant for me. He said it was "just his friend." Her name was Taylor. Unisex too. He swore I was "crazy." Until I found screenshots. Until I found their late-night phone logs. Until I found the messages that started with "Hey bro," and ended with "I miss you."

I remembered the way betrayal doesn't walk in. It seeps in through doubt disguised as paranoia.

Suddenly, I was no longer talking to this man in front of me.

I was arguing with a ghost wearing his face.

"You seemed real happy," I said sharply, folding my arms.

He blinked. "Babe... are you okay?"

Wrong question. Fire lit.

My heartbeat became anger. My fear became defense. My trust issues became attack mode.

"Just thought it was funny," I snapped. "How you got jokes for phone calls but not for me."

Now he looked more hurt than confused. I could see him trying to wrap his mind around the shift.

"You're mad... because I laughed on the phone?" he asked slowly, like he was afraid of stepping on a landmine he didn't plant.

I wanted to stop. I wanted to calm down. But once fear becomes anger, it's hard to put it back quietly.

"That's not what I said," I muttered—a classic dodge.

He exhaled. "Can you just tell me what's actually wrong?"

That's when I said it. Without meaning to. Without filtering.

"I don't trust that shit."

Instant silence.

We both knew this was the first crack.

His jaw tightened... not in anger, but disappointment. Maybe fear. Maybe the sinking realization that he was being punished for someone else's crimes.

"You don't trust me?" he finally asked.

I opened my mouth to explain. But I didn't have an "I don't trust you"... I had an "I don't trust love anymore."

But that wasn't what I said.

Instead, I stayed quiet.

And silence can sound a lot like a guilty verdict.

"Sometimes the fight isn't between two people... it's between one person and their past, while the other just ends up collateral damage."

Now we enter his head for the first time... the moment where her unspoken trauma becomes his unexpected punishment. We'll let the argument build, but not explode into something irreparable yet. Just enough to shake them both.

He Feels the Shift

He had never seen her eyes look at him like that—not like he'd hurt her... but like she was waiting for him to.

She walked away after dropping that statement: "I don't trust that shit."

Now he stood in the living room, keys still in the bowl, jacket still on, trying to figure out what crime he'd committed without knowing the law.

His Inner Thoughts:

She thinks I'm lying. Over a laugh. Over a damn phone call with my boy. How did we get here in five seconds?

He ran a hand over his face and exhaled the kind of breath that comes when confusion starts turning into pain.

He didn't grow up with guesswork. If there was a problem, you talked it out. But right now, communication felt like walking across a bridge he didn't build, hoping it didn't collapse from something he didn't cause.

He found her in the kitchen, pretending to be busy with dishes she'd already washed.

"Can we talk?" he asked, voice calm but not soft. It carried the weight of a man who felt something fundamental shifting beneath him.

She didn't look up. "Nothing to talk about."

That sentence hit him harder than she knew.

His Memory:

He remembered loving someone once who shut down every time he tried to fix things. He remembered fighting alone in a relationship with someone who made him chase ghosts he didn't believe in. He swore he'd never love someone who turned silence into punishment again.

Now he felt familiar anxiety in his chest. The kind he thought he'd healed from.

"Look," he said carefully, "help me understand what just happened. If I did something wrong, I'll own it. But I'm not gonna keep explaining myself for something I didn't do."

She finally turned around, eyes filled with heat she couldn't place.

"You were laughing like someone made you real happy," she said.

"It was Chris," he repeated. "You know, the same Chris I've mentioned a hundred times."

"And I'm just supposed to believe that?"

He stared at her for a long second. It wasn't anger that flickered in his eyes. It was hurt. Disbelief.

"I haven't given you a reason not to," he replied quietly.

The quiet in his voice shook her more than yelling ever could.

She shrugged like she didn't care, but that shrug was armor, and he could tell.

"So what... you're gonna flip this on me now?" she asked.

He stepped back slightly... not from fear, but from the feeling of being pushed into a courtroom without a chance to testify.

"This isn't a flip," he said. "It's a statement. I can't keep reassuring you if your mind is already made up."

Her jaw tensed. "So now I'm crazy?"

He rubbed his forehead. "I never said that. But you're fighting me like I cheated, and I didn't."

Silence. Heavy. Thick. Like two people trying to breathe underwater.

Then he said the sentence that would shake her:

"I love you... but I won't keep apologizing for things I haven't done. I'm not him."

That line hung in the air. *I'm not him.* And with it came the terrifying truth:

She wasn't just arguing with him. She was arguing with history. And he was losing a fight he never entered.

"He didn't walk out... but something in him stepped back. Not out of love... but out of self-protection."

Where Silence Sounds Like Goodbye

They didn't sleep in separate rooms.

But they may as well have.

She lay on her side, back turned to him, staring at a wall, feeling every inch of space between their bodies like a punishment she gave herself.

He lay behind her, awake... not touching her, not reaching, replaying everything in his head like he was trying to find proof that he did something wrong... and coming up empty.

His Thoughts: Quiet, Heavy, Exhausted

I love her.

But damn... I can't love a version of myself she made up to match her fear. I can reassure, but I can't constantly defend myself against things I've never done. Do I keep trying? Or do I save myself before she makes me bleed for someone else's betrayal?

He stared at the ceiling.

Wondering if love was supposed to feel like constantly waiting to be misunderstood.

Her Thoughts: Racing, Defensive, Drowning

I shouldn't have said it like that.

I could fix this... right now.

All I have to do is turn around and say, "I'm scared, not angry."

But what if I open up, and he thinks I'm too much?

What if my truth becomes the reason he leaves?

So instead of saying any of this... she said nothing.

Self-sabotage in silence format.

Hours passed. Emotions fermented.

Finally, she muttered, "You're really not gonna say anything?"

He paused before answering carefully, because one wrong word could ignite her again.

"I've tried," he said quietly. "But I can't keep chasing you after you push me away."

Her chest stung. That should've been her chance to be soft. Vulnerable. Honest.

Instead... she put her armor back on.

"What if I'm not pushing you away?" she said. "What if I'm just not convinced?"

His heart sank... not in anger, but disappointment.

She thought she was explaining.

He heard: "You haven't earned me yet, even though you've done nothing wrong."

He turned onto his back, staring at the ceiling again. "I don't know what else I can do to prove I'm not someone I never was."

She felt exposed. Threatened by vulnerability. So she defaulted to damage.

"So you wanna leave now?" she snapped, as if he'd said he would.

He rubbed his temples. "I never said that."

"But you thought it." Her voice cracked. A mix of fear and false confidence.

"No," he said softly. "I'm thinking... I don't know how to love you through a war I didn't start."

That line hit her like a gunshot.

She wanted to cry. Instead... she scoffed.

"Well, if you can't handle me when I'm scared, maybe you're not the man I thought you were."

There it was. The bullet. Fired from her fear... straight into his trust.

He closed his eyes... not to sleep, but to protect himself from the urge to fight.

In that moment, they weren't lovers.

They were wounds arguing about whose scar hurt more.

He rolled away from her this time.

Not dramatically.

Quietly.

Like a man pulling his hand back from a flame that already burned him once.

And this time... she felt it.

Not distance.

But disappointment.

The silent kind that feels like a door slowly closing.

"She wanted him to fight for her but pushed him so far back that he started fighting for himself instead."

Love on Mute

He didn't leave.

He just shut down quietly like someone who found the emergency exit in his own emotions and stood next to it... just in case.

She lay there, eyes wide open in the dark, hearing his breathing shift into a soft, steady rhythm. Sleep came for him eventually. It didn't come for her at all.

Her Breakdown... Done In Silence

Tears slid down her face in slow betrayal... not loud, gasping sobs, just silent streams of regret.

She wasn't crying because he was gone. He wasn't.

She was crying because for the first time... she could feel him preparing to be.

She pressed her hand to her chest like she was trying to stop something from falling apart inside her.

What if I pushed too far this time? What if he's done trying to prove he's not guilty? What if I turned a good man into a tired one?

She wanted to curl into him. Apologize. Explain that everything she accused him of was really just past ghosts wearing his name.

But she didn't move. Because pride said, *If you break first, you look weak.* Fear said, *If you open up and he leaves anyway, you'll fall apart completely.*

So she lay there. Crying silently beside the man she loved, who now felt two lifetimes away.

His Thoughts, In The Half-Sleep

He wasn't fully asleep. He drifted in and out, thoughts heavy.

I love her... but am I slowly becoming her emotional punching bag? Will every time I laugh, smile, or speak to someone else turn into a trial? How long until I start resenting her for seeing me as a villain? Can love survive if one person always has to defend their innocence?

The saddest part?

He didn't want to leave her.

He just didn't want to lose himself trying to prove he was worth being trusted.

And somewhere between questioning and caring... he emotionally stepped half a foot back.

Morning: A Stranger In Familiar Skin

She woke up early. Earlier than usual... not because she slept... but because fear won't let you rest when you think love is slipping.

He got up a few minutes later.

He said, "Morning," with a tone that wasn't cold... but wasn't warm either. It sounded like a word wrapped in caution.

She tried to smile, but it trembled. "You hungry? I can make something."

"I'll grab something on the way," he said.

He always loved her pancakes. He never skipped breakfast at home.

Today he did.

The sound of the front door shutting wasn't loud...

...but to her, it felt like a warning shot.

Her Unsent Text. A Confession She Can't Send

She sat on the edge of the bed holding her phone, typing and deleting three times before finally writing:

"I don't think you did anything wrong yesterday. I think my past did. I'm sorry for making you fight shadows. I just... get scared. Not because of you, but because of what people before you did when I trusted them. I'm trying to unlearn fear before it ruins something real. Please don't give up on me before I figure out how to stop self-destructing."

She stared at it.

Thumb hovered over "Send."

Heart screaming, *SEND IT, PLEASE.*

Fear whispering, *What if he thinks you're too broken?*

She saved it in her Notes app instead......and whispered to herself, "Maybe later."

"She didn't lose him that morning...but he stopped being hers without question.

And love on edge is just love counting heartbeats, wondering when it will break."

When Silence Becomes Proof (Even If It Isn't)

She told herself she'd stay busy today. Focus on work. Drink water. Eat. Breathe.

But by 9:15 AM, she'd already opened her messages five times to see if he'd texted first.

Nothing.

By 10:03, she started justifying it. *He's busy. He said he had an early meeting. He never texts this early anyway. He's fine. We're fine. Right?*

By 10:47, panic started whispering. *What if he's rethinking us? What if I made him feel unsafe? What if he's slowly detaching?*

By 11:21, her chest was tight, and she wasn't sure if she was anxious... or already grieving something that hasn't even left yet.

She checked her Notes app. Reread the unsent apology. Felt it sting.

"Please don't give up on me..." That sentence alone made her feel small. Desperate. Exposed.

She hovered over it, debating if today was the day she swallowed her pride. Then...

What if I send it and he pulls away anyway? What if I get vulnerable and he takes it as confirmation I'm too much? What if I make it easy for him to decide I'm damaged?

Her fear started twisting the narrative again.

What if now I should pull back too? Maybe he needs to feel me gone a little. Maybe I shouldn't chase. Maybe this time, I should make him come to me.

She wasn't sure if she was making a strategy... or building another self-destruct button.

12:14 PM: His message finally came.

Him: "Hope your day's going okay."

That was it.

No heart. No nickname. No "Miss you." Just ...okay.

And she felt it.

Not an absence of love. But a withdrawal of warmth.

Her Thoughts Start Cracking:

He's being polite. He's creating distance. He's playing it safe now. He's talking to me like he's testing how much energy to give... because he doesn't know if it's worth it anymore.

Her fingers moved quickly:

Her: "It's fine. Yours?" *She deleted it.*

Her: "Good." *Deleted.*

Her: "It's ok." *Deleted.*

Her: "Yeah." *Deleted again.*

She typed nothing. Locked her phone. Unlocked it again. Reread his message 12 more times like looking at it differently might reveal a hidden tone.

Now came the dangerous shift: He didn't seem mad... but he didn't seem entirely here, either.

And that gray area became its own torture chamber.

She opened her Notes app again. Stared at the apology.

For a moment, a heartbreakingly genuine moment, she was ready to send it.

Then pride whispered: *What if he's already halfway gone? What if you send it and he already decided you're unstable? What if the apology makes you look like you're chasing someone who's slipping?*

Fear whispered too: *And what if sending this means he has the power to reject you completely?*

So instead of sending something honest...

She decided to send nothing.

And in that silence... her heart convinced itself he must already be giving up.

"She didn't respond out of fear of losing him...but the longer she stayed silent, the more she started believing she already had."

"My Past Taught Me to Bleed First Before Someone Else Makes Me"

I wanted to tell him the truth. That I'd been operating like love was a battlefield and survival meant striking before being struck.

I opened my mouth to say, "I'm sorry." But fear grabbed the words before they came out.

MY MIND (cold, familiar): "If you admit you're wrong, you give him power."

ME: "But I already hurt him."

MY MIND: "You were hurt first. Don't forget that."

ME (hesitating): "Yeah... I remember."

And suddenly, I was pulled back to the first time love made me stupid enough to trust someone who broke me.

Flashback (not poetic, just real):

I remember being 17 and begging a boy who already emotionally left me to explain why. I remember checking his phone and finding "I love you too" typed to someone who wasn't me. I remember choking on silence because I didn't want to seem crazy. I remember staying so I wouldn't feel abandoned, even though staying was just a slower version of leaving. I remember saying "it's fine" while my soul cracked open.

And after that... every relationship became a crime scene until proven safe. Every man was put on trial for someone else's sins.

Back in the present, he's sitting there looking at me with those tired eyes.

He says softly, "Talk to me."

I want to. God, I want to. But my throat closes like confession might kill me.

MY MIND (firm, almost parental): "He'll think you're unstable."

ME: "I am unstable right now."

MY MIND: "And now you want to hand him the weapon by admitting it?"

ME (small whisper): "What if admitting it is the key to putting the weapon down?"

Silence.

Even my trauma paused like it wasn't programmed for healing.

He reaches out and puts his hand on mine. It's gentle. Too gentle. It makes me feel seen and safe and... unworthy.

So I pull my hand back before comfort makes me cry in front of him.

"I'm tired," I say.

He nods. Not hurt, not angry... just sad. Like he knows I'm fighting a war that started long before he arrived.

When he turns off the light, I lay there staring into darkness, hearing my past whisper:

"You'll lose him if you don't fix this."

But another voice, one I barely recognize yet, whispers:

"You'll lose you if you don't try."

"I wasn't afraid he would hurt me. I was afraid he would love me enough to see where I was already bleeding."

"I Finally Broke In a Place Nobody Could See Me"

I didn't cry next to him.

I waited until I was alone.

Not even in my room... too many memories there. Not in the shower... water doesn't hide pain as well as people think.

I cried in my car.

Parked outside a gas station like I just needed a moment before going inside. Engine off. Silence too loud.

And that's when everything I'd been holding together started to shake loose.

At first, it wasn't even tears. It was this tightness in my chest like I was being smothered by my own thoughts. Then the memories rushed in like they'd just been waiting for the signal.

MY MIND (soft but cutting): "You did it again. You pushed him away before he could prove if he was safe."

ME (cracking): "Why do I keep doing this to people who love me?"

MY MIND: "Because you were taught that being loved is temporary... and abandonment is guaranteed."

ME: "So I abandon first?"

MY MIND (almost proud): "Exactly. Survival."

ME (breaking further): "This isn't survival anymore. This is self-destruction."

Silence.

That was the first time I said it out loud like it was a diagnosis.

And then I started crying, the kind that makes no sound.

Just tears falling with the weight of a confession I'd never admitted:

"I am emotionally dangerous to the people who try to love me."

Not intentionally. Not maliciously. But because I'm still fighting wars with people who aren't even here anymore.

MY MIND (now uncertain): "He still loves you... for now."

ME (sobbing quietly): "How long until 'loving me' becomes 'surviving me'?"

MY MIND: "...Maybe sooner than you think."

For once, I didn't argue with the voice. I didn't defend myself. I didn't perform strength.

I just sat there, forehead pressed against the steering wheel, whispering to no one:

"I don't want to lose him. But I don't know how to keep him without hurting him."

And that right there was my rock bottom disguised as awareness.

Because before I could heal...

I had to finally admit:

It's not always them. Sometimes... it's me.

"I kept waiting for him to hurt me like the others, never realizing I had slowly become 'the others' in my own story."

"I Typed the Truth Into Google, Then Sat There Too Afraid to Press Enter"

I sat in my car until the tears dried into that tight, salty feeling on my cheeks... the kind that makes your skin feel stiff like it's holding your guilt in place.

My mind wouldn't shut up.

Not the screaming part. Not even the crying part.

Now it was whispering like it was ready to negotiate.

MY MIND (softly, almost reasonable):

"You know something's wrong. You can't keep doing this."

ME (exhausted):

"I know."

MY MIND:

"So... maybe look it up? Figure out what this is?"

ME (nervous laugh):

"You want me to Google 'how to not be emotionally insane?'"

MY MIND:

"Something like that."

So I opened my phone.

Went to Google like it was a confessional booth.

Sat there... staring at the blinking cursor like it was daring me to be honest.

I typed:

Why do I ruin good relationships even when I love him?

Then deleted it.

Typed again:

Self sabotage in love.

Then deleted it.

Tried again:

Why am I scared when someone actually loves me?

Then... just stared.

MY MIND (taunting now, panicked):

"You sure you wanna know? What if it tells you you're broken?"

ME (whispering):

"What if it tells me I'm not... but I just refused to heal?"

I hovered over the search button with my thumb.

Froze.

Pressing that button felt like opening a door I couldn't close again.

Because once the truth had a name... I'd have no excuse left.

No more "this is just how I am."

No more "they always leave."

No more "I'm just protecting myself."

It would turn my trauma into a mirror.

And I wasn't sure I was ready to look at what I'd become while trying to survive.

So I backspaced everything.

Locked my phone.

Sat there in silence.

Not healed. Not okay.

But scared enough of myself to realize I couldn't keep pretending I didn't see the damage.

"I didn't hit search because once I knew the truth about myself, I'd have to choose: stay broken or try to change."

"The Algorithm Tried to Heal Me But I Ran to Someone Who Wouldn't Challenge My Damage"

I didn't press search...

But my phone wasn't done with me.

Hours later, I opened TikTok just to numb out. Scroll, laugh, forget.

The second video that popped up wasn't a dance or a meme.

It was a girl crying to audio that said:

"Some of you don't fear abandonment. You expect it. So you destroy love before it has the chance to leave you first."

My stomach dropped like the universe just threw a brick at my chest.

I scrolled fast.

Didn't even let it finish.

MY MIND (panicking):

"Nope. That wasn't about you."

ME (quiet):

"It kind of was."

MY MIND:

"Don't go there. You're just emotional right now."

ME:

"Yeah… emotional."

But then the next video was a therapist saying:

"If you were taught that love equals pain or unpredictability, you might push away healthy love because it feels unfamiliar and unfamiliar feels unsafe."

Scroll.

Scroll faster.

Scroll like I'm running.

Now every video feels like a personal attack:

"How to stop sabotaging healthy love."

"Signs you're recreating your trauma in your relationship."

"Loving someone but being afraid they'll wake up and realize they can do better."

It was like TikTok had been waiting for me to emotionally admit something just so it could drag me by the soul.

I slammed the app shut and called the one person who would understand...

not understand me healing,

but understand me staying broken.

My friend Maya.

Big on "men ain't shit" energy.

Certified member of the "make him suffer before he gets the chance to hurt you" community.

When I told her how I felt like I'd overreacted, she didn't let me finish.

She jumped in quick:

"Nah, girl. Your intuition is strong. If you felt something was off, it was. Never doubt that. Men will play you if you give them too much trust."

I wanted her to be right because it felt safer.

MY MIND (exhaling in relief):

"See? Someone gets it."

ME (weakly):

"But what if I didn't trust him because I don't trust anyone?"

MY MIND:

"She said intuition. Stick with that. 'Trauma' sounds like you did something wrong."

ME:

"I did."

MY MIND:

"No. He might still hurt you. Better to stay guarded."

But it didn't feel like reassurance this time.

It felt like relapse.

Because while she was talking, I realized something:

She wasn't protecting me.

She was feeding the version of me that ruins things to feel safe.

And the worst part?

I almost let her.

"Some people don't comfort you. They comfort your demons so you stay the same."

Scroll, Freeze, Speak

I opened TikTok again, against my better judgment.

I said I'd scroll for distraction. Just five minutes.

But the universe apparently didn't get that memo.

The first video I saw wasn't funny.

It was a therapist saying, calmly, directly:

"When you push someone away for their safety, remember: you're often pushing away the people who would never hurt you."

I froze.

Like a deer caught in headlights, my thumbs hovering over the screen.

Scroll? Keep moving? Ignore?

No. I couldn't.

I watched it all.

Every word felt like a mirror I didn't want to admit I needed.

Then my phone buzzed.

I nearly dropped it.

Him: "Are we okay?"

My chest slammed into my ribs.

My stomach flipped.

My brain scrambled for cover.

MY MIND (panicking):

"Don't respond. Play it cool. He's already seen too much."

ME (hesitating):

"But... he's reaching. He cares."

MY MIND (cold, warning):

"Careful. If you answer too honestly, you'll scare him. If you answer too cold, he'll pull back."

ME (softly, trembling):

"I can't get this wrong."

I started typing:

"I... I want to say..."

Then deleted it.

"Look, I just..."

Deleted again.

"I'm sorry if..."

Stopped. My heart raced.

Every word felt like walking on glass. One wrong step and I'd shatter him or myself.

MY MIND (almost smug):

"See? You're too much. Better to leave it unsent."

I stared at the cursor.

Blinking. Silent. My thumb hovered.

I wanted to tell him everything:

That the fight wasn't about him.

That it was about ghosts and fear and my own inability to trust.

That I was scared of losing him... but mostly scared of myself.

But fear whispered:

Say it wrong, and you'll make him leave.

Say it right, and you'll finally have to own your mess.

So I froze.

Unread. Unsure.

A silent apology trapped in my chest.

And the algorithm kept playing:

"The ones you push away are often the ones who would never leave you."

I couldn't scroll. I couldn't move.

I couldn't breathe.

Because the truth was finally visible.

And the choice was mine: speak or destroy what little peace was left.

"I could feel love reaching out, but my fear was still louder than my courage."

The Call That Made Me Choose

I had my phone in my hand, frozen, when TikTok threw another video at me.

"Some of you are scared to be loved because you think the wrong move will ruin everything... but the wrong move is staying silent."

My chest tightened. My fingers trembled.

This wasn't just advice anymore. It was a mirror. A warning.

Every unread message, every frozen text, every hesitation. It all hit me at once.

And then my phone rang.

His name on the screen. Not a text.

A call.

I dropped the phone into my lap. My heart hammered like it was trying to escape.

MY MIND (panicking):

"Don't answer. You'll mess it up."

ME (small whisper, trembling):

"But... he's reaching. He wants to hear me."

I swiped. Answered.

"Hello?" My voice quivered.

"Hey," he said softly. "I... I wanted to hear your voice. Are we okay?"

I froze.

All the walls I had built came crashing down.

All the rehearsed defenses, the deleted words, the TikTok truths, all of it threatened to pour out, and I wasn't sure I could stop it.

MY MIND (warning, sharp):

"Say something safe. Don't get too real."

ME (panicked):

"Safe won't work. He'll know."

I swallowed hard. "I… I don't know. I don't know if we are."

He paused, breathing steady, patient.

"You don't have to say it all at once. Just… talk to me."

I glanced at the phone, at the TikTok video still open in my mind.

"The wrong move is staying silent."

And something inside me snapped.

Something that had been hiding behind fear and self-sabotage finally forced me to act.

"I've been… pushing you away. Not because of you… because of me. My past, my fear, my…"

I choked.

"… my demons. And I'm scared I'll ruin this… before it even grows."

He didn't interrupt. He just waited.

And I realized that waiting wasn't judgment.

It was love.

It was patience.

It was a chance… one I might have thrown away so many times before.

"I don't want to lose you," I whispered.

"Not because of them, not because of anyone. Because of me, I might have… but I don't want to."

Another pause. Then his voice, soft but certain:

"You won't. Not if we do this together. I'm here. I'm not going anywhere."

I let out a shaky laugh.

Tears threatened but this time... they felt like relief, not defeat.

The algorithm, the friend, the fear none of it mattered anymore.

I had two choices: fight for love... or run.

And for the first time in a long time, I chose fight.

"I finally spoke. And in that one breath, I decided that love deserved more of me than fear ever would."

Healing Is Messy

We sat across from each other on the couch, the air heavy with weeks of silence, unspoken fears, and unsent words.

For a moment, it felt like staring at a stranger.

"I want to try," I said, my voice cracking, "but I don't know how to stop myself from... from messing it up."

He reached for my hand, gentle, steady. "You don't have to do it perfectly. You just... have to try. That's all I ask."

I nodded, swallowing a lump in my throat.

Trying felt like standing on a cliff. One wrong move and I'd fall into old habits again.

The First Honest Conversation

"I've been terrified of losing you," I admitted.

"Not because of anything you did... but because I keep bringing my past into us. I sabotage... I overthink... I..."

"Stop," he interrupted, softly.

"I don't want apologies that make you feel small. I want honesty, even if it's messy. I want you... all of you."

I let out a shaky breath.

All the fear, the shame, the "I'm too much" thoughts. Rhey were surfacing, and I let them.

Old Habits Resurface

And then, just as relief started to settle, my mind tried to sabotage again.

"What if I say the wrong thing?" I whispered.

"What if this isn't enough? What if he thinks I'm still broken?"

"I'm not thinking that," he said.

"But I can tell when you're shutting down. Don't do that, not now. Talk to me."

I flinched. My fingers curled into mine.

My old impulse screamed: withdraw, hide, protect myself before I get hurt.

He noticed.

"Stop thinking about what you might do," he said.

"Just be here. With me."

I closed my eyes, fighting the urge to retreat, the fear of being too much, the voice in my head telling me to protect him from me.

We talked for hours.

Raw. Messy. Imperfect.

I stumbled over my words.

He corrected me gently.

I cried.

He held my hand.

I almost pulled away.

He didn't let me.

It wasn't easy.

It wasn't calm.

It wasn't perfect.

But for the first time, it felt like we were speaking the same language: honesty, not fear.

"Healing isn't about perfection. It's about showing up, even when your past screams at you to run."

Testing the Calm

It was Saturday afternoon when the first stress hit.

A friend of his stopped by unexpectedly, the one who always had an opinion about us.

She smiled too wide, eyes flicking between us like she was evaluating a test she already expected us to fail.

I could feel my old instincts twitching.

Analyze. Judge. Defend. Pull away.

He caught my gaze.

A small, calm reminder: Talk. Don't assume. Don't sabotage.

I took a breath and forced a smile.

The External Stressor

"Hey, you two!" she said, leaning in.

"Wow, you guys are... quiet. Everything okay?"

I felt the walls creep up around me.

She's going to judge. She's going to think we're broken. She's going to see me as the problem.

He squeezed my hand under the table.

A grounding touch.

I swallowed my fear and said, "Yeah, we're fine. Just... catching up on life."

And that was it.

No overexplaining. No hiding. No anger.

Just honesty.

The Intimate Victory

After she left, the room was quiet.

I exhaled, the tension still lingering but lighter.

He leaned over and whispered, "See? You didn't explode. You didn't shut down. You were calm."

I laughed softly. "It didn't feel like calm."

"Sometimes calm is choosing not to react the way your past wants you to," he said.

"And that? That's progress."

I let his words sink in.

He brushed a stray hair from my face.

For the first time in weeks, I didn't flinch.

I didn't pull away.

I leaned in. Kissed him softly.

No drama. No manipulation. Just presence.

Just trust.

It was a small victory.

But victories like this aren't measured in fireworks. They're measured in moments you don't run, don't sabotage, don't hide.

And I stayed.

And he stayed.

And for once, love didn't feel dangerous.

"Progress isn't loud. Sometimes it's just holding someone's hand without needing to protect yourself from the world or them."

The Test of Truth

I scrolled through my notifications, trying to ignore the tight knot in my stomach.

A comment from someone on social media caught my eye:

"Are you sure he's really good for you? Heard some things..."

My chest tightened. My hands trembled.

The old instinct whispered: Hide. Defend. Attack first.

I felt the panic creeping in. The same panic that used to have me shutting down, pushing him away before anyone could hurt me.

The Old Habit Surfaces

I glanced at him.

He noticed immediately.

"You okay?" he asked, calm but concerned.

My fingers curled into mine.

"I... I don't know," I admitted.

"My mind is spinning."

MY MIND (warning, familiar):

"Say something safe. Don't let him see how fragile you are."

ME (softly, trembling):

"No. He deserves honesty. I can't... I can't lie anymore."

I told him everything: the comment, my anxiety, my fear of being judged, my fear of overreacting.

The External Test

He listened.

Really listened.

No judgment.

No immediate solution.

Just presence.

Then he said, quietly:

"Thank you for telling me. I could have assumed you didn't trust me. But you did. And that matters more than anything."

I exhaled, a tension I hadn't realized I'd been holding releasing in slow waves.

The panic didn't disappear, but it didn't control me either.

Choosing Honesty Over Defense

Instead of reacting with suspicion or shutting down, I asked:

"What do we do about it? How do we handle this?"

He smiled softly.

"Together. We talk. We clarify. We don't assume the worst. And we don't let outside voices dictate our love."

I nodded.

A small smile broke through my anxiety.

We had faced a trigger, a rumor, a test... and instead of retreating into old habits, we spoke.

It wasn't perfect.

It wasn't instant trust.

But it was a step toward building a foundation strong enough to withstand both my fears and the outside world.

"The real test isn't when everything's easy. It's when your past and the world try to make you doubt love, and you still choose honesty over defense."

Breaking the Silence

He was sitting across from me in the kitchen, coffee in hand, eyes soft but steady.

I felt a knot in my chest tighten like a vice.

This was it.

The moment I either stayed buried in fear... or finally spoke.

Vulnerability: The Backstory

"I... I need to tell you something," I whispered.

He nodded.

"Everything that made me this way... the way I push people away before they can hurt me... it didn't start with you. It started long before I met you. I just... I never learned how to trust love without feeling like I'm going to get hurt."

I paused, tears threatening.

"My first love left me when I was seventeen. I checked his phone. I begged him to stay. He lied. I stayed anyway. And after that... I built walls. And every man after him was tried against the ghosts of that one. I... I learned to push first, so no one else could ever leave me by surprise."

His hand reached across the table, holding mine.

"I didn't know," he said softly.

"You don't have to. But now you're telling me, and that's enough for me to know where you're coming from."

External Pressure: The Crisis

Then my phone buzzed.

A work email. A friend in crisis. Something urgent that demanded attention, pulled me out of this intimate moment.

I felt panic creeping in. Old habits screaming: Withdraw. Protect yourself. Push him away before he sees the mess.

MY MIND:

"Step back. Don't let him see your chaos. They'll leave."

ME:

"No. Not this time."

I took a deep breath, exhaled slowly, and turned to him.

"I need to handle this. But I... I don't want to do it alone."

He nodded.

"I'm here. We do it together."

Interrupting Self-Sabotage

The email was a mess, demanding, chaotic... exactly the kind of situation where I'd normally spiral and make things worse.

But this time, I paused.

Instead of letting fear or pride dictate my actions, I asked for his guidance, let him speak, and stayed present.

Instead of retreating, I let him in.

Instead of sabotaging, I collaborated.

We navigated the crisis as a team.

And in that moment, I realized: old habits might still whisper, but they don't have to win.

"I could have pushed him away, blamed the world, blamed myself... but this time, I chose honesty, trust, and partnership over fear."

First Calm, First Test

We drove out of the city without a plan, just him, me, and the hum of the tires on the road.

No schedules. No expectations.

Just space to breathe, together, without ghosts whispering in my ear.

For the first time in months, I felt it: calm. Safe.

The kind of safety I had always avoided because I was scared I didn't deserve it.

A Quiet Emotional Milestone

We found a little diner tucked between two trees on a back road.

We sat in a booth, shared fries, laughed at dumb jokes, and just... existed.

I realized that love didn't always have to be a war.

It could be this quiet, soft thing.

It could be laughter and hand-holding and stolen glances.

"I can't believe this," I said, smiling, "I feel... normal. Not anxious. Not paranoid."

He reached across, brushing my hand.

"You've earned this calm. You've been fighting so hard, not just for us, but for yourself."

A Minor Conflict

Then my phone buzzed.

A comment from an old "friend," the one who used to encourage my worst instincts:

"I hope you're not letting him walk all over you like every other guy."

I felt my chest tighten.

The familiar panic threatened to pull me under: Say something sharp. Protect yourself. Push him away.

But I paused. Took a deep breath.

ME (thinking):

"No. I'm not her anymore."

Instead of reacting, I closed the app, turned to him, and said:

"Someone from my past tried to stir trouble. I'm ignoring it."

He smiled, proud but relieved:

"That's progress. You didn't let it ruin this moment."

Confronting the Past

Later that night, I texted her directly.

"I don't need your opinions or advice anymore. I'm not the person you used to know, and I'm choosing to protect my peace."

No explanations. No debates. Just boundaries.

When I hit send, a weight lifted.

For the first time, I realized: I could step out of old cycles, protect myself, and still be capable of love.

"The old voices still whisper, but this time I'm choosing calm over chaos, honesty over fear, and boundaries over sabotage."

Receiving Love, Owning Power

I woke up that morning with a strange lightness.

Not excitement. Not anxiety. Just... calm.

He leaned over, brushing a strand of hair from my face.

"Morning," he whispered.

Normally, I would have flinched, pulled back, or given a sarcastic smile to hide how vulnerable I felt.

But today, I didn't.

I leaned into him.

Breathed.

Felt his warmth without questioning his intentions.

Without plotting my defense.

For the first time, love didn't feel like a trap.

It felt... safe.

Quiet, Intimate Victory

We spent the morning talking softly, sipping coffee, and sharing dreams we'd never dared to voice.

I realized that love isn't just about giving. It's about receiving.

And I allowed myself to receive it fully.

"No games. No walls," I whispered.

He smiled, reading the unspoken admission: I'm here. I'm staying. I trust you.

That was victory enough.

A small, quiet one but monumental.

Confronting the Past

Later that day, I drove to see my mother. The one whose neglect and harsh words had taught me fear, doubt, and self-sabotage.

I had rehearsed this conversation for years.

I wasn't sure I'd have the courage.

But the lessons of love, boundaries, and self-trust had built something strong inside me.

"I need to tell you something," I said, calm but firm.

"You hurt me. You left me doubting myself, doubting love, and fearing the people who cared. I can't change the past, but I can choose my future. And I'm choosing me."

Her eyes widened.

She opened her mouth to respond, but I shook my head.

"No. Listen. I'm not asking for apology. I'm not asking for anything. I'm telling you: I am stepping into my power. And I won't let old wounds dictate who I am anymore."

I left her house feeling lighter than I had in decades.

I had received love at home, and now I had reclaimed my own voice from the source of my deepest pain.

"I've learned that true power isn't taking from others. It's letting love in, setting boundaries, and choosing yourself without guilt."

The Day I Chose Us

The morning sun spilled through the kitchen window, painting the room gold.

I brewed coffee, humming quietly, feeling... normal. Not tense, not guarded. Just present.

He walked in, stretching, smiling at me like he'd discovered a secret I hadn't known existed.

"Morning," he said.

"Morning," I replied, soft, steady.

No walls. No fear. No rehearsed defenses.

Planning a Future

Over breakfast, we talked about the future.

Not hypotheticals. Not conditional dreams. Real plans: a trip together, moving in, even talking about what kind of life we wanted to build.

I felt the old panic creep up... what if I mess this up? What if it all falls apart?

But I didn't retreat. I didn't sabotage.

I spoke freely, laughed easily, and listened to him with the same openness I'd demanded from myself for years.

This was a milestone: for the first time, we planned together, without fear steering the conversation.

Testing Growth

Later, I ran errands alone. Usually, a text from a friend could spark panic or doubt.

And today, of course, a message appeared:

"Be careful giving him all your trust. You know men always... blah blah."

Normally, I would have spiraled, called him in a panic, or argued with the friend.

Today, I paused. Breathed. And deleted the message without response.

I felt my heartbeat slow, my old instinct to defend or prove herself fading.

Standing Firm

When I saw the friend later, she tried again.

"You're really letting him get away with everything. Are you sure?"

I looked at her, calm but resolute.

"I'm sure. I've made my choice. This isn't about what you think. It's about what I need. And I'm not going to let old patterns control me anymore."

She blinked, surprised, then walked away.

And for the first time, I didn't feel guilty.

I didn't feel anxious.

I felt empowered.

"A milestone isn't just what you plan with love. It's the day you refuse to let fear, habit, or old voices dictate who you are or who you choose to be with."

Trust in Action

The day started ordinary enough, sunlight spilling through the windows, coffee brewing, a quiet hum of domesticity.

But something in the air felt different.

We were calmer. Safer. Connected.

I watched him across the kitchen, his hands wrapped around his mug, eyes soft and steady.

I realized I could look at him without fear.

Without walls. Without rehearsed defenses.

A Moment of Intimacy

Later, we sat on the couch, feet tucked under us, talking about the little things: favorite songs, childhood memories, silly habits.

I leaned into him, feeling his hand find mine, and I didn't pull away.

For the first time in years, I allowed myself to receive love fully, not just give it back in fear or preemptive defense.

He kissed my forehead, whispered,

"You're safe with me. You always have been."

And I believed him.

I didn't doubt. I didn't flinch.

I simply let it in.

The External Challenge

The calm didn't last long.

A phone call came, urgent news about a close family member.

Sudden, chaotic, emotionally charged.

My first instinct: panic. Withdraw. Self-sabotage.

But I caught myself. Took a breath. Looked at him.

"We handle this together," I said.

He nodded, and we sprang into action: coordinating calls, arranging help, checking in on details.

We communicated clearly, divided tasks, and leaned on each other.

The chaos tested our patience, our trust, our ability to stay grounded.

And for the first time, I realized: we weren't just surviving together.

We were functioning as a team.

Victory in Trust

That night, exhausted but connected, we sat side by side in silence.

No words were needed.

I rested my head on his shoulder, his arm around me, and felt the truth in my chest:

We had faced the storm together.

And it hadn't broken us.

"Love isn't proven in perfect moments. It's proven in how you weather chaos together, hand in hand, without fear."

Building Us

We sat on the small balcony of our apartment, the city lights twinkling below, a soft breeze carrying the quiet hum of life.

For the first time, I felt truly settled.

Not because everything was perfect but because we were facing the future together.

Planning the Future

"I've been thinking," he said, voice low but steady.

"What if we finally move in together? Take the next step?"

My chest fluttered. My old instincts whispered: Pull away. Wait. Protect yourself.

But I didn't. I looked at him and felt only trust.

"Yes," I said, softly but firmly.

"Yes, let's do it. Together."

We spent the next hour laughing, planning, imagining:

Furniture, routines, favorite meals, even how we'd handle the little disagreements without fear or overreaction.

It wasn't just planning logistics.

It was planning a life together, built on honesty, boundaries, and love we'd fought to preserve.

The Intimate Milestone

Later, we sat on the couch, wrapped in blankets, the soft glow of the lamp illuminating his face.

I leaned against him, resting my head on his chest, and felt the steady rise and fall of his breathing.

"I love this," I whispered.

"Not the moving or the planning... this. Being here, feeling safe, feeling loved."

He kissed the top of my head.

"I've always loved this. I've just been waiting for you to believe it too."

And in that moment, I finally did.

I let myself fully receive love, not guarded by fear or shaped by trauma.

I let myself be happy.

Truly happy.

We stayed like that for a long while, simply existing in our closeness.

No drama. No walls. No ghosts of the past.

Just us, fully present, fully committed, and fully in love.

"Love isn't just surviving each other's fears. It's choosing to build a future together, unafraid, unguarded, and fully present in the moment."

Quiet Anchors

It was late evening, the city quiet beneath the hum of streetlights.

We sat on the balcony, wrapped in a single blanket, shoulders touching, feet dangling over the edge.

No words at first. Just presence.

Just breathing together.

Just the feeling of being safe in each other's space.

The Intimacy

He reached over and traced the back of my hand with his thumb.

A simple gesture but it carried everything: patience, trust, devotion.

"I've never felt like this before," I whispered.

"Like... I can just be me. Without fear. Without hiding. Without planning my next move to protect myself."

He turned toward me, his face soft.

"You've always been enough. You just needed to see it too."

I smiled against his chest.

And for the first time, I believed it fully.

No walls. No hesitation. No ghosts.

Bond Cemented

We talked quietly after that. About our day, about silly memories, about dreams we hadn't dared share before.

Every word, every laugh, every brush of fingers over knuckles was a reminder:

We had built this. A love grounded in honesty, vulnerability, and choice.

It was quiet. Simple. Intimate.

But it was monumental.

Because in that moment, I realized:

Love doesn't have to be loud to be true.

It doesn't have to be perfect to be lasting.

It just has to be present.

And we were.

"True intimacy isn't fireworks or grand gestures. It's the quiet moments where you feel seen, safe, and fully loved."

4

The Prescription

Full circle the cost

Ty Brooks had never been inside a clinic like this before. White walls, bright fluorescent lights, and the faint antiseptic smell made his stomach twist. He fidgeted in the waiting room chair, glancing at the small television mounted in the corner, looping a cheerful ad about "managing pain responsibly."

When his name was called, he followed the nurse into Dr. Marcus Hale's office. Hale was in his mid-forties, neatly dressed, calm, but there was something in his eyes that suggested he'd seen more pain than he cared to admit.

"Ty Brooks?" Hale asked, glancing at the chart. "I hear you hurt your shoulder pretty badly. How's the pain?"

"Uh... bad," Ty said, shrugging. "Hurts all the time."

Hale nodded, making notes. "We'll start you on something that helps. Just follow the instructions exactly, okay?"

He pressed a small prescription pad across the desk. The handwriting was neat, professional. Beneath it, the name of a powerful opioid: Oxyzene.

Hale's office phone buzzed briefly, an alert from Liam Ward, the pharma rep who kept him "incentivized."

"Tier three bonus activated. Teens under 18 showing high engagement. Keep refills compliant."

Hale ignored it, rationalizing: I'm just doing my job. Managing pain. Helping kids.

But the truth was clear: every prescription, every refill, every "manageable pain" patient fed the empire built by Vivian Roth and her directors. An empire designed to profit from dependency.

Ty stepped outside into the crisp afternoon, pills safely tucked in his backpack. His mother, Elena Cruz, waited in the car.

"You got the prescription?" she asked.

Ty nodded, sliding the bag across the seat. "The doctor said it'll help."

Elena studied him. Something felt off... not just the pain, but the way he hesitated, like he didn't entirely trust the medicine, and neither did she.

Back in the clinic, Nurse Kelly reviewed patient charts for the day. She noticed Ty's file flagged unusually early.

Observation: Teen male, prescription initiation, high dependency risk.

She frowned. Hale signed the refill without hesitation. Kelly scribbled a note in her personal log, a quiet alarm she wasn't sure anyone would hear.

At a nearby café, Liam Ward reviewed regional metrics on his tablet. Teens like Ty, early refill compliance, high engagement. Every number a potential bonus.

He smirked. "Field operatives are responding well. This is going to be a big quarter," he muttered to himself.

Every prescription was a calculated step in a hierarchy designed for profit:

- Vivian Roth: Kingpin, remote control of expansion
- Directors: Executing strategy and quotas
- Enforcers: Incentivizing doctors
- Field Operatives: Administering prescriptions
- Patients like Ty: The unwitting foundation of the machine

Ty took the first pill that night. Relief flooded through him... warm, euphoric, dangerous.

Elena kissed his forehead. "Rest, honey. It'll help."

He nodded, eyes heavy. But beneath the temporary comfort, a subtle voice whispered in his mind: This is only the beginning.

The prescription was more than medicine. It was the first link in a chain he wouldn't easily escape.

Death

Helena Briggs tapped the touchpad, pulling up the quarterly data. Charts exploded onto the wall: rising profits, rising prescription rates, rising dependency masked as "customer retention."

"Adult market is plateauing," she said. "We need new consumers with longer dependency potential."

Roger Kane added, "Teens are responding well to recovery narratives, anxiety management campaigns, and sports injury outreach."

Sports injury. Two harmless words masking the start of a slow death spiral.

Vivian didn't flinch. "Risk?"

Helena: "Media backlash... manageable with mental health messaging. Parental pushback, minimal. If we frame it as healing."

Roger: "Dependency rates in test regions already exceeding projection curves. They're staying on. They're hooked early."

A moment of silence. Vivian raised one eyebrow.

"Projected annual revenue if we fully throttle teen expansion?" she asked, voice soft as a surgical blade.

Liam Ward answered, smiling: "Two-point-eight billion increase minimum."

Vivian leaned back slowly. She didn't smile. She didn't need to. When she finally spoke, the words were quiet, measured, surgical:

"Extend Phase II to all teen-approved regions. I want new prescription leads, influencer partnerships with recovery-facing subjects, and sports rehab referral funnels. Incentivize field operatives accordingly."

She paused. The room didn't breathe.

"Dependency is retention. Retention is revenue."

Silence bloomed. Morality died.

She tapped the table once, a kingpin's gunshot.

"Phase II is greenlit."

No applause. Just a flurry of silent nods, obedient soldiers following their queen into war.

As the meeting progressed, Helena briefed the table on "Narrative Engineering." A sanitized way to say they would emotionally manipulate struggling teens.

Key internal strategy points flashed across the display:

- "Pain is isolation — we provide connection."
- "Frame Oxyzene as emotional relief, not addiction risk."
- "Use language like 'belonging,' 'hope,' 'relief' to reduce fear."
- "Provide free 'wellness events' hosted by sponsored doctors."

Each bullet point was a loaded syringe aimed at the young and unaware.

Roger added casually, "We'll need tighter control over field operatives. Some doctors hesitate."

Vivian's expression hardened. "Then pressure them. Compliance or displacement."

Liam Ward nodded. A loyal enforcer, ready to whisper, threaten, or bonus as needed.

Vivian stood alone in the boardroom as others filed out. She looked out at the city, millions of people going about their lives, unaware their children had just been entered into a high-profit death funnel.

She whispered, almost to herself, "Customers for life."

Then she turned away, already on her way to her next call with an investor group that would soon toast unseen casualties with champagne.

Phone in hand, Liam began sending "motivation" to compliant doctors like Dr. Marcus Hale.

"Big quarter ahead. Refill momentum expected. Teens recovering need emotional continuity. Don't let them fall off."

He also sent a separate message to field reps:

"New bonuses rolling for under-18 Oxyzene patients. Loyalty pays."

Back at home, Ty popped his second pill. The warmth rushed in.

He didn't know he had just become a number on Vivian Roth's wall.

The greenlight had already claimed its first soldiers.

He exhaled, unaware he was now enlisted in a war he never chose.

White Coat Blood Money

The fluorescent lights buzzed low and steady in Dr. Marcus Hale's clinic, casting everything in a sterile white glow. It was late afternoon, but the sun outside had long disappeared behind a gray curtain of clouds. The faint hum of air conditioning was the only sound, except for the occasional ping of Hale's laptop... a constant reminder that his life was now measured in metrics.

Hale sat at his desk, hands clasped, staring at the prescription dashboard. He scrolled through patient after patient, and then Ty Brooks's name appeared again. Another refill request. He exhaled slowly. It was just a pill, he told himself. Just another dose of relief for a kid who had a hurt knee. No harm, no foul.

A notification popped up from Lucas Ward, the regional pharmaceutical representative, the enforcer behind the numbers.

"Excellent numbers this week, Doc. Keep them coming. High engagement in your 15–18 bracket. Don't let the kids fall off."

Hale's hand hovered over the refill button. He could feel a pulse of guilt that was almost tangible, like a vein thumping in his temple. He clicked. The order processed. Another statistic added to the empire. Another life nudged closer to dependency.

The moral erosion wasn't dramatic. It was subtle. Each click, each signature, each reassurance to himself that he was helping... it built a lattice of lies so tight he could barely see the truth.

The Enforcer Arrives

Downstairs, in a dimly lit private bar, Liam Ward tapped his fingers on a polished walnut table. He had the charm of a man who could sell happiness to the hopeless, but underneath the tailored suit and practiced smile, he carried a weapon more powerful than a gun: fear disguised as professionalism.

"Some doctors hesitate," he muttered to a junior rep. "Numbers are lagging. We need compliance." He leaned back, sipping his scotch. "Gentle pressure, subtle nudges. Incentives first, consequences second but consequences are waiting."

He thought of Dr. Hale. Hale was good at his job, but he wasn't bulletproof. The boy's conscience could be exploited. Ward grinned faintly. A reluctant soldier is still a soldier.

The Conscience of a Nurse

Nurse Kelly walked the halls of Hale's clinic, her shoes soft against the tile. She had seen patterns forming. Three teenage boys, same prescription, same return visits. Ty among them. Something in her chest tightened when she noticed how quiet he had become, how his hands shook ever so slightly as he waited for the nurse to hand him the pills.

She approached Hale quietly. "Marcus... maybe we should flag these cases? Early intervention, just in case?"

Hale gave a tight smile, not meeting her eyes. "Kelly... it's manageable. They're being monitored. Nothing to worry about."

But she noticed Lucas Ward laughing in the staff breakroom, joking about how "kids hooked on feeling good" were the easiest to maintain. Kelly's stomach turned. She began keeping her own notes, documenting quietly. Every chart, every refill, every symptom became a piece of a puzzle she couldn't yet articulate.

Ty's Quiet Transformation

At home, Ty sat on the edge of his bed, the second pill glinting in the soft light of his desk lamp. He flexed his knee experimentally, testing the limits of his pain. It was fine, really. He didn't need the pill physically but something in his chest demanded it.

He swallowed it anyway. The warmth rolled through him, a slow release that whispered, this is better than before. His thoughts slowed. The game tomorrow seemed less intimidating. Homework seemed lighter. The world, for the first time in months, felt like a place he could navigate.

Unseen and unheard, the pill planted a seed. One that would grow quietly but relentlessly.

Corporate Shadows

In a penthouse somewhere, Vivian Roth reviewed the week's metrics. Phase II was performing ahead of schedule. Teen engagement in pilot regions was surpassing expectations. Each statistic represented a life unknowingly entering her empire, a body quietly reshaped to serve her bottom line.

She didn't care about the moral implications. Metrics were truth. Numbers didn't cry. Numbers didn't bleed. Humans did.

Her phone buzzed. Liam Ward reporting in. "All field operatives aligned. Compliance improving. Doctors responding well."

"Good," she said. Leaning back, she studied the skyline. "Keep the pipeline steady. Phase II is just the beginning."

The First Ripples of Consequence

Back in his room, Ty's eyelids grew heavy. He felt a brief flicker of guilt, a whisper that he shouldn't rely on this. But the warmth, the comfort, drowned it. He didn't yet realize that every pill, every refill, every promise of relief was wiring him deeper into the system.

In that moment, he was blissfully unaware he was now a player in a corporate war. A pawn in a hierarchy that stretched from the gleaming towers of Roth Global Pharmaceuticals down to the fluorescent-lit clinics of suburban streets.

Dr. Hale sat at his desk, staring blankly at the screen, his hand trembling slightly. Nurse Kelly's quiet notes awaited the day she would expose the truth. Lucas Ward checked his tablet again, the enforcer's grin growing. Vivian Roth plotted her next expansion. And Ty... Ty had just taken his first real step down a road he didn't yet see, but could never turn back from.

The white coats and the blood money were in motion. The game had begun.

"The Craving"

The first taste of relief had been subtle, almost innocent. Ty Brooks felt it again that night, lying on his bed, the pill pressed between his fingers. This time, it wasn't just his knee that hurt. It was the quiet emptiness in his chest, the unease he didn't yet have words for. The pill melted like a secret against his tongue, and warmth spread through him, a slow, seductive comfort that whispered, "You're okay now."

Outside, the streetlights flickered against the quiet suburban street. Inside, the world felt smaller, simpler, safer. But that safety was an illusion, a carefully constructed lie, and Ty couldn't see it yet.

Hale sat alone in his office, the clinic dark around him. He stared at the patient dashboard, Ty's name glowing like a beacon. Each refill request, each new symptom report, each subtle change in the teenagers' behavior weighed on him like an invisible weight.

He ran a hand through his hair. I'm helping them, I swear... Yet, the numbers told another story. Teen prescriptions were climbing. Dependency signs were increasing. The field reps celebrated compliance and loyalty bonuses while he quietly calculated the cost in human terms.

Hale had always believed in doing the right thing. Now, he was beginning to understand: in this game, right and wrong were determined by revenue, not morality.

Across town, Liam Ward met with other field operatives in a quiet café. Laptops open, spreadsheets glowing, regional metrics laid bare. Ward didn't raise his voice. He didn't need to. Authority dripped from his suit sleeves like oil.

"Some of you are slipping," he said, tapping the screen. "Compliance is not optional. Incentives are real. Consequences are real. Understand the difference."

He walked the room, his gaze sharp and unyielding. A doctor had tried to resist a refill schedule last week. Ward ensured it never happened again. This was the subtle violence of the corporate enforcer: data-driven, measured, merciless.

Nurse Kelly noticed Ty's behavior shifting. He arrived earlier than usual, restless, hands shaking slightly as he handed over his pill bottle. She saw the flicker of dependence forming in his eyes, a quiet hunger he didn't yet recognize.

She pulled Hale aside. "Marcus... something is happening. Ty's different. The other kids too. The pattern... look at it."

Hale shook his head, unwilling to fully confront the reality. "Kelly, we're following protocol. We monitor them. That's all we can do."

Kelly frowned, frustration mounting. She had always trusted the system to protect patients. Now she realized the system was feeding them into the fire.

Ty's second week on Oxyzene was a slow, imperceptible transformation. Tasks he once tolerated became easier. Anxiety he never knew how to name faded like smoke. Homework was lighter. Conversations smoother. But the relief was addictive not because of physical pain, but because it rewired his emotional baseline.

He didn't crave the pill consciously. He craved the feeling of normalcy it gave him. One pill became a ritual. One pill became a tether to an invisible safety net.

In Roth Global's gleaming tower, Vivian Roth reviewed the weekly expansion reports. Teen engagement metrics were climbing faster than anticipated. The numbers were perfect. Every metric represented a young life subtly altered, a dependency forming, a profit secured.

She didn't think of them as people. They were nodes in a machine, predictable and malleable.

Her phone buzzed. Liam Ward's report: field operatives had enforced the refill quotas. Doctors were aligned. Metrics stable.

Vivian smiled faintly. "Good. Keep the current velocity. Phase II is solidifying."

Ty lay in bed that night, staring at the ceiling, fingers resting on the empty pill bottle. He felt a craving he didn't fully understand yet... not pain, not desire, just a whisper of longing for the calm, the safety, the control the pill offered.

Across the city, Hale sat in his office, guilt gnawing at him but buried beneath the weight of responsibility. Nurse Kelly documented quietly, building her record of what was happening. Liam Ward prepared his next round of field compliance, and Vivian Roth already planned the next expansion phase.

The machine was humming. Lives were shifting. And no one at the top would ever touch the consequences they were creating except in numbers, charts, and spreadsheets.

Ty's journey had officially begun. The craving wasn't loud yet, but it was persistent. It was patient. And it would not be ignored.

The Numbers That Don't Cry

The room was quiet, almost violently so, the kind of quiet that made the fluorescent lights hum louder than they should. Marcus Hale sat at his desk, hands steepled, eyes scanning the spreadsheet glowing on his laptop. Each row, each column, each number was a pulse of someone's life. Ty Brooks. Emma Santos. Javier Ruiz. Names like entries in a ledger, lives measured in dosage, frequency, refill compliance, risk scores.

Marcus breathed slowly. The numbers were perfect. Clean. Predictable. The bloodless arithmetic of addiction.

Ty Brooks, age 16, week 3: emotional baseline below expected, pill intake stable, dependency potential rising 12%.

He tapped the screen. Twelve percent. It was a fraction, a decimal, but it meant more than he wanted to admit. He saw the warmth of the pill in Ty's hand, the subtle glow of relief in his eyes, the quiet tether forming that neither mother nor nurse could yet detect. The numbers didn't cry. They didn't gasp. They didn't plead. They simply existed... silent testimony of control.

Exhibit A – The Pattern Report

Marcus's mind mapped the sequence. Each teen was a line chart. Peaks of relief. Valleys of withdrawal. His notes scrawled on a sticky pad: "Week 4 spike in emotional dependency, correlate with family absence and sport pressures. Watch for refill anxiety."

He shook his head. The cold logic was easier. Easier than feeling the weight of guilt pressing against his chest, the subtle horror of watching a young boy become tethered to a synthetic calm. He rationalized. We're managing pain. We're providing relief. This is clinical.

Yet every so often, a flash of something raw crept in. Ty's smile after practice, the way he laughed with Elena Cruz, unaware of the calculus surrounding him. Marcus looked away, squinting at the chart. Numbers didn't laugh. Numbers didn't cry. Numbers were merciless.

Exhibit B – Present Tension

Ty sat on the edge of his bed, fingers resting on the empty bottle. One pill gone. One missed moment of relief. The craving buzzed in his chest like static. His mind traced the pattern: last week, two pills brought calm, warmth, focus. Tonight, nothing. Anxiety unfurled quietly, insidious. He wanted, needed, feared.

Marcus watched, not in the room, but in his mind. Each reaction a data point. Heart rate increases. Behavioral shifts. Restlessness measured against his own moral dashboard. Marcus did not intervene. He was a silent observer, tallying outcomes, recording compliance, noting dependency.

Ty's eyes shifted to the ceiling. Just one. A whisper. Just enough to feel normal. The silence pressed in, punctuated by the soft hum of the lamp. The numbers never judged. They never warned.

Exhibit C – Emotional Market Collapse

Somewhere in a gleaming tower, Vivian Roth poured over regional reports. Teen engagement: 73%. Retention: 88%. Compliance: 92%. Every figure a testament to control. A profit built on the quiet desperation of bodies and minds.

Her phone buzzed. Liam Ward's message: "Phase II expansion ahead of projection. Teens responding as predicted. Doctors fully compliant."

She smiled, cold and sharp. Phase II was proof of concept. Addiction normalized. Metrics rising. Profit undeniable. Human cost invisible. Numbers didn't cry. Numbers didn't scream. Numbers were the language of empire.

Meanwhile, Marcus documented Ty's subtle shift: slight restlessness, obsessive checking of the bottle, moments of impatience with friends, increased irritability. Each observation entered into his log like a forensic report. Clinical. Cold. Precise.

Nurse Kelly had started compiling her own records, comparing patient behavior against prescription logs. The discrepancy was glaring. Ty and others were exhibiting signs that defied "normal recovery" metrics. She typed notes, careful, quiet. She knew that when the record hit the right eyes, consequences would follow.

Cause of Death – Pending

Ty's bedroom smelled faintly of sweat and desperation. He held the bottle, turned it in his hands, fingers tracing the label. His lips pressed lightly against the cap as though seeking comfort. The craving was not loud.

It was quiet, patient, persistent. It had been creeping in for weeks, invisible to everyone but Marcus and Kelly.

Marcus exhaled. He did not intervene. He could not intervene. Intervention would disrupt the experiment. Intervention would skew the data. Intervention might expose the truth he was silently recording: the ease with which a life could be catalogued, predicted, and manipulated.

The pill was temptation, anchor, whisper of normalcy. Ty's hand hovered. Marcus watched, noting heart rate fluctuation, micro expressions, micro hesitation. Kelly would record the same when she returned tomorrow.

Vivian Roth would note the aggregate numbers in her next board meeting. Phase II metrics: flawless.

And still, no one cried.

The Quiet Apocalypse

The room was still. Numbers glowed cold on screens. Adolescents lay in beds, unaware of the architecture of control forming around them. Doctors rationalized. Nurses documented. Reps enforced. Executives planned.

The machine hummed. Data was law. Compliance was devotion. Dependency was profit.

Ty swallowed the pill. The warmth spread. He closed his eyes, unaware that he had just joined an empire measured in decimals and percentages.

Marcus typed a note: "Patient shows early signs of emotional reliance. Continue monitoring. No intervention unless severe."

He leaned back, eyes tired, hollow, aware that every calculation, every number, every chart represented a human being he could no longer fully see.

Numbers didn't cry. But in their silence, the truth screamed.

Breaking Points

The first cracks always come quietly. A misstep, a skipped pill, a delayed refill. Small tremors in a system designed to seem unshakable. But for Ty Brooks, the tremor became a quake.

He woke that morning with his chest tight, hands clammy, stomach twisting in a knot he couldn't name. The pill he usually took before breakfast was gone. He pawed through the bottle, only to find emptiness. Panic rose like smoke, filling every thought, spreading faster than his rational mind could contain. I need it. I need it. I need it.

Across town, Dr. Marcus Hale reviewed Ty's log, already flagged for early warning signs. He frowned, noticing patterns he had once ignored. Missed doses, increased irritability, subtle obsessive behaviors. Each number now felt heavier, more urgent. He couldn't save Ty, not really but he could watch, record, calculate. Observation had become his shield and his prison.

Marcus pressed his hands against his desk, eyes fixed on the glowing screen. His mind raced. Every intervention he had withheld now screamed in his head. He remembered the moment he clicked approve refill the first time, the rationalization, the silent permission he had given himself.

Where did this start? he asked silently. And how many kids have already fallen through the cracks?

He couldn't admit it aloud. Not to anyone. Not to Nurse Kelly, who had been quietly documenting concerns, or to Lucas Ward, who celebrated compliance with the glee of someone counting gold. This was bigger than him, bigger than morality. It was a machine, and he had become a cog.

Kelly had been watching Ty's subtle changes with growing alarm. She saw the jitter in his fingers, the shallow inhale, the way his gaze darted toward the bottle the moment he entered the clinic. Her notebook was full of observations, charts, and notes... evidence, meticulous and uncompromising.

She approached Marcus quietly. "Marcus, it's worse than I thought. Ty's not alone. The pattern is repeating across other patients. We can't ignore this anymore."

Marcus shook his head, voice low. "Kelly... intervention risks exposure. Compliance audits, corporate oversight... it's not just numbers. It's insurance, legal, my license... You know that."

She leaned in, voice sharp. "And what about their lives? Do we have to wait until one of them breaks completely before we act?"

He looked at her, realizing he had already crossed a line, the point of no return. Words failed him. Numbers, however, didn't. They never failed.

By mid-afternoon, Ty could no longer mask the craving. His focus at school shattered. The warmth and calm he associated with the pill had become a necessity, not a comfort. Thoughts looped: Just one. Just enough. One small dose.

The withdrawal tremors were subtle at first... a quiver in the hands, tension in the jaw but they escalated. Anxiety churned, panic teased the edges of control. Each moment he waited felt infinite, stretching minutes into hours.

He couldn't concentrate. He couldn't eat. He couldn't convince himself that he was safe without it. The numbers Marcus recorded earlier flashed in his mind, not as figures, but as predictions of his own inevitable spiral.

Meanwhile, Liam Ward moved methodically, ensuring every doctor remained compliant. He wasn't violent, not in the traditional sense. His enforcement was quiet, relentless, surgical. A text, a polite reminder, a hint of corporate consequences, nothing overt. But every doctor knew the cost of defiance, even if it was unspoken.

He called Marcus. "The refill quotas are slipping. I need assurance that your patients remain on track. Ty Brooks, for example, his adherence is critical to regional metrics. Are we aligned?"

Marcus hesitated. "Yes... yes, we're aligned."

Liam's eyes narrowed, voice calm but lethal in its precision. "Good. Keep it that way. Numbers don't wait."

Vivian Roth didn't care about the human tremors beneath her empire. Phase II metrics were slightly off, and the board wanted explanations. Her team presented graphs, charts, compliance tables. She scanned them, eyes cold, calculating, untouchable.

She smiled faintly. "Performance is steady. Adjust incentives. Re-engage non-compliant patients. And make sure all physicians are aware, numbers are sacred. Human error is irrelevant if metrics are met."

Her tone carried no empathy. Only profit. Only precision. Only survival of the system.

Ty's afternoon ended in quiet desperation. He sat in his room, tears threatening, fingers trembling. One thought dominated: I can't feel normal without it. The craving was now a roaring undercurrent, subtle at first, but undeniable.

Marcus sat at his desk across town, watching the logs, noting the escalation. He realized, painfully, that Ty had passed a threshold. The system he had helped manage had created its own gravity, pulling children into dependency with mathematical inevitability.

Kelly stood at the edge of Marcus' office door, notebook in hand, exhaled sharply, and said, "We have to do something before someone breaks completely. Before the numbers stop just being numbers and start being lives."

Marcus stared at her. The spreadsheets. The numbers. The patterns. For the first time, he saw the human faces behind the decimals. Faces he had almost forgotten existed.

The clinic remained eerily quiet as night approached. Ty's bedroom light flickered, shadows trembling on the walls. Marcus leaned back, knowing the next few hours would define trajectories: addiction versus intervention, morality versus compliance, humanity versus empire.

Liam Ward's call had ended. Vivian Roth's boardroom had adjourned. Nurse Kelly's notebook brimmed with silent warnings. And somewhere in the suburban night, Ty's trembling hands hovered over the pill bottle, unsure if he could wait or if the numbers had already decided for him.

Breaking points had been reached. Lines had been crossed. And nothing, neither authority, conscience, nor corporate empire would ever look the same again.

Collateral Damage

The first sign came quietly... a missed call from Ty's mother. Then another. His phone vibrated endlessly, the messages blurring into a haze of worry and confusion. At school, he was irritable, distracted, eyes darting toward his empty bottle, a tether that had once offered comfort now only whispered threat.

Marcus Hale noticed the spike in behavioral anomalies immediately. His dashboard flagged Ty as "critical risk," a term clinical and cold, yet packed with human consequence. It wasn't just Ty. Others were showing signs: absenteeism, mood swings, arguments, accidents. The data points multiplied, each one a tiny body crashing into the harsh machinery of numbers and compliance.

Kelly stood in the clinic, reviewing her notes. She had spent hours cross-referencing charts with observed behavior. Patterns were emerging, frightening in their clarity. One teen fell behind on homework, another skipped practice, yet another was suddenly hyper-focused, jittery, volatile. The pills had become a silent puppet master.

She looked at Marcus. "It's not just Ty. It's the others. They're all starting to crumble. We can't pretend this is manageable anymore."

Marcus rubbed his temples. "I know. I see it. But what can we do? Every step we take feels like a step into a storm we can't control."

Kelly slammed her notebook down. "Then maybe we start with one. One before the storm consumes them all."

Liam Ward visited the clinic that afternoon. His presence was precise, almost surgical. He didn't raise his voice. He didn't need to. The aura of authority alone was enough to bend behavior.

"Compliance is slipping," he said. "Metrics must remain intact. Ty Brooks, keep him within range. Other patients, same. You know the consequences of deviation. I don't like repeating myself."

Marcus nodded, silent. He knew that deviation didn't just threaten profit. It threatened careers. And in this corporate cartel, careers and lives were fungible, expendable, replaceable.

Ty's afternoon dissolved into chaos. His hands shook as he tried to focus on homework, the warmth of a normal day unreachable. Anxiety and craving battled violently inside him. Thoughts looped: I need it. I need it. I can't wait.

He lashed out at friends. Misunderstood their concern. Pushed people away. Each reaction a reflection of the subtle chains forming around him. Chains forged in a clinic, reinforced by numbers, overseen by executives.

He didn't know yet that he was the center of an empire of control. That his body, his mind, his cravings, were now catalogued, monitored, and exploited.

At home, Ty's mother sensed the shift. She watched her son, noticed the tremors, the distracted glances, the irritability. She didn't know why, didn't understand the mechanisms, didn't know the quiet empire building around her child.

Calls to the doctor went unanswered. Texts were polite but distant. Ty's father, absent most days, shrugged off concern with corporate-like efficiency. The family, unaware, was beginning to fracture. Collateral damage was not just a term. It was life.

Marcus watched the dashboard, noted each spike, each anomaly, each deviation. Each number screamed consequences he could no longer ignore. One patient had fainted from withdrawal. Another had a minor accident. Another had a panic attack in school. All numbers, precise, clean, factual yet screaming with human pain he had helped enable.

He closed the laptop. Staring at the ceiling, he realized he was complicit. Every click, every approval, every rationalization had fed this machine. And now it was eating children, one by one.

Vivian Roth's office overlooked the city, skyline glittering like controlled chaos. Her phone buzzed. Field reports arrived. Metrics slightly off. Minor anomalies. Not alarming. Not enough to disrupt profits. Not enough to matter.

She sipped her espresso. "Adjust marketing. Increase compliance outreach. Make sure the doctors feel the incentives. The numbers must remain intact."

Lives, collapse, panic, craving. Irrelevant. Numbers never cry. Metrics never break. Profit never hesitates. Humanity is incidental.

Ty sat on his bed that night, staring at the empty bottle. Tears rolled silently down his cheeks. Craving and despair battled inside him. Outside, the suburban street was quiet, unaware of the storm building inside homes, schools, and clinics.

Marcus sat across town, heart heavy, staring at the dashboard. Every number now screamed guilt. Every metric whispered consequences. He realized too late that he had been cataloguing lives, not helping them.

Kelly compiled her final notes for the day, knowing intervention was necessary. She had the evidence, the observations, the documentation. But would it matter against the machine? Against Liam Ward's enforcements? Against Vivian Roth's empire?

Breaking points had been reached. Collateral damage was no longer abstract. It had names, faces, trembling hands, hollow eyes. And no one corporate, medical, or otherwise was prepared for the storm their system had set in motion.

The Fall of Innocence

The morning light hit Ty's bedroom window like a cold interrogation lamp. He lay in bed, staring at the ceiling, hands shaking, stomach twisting. The bottle was empty. The calm, the warmth, the comfort he had relied on was gone, and with it, a fragile illusion of control.

Every shadow in the room seemed to mock him. Every tick of the clock measured the seconds of longing and panic. He tried to breathe, tried to distract himself with homework, music, scrolling through social media but the craving was insistent, insidious, and unforgiving.

I need it. I need it. I can't be normal without it.

Marcus Hale sat at his desk, staring at Ty's latest logs, heart rate spikes, missed doses, and behavioral anomalies. He could no longer hide behind spreadsheets and numbers. The evidence was raw, human, undeniable.

He pushed his chair back and walked to the phone. Calling Ty's mother was necessary, but he hesitated, knowing the truth would terrify her. Yet silence felt like complicity. The line rang, and her voice answered, worried, tired, unaware of the depth of the storm surrounding her child.

"Mrs. Brooks," he began carefully, "I... I think Ty needs help beyond the clinic. He's showing signs of serious dependence. I believe intervention is urgent."

There was a pause. Then a shaky, "I. I didn't realize it was this bad."

Marcus exhaled slowly. It was worse than she knew. Worse than even he could quantify. Numbers could track doses, heart rate, behavior but not despair, panic, or the slow unraveling of innocence.

Kelly entered Marcus' office, notebook in hand, determination flashing in her eyes. "We can't wait for numbers to adjust. The system is failing them. All of them."

Marcus rubbed his temples. "And what do you suggest?"

"Immediate intervention. Home visits. Counseling. Therapy. Remove them from the system's constant pressure. Stop the pipeline while we still can."

He shook his head, conflicted. "Do you know how big this is? We're talking corporate oversight, audits, compliance... I can't just walk away from my license, my career. You know that."

Kelly leaned forward, voice fierce. "And do you know how big the damage is? Look at Ty. Look at these kids. Careers don't bleed. Innocence does."

By afternoon, Ty could no longer contain the panic. He ransacked his backpack, drawers, pockets... anywhere that might contain a pill. Nothing. The craving burned hotter, a fire spreading through his chest. Tears blurred his vision, fists clenched, teeth gritted.

He screamed into the empty room, a sound raw and animalistic. Pain without relief. Craving without comfort. Fear without support. The fall of innocence was complete, quiet, and relentless.

Meanwhile, in the gleaming towers of Roth Global, the world continued in its cold, measured rhythm. Vivian Roth reviewed regional reports, noting slight deviations. Teen engagement down 3%, retention steady, compliance 90%. The numbers didn't worry her.

"Adjust the field reps," she instructed. "Metrics must remain intact. Deviations must be corrected. Lives are irrelevant as long as numbers stabilize."

Liam Ward nodded, the enforcer's calm smile never flickering. He would ensure compliance. He would ensure the numbers never faltered. He would not see the faces, the panic, the trembling hands. That was not his problem. That was not the system.

Marcus returned to Ty's dashboard, every metric flashing like warning lights he could no longer ignore. His moral equilibrium had collapsed. Numbers didn't scream, but he felt their echoes in the reality they represented. Every spike, every deviation, every sign of craving was a human life fraying at the edges.

Kelly handed him a folder. Charts. Logs. Notes. Observations. All pointing to the same truth: intervention wasn't just necessary. It was urgent.

He looked at her, silent, realizing that the system had failed. And that in failing, it had destroyed the fragile innocence of the children it claimed to help.

Ty curled on his bed, exhausted, sobbing silently. His mind raced: I can't be normal. I can't. Everything feels wrong. Nothing feels right. I just need... something...

The door opened. It was his mother. She knelt beside him, holding out her hands, trying to reach across the chasm he felt inside.

Marcus and Kelly watched from the doorway, both aware that the intervention would only succeed if human connection outweighed the system's machine. The numbers could guide, predict, warn but only love, presence, and action could stop the fall.

Ty looked up, eyes wide, desperate. For the first time, he wasn't alone in the numbers. He wasn't just a data point, a metric, a statistic. He was a child being pulled back from the edge.

Intervention and Reckoning

The morning sun felt heavy, almost oppressive, spilling gold light across Ty's room. He sat on the edge of his bed, hands clenched, the empty pill bottle a silent monument to the past weeks of quiet erosion. His mother hovered nearby, tentative, afraid, knowing she was too late and too early at once.

The door opened quietly behind her. Nurse Kelly stepped in, notebook clutched tightly, her eyes sharp with determination. Marcus followed, weary but resolute. They were here not as clinicians, not as enforcers, but as human beings finally confronting what the numbers had always hinted at: the machine had failed, and it had taken its toll.

Ty looked up at them, panic flaring in his eyes, the craving a tangible, almost visible force pulsing through him.

Marcus knelt beside Ty, voice steady but soft. "Ty... we're going to help you. You're not alone in this. The system failed, but that doesn't mean you have to fail too."

Ty's breathing hitched. "I... I can't... I can't do it... I just need it..."

Kelly stepped forward. "No. You can do it. You've already survived more than you realize. We're going to guide you through this, but you have to fight with us not against us."

It wasn't persuasion. It was presence. It was human contact replacing the emptiness the pills had filled. For the first time in weeks, Ty felt an anchor beyond chemicals. Someone seeing him, someone caring, someone acting.

Meanwhile, miles away, Vivian Roth and Liam Ward reviewed regional compliance. Deviations had risen slightly, teen engagement slipping. Metrics were falling. The board demanded explanations.

"Bring the doctors back in line," Vivian said coolly. "Reinforce protocols. Ensure metrics are restored. Human error is irrelevant."

Liam nodded, calm but uncompromising. "They will comply. The numbers must recover."

They didn't see Ty. They didn't see the trembling hands, the hollow eyes, the family finally awake to the consequences of their empire. For them, the reckoning was in percentages and graphs, not hearts and futures.

Back at Ty's house, Marcus and Kelly guided him through a small ritual: deep breaths, gentle conversation, distraction techniques. The craving roared inside him like a storm, but it had a form, a shape, a channel now. Human guidance. Presence. Accountability.

Ty's mother held his hands. "We'll get through this. I promise."

Ty nodded weakly, tears mixing with the faint relief of feeling seen. For the first time, the machine's cold logic and corporate calculus met resistance... not in charts, not in audits, but in human action, empathy, and immediate intervention.

Other teens, other families, other nodes in the corporate system were beginning to feel the impact of intervention, subtle but significant. Marcus began mapping intervention strategies. Kelly coordinated outreach. Families were being educated, supported, empowered.

Ty's crisis was no longer just his. It was a wake-up call. The ripple spread outward, small, fragile, but undeniable. Even Liam Ward noticed anomalies in field compliance reports. Numbers, once predictable, began to wobble under the weight of human unpredictability.

Marcus sat alone later that evening, dashboard open, fingers tracing Ty's metrics, his heart heavy. The numbers had once been clear, precise, silent. Now they screamed consequences, warning lights that no spreadsheet could erase.

He realized the machine could be disrupted, that the human element... care, attention, moral courage was stronger than the charts, stronger than the enforcement, stronger than the cold logic of corporate greed. But the cost had been high. Too many kids had already been affected. Too many families had begun to fracture.

Ty lay in bed that night, exhausted, trembling, yet calmer. The craving hadn't disappeared, but it had been acknowledged, faced, guided. Marcus and Kelly watched quietly from the doorway, knowing this was the first night he had slept without chemical sedation, without the machine's influence dictating his emotions.

It was small. It was fragile. But it was real.

Outside, the corporate empire hummed, unaware, unfeeling. Inside, human connection had begun to reclaim its power, threading through the cracks of a machine built to ignore it.

Aftermath and Accountability

The morning was heavy with the scent of rain, wet asphalt bleeding into the sterile air of the clinic. Ty sat quietly, knees pulled to his chest, the trembling that had plagued him now faint, almost manageable. The pills were gone... not stolen, not forgotten, but removed, replaced with guidance, presence, and structure. The craving still hummed, low and persistent, but no longer an uncontrollable force.

Marcus Hale watched from across the room, exhaustion etched into his face. He had spent sleepless nights reviewing charts, observing patterns, tracking anomalies, but tonight he felt something the numbers could not quantify: relief. Ty was here. Alive. Slowly reclaiming himself.

Across the city, Vivian Roth stood in her office overlooking the skyline, briefcase in hand, eyes scanning the latest compliance report. The numbers were off slightly, enough to disturb the illusion of perfection. Field reps had reported anomalies, patient retention dips, and a few internal whistleblowers had submitted troubling observations.

She frowned. Deviations like this were unacceptable. The machine could tolerate minor variance, but systematic flaws threatened control. She summoned Liam Ward.

"Metrics are failing in multiple regions," she said. "I want explanations. Full audits. Heads will roll if this isn't corrected."

Liam nodded, cool, precise, unflinching. "Understood. I'll ensure compliance is restored. And the physicians?"

"Remind them that metrics are non-negotiable," she said. "Human cost is irrelevant."

For Roth, accountability existed only in charts, percentages, and results. The faces of those affected didn't matter.

Back at the clinic, Marcus finally allowed himself to confront the personal toll of his complicity. He reviewed Ty's progress, noting subtle improvements, small victories, but also the collateral damage: other patients, other families, the ones who had already fallen too far.

Kelly watched him, steady and unwavering. "You can't fix all of it, Marcus. But you can start somewhere. Intervention matters. Care matters."

He nodded. "I know. I just... I see what we've allowed to happen. I see the lives we've quietly cataloged and manipulated. And I wonder... are we accountable only to numbers, or to them?"

Kelly's eyes met his. "Both. One is the machine. The other is human life. Choose."

He exhaled, feeling the weight of every spreadsheet, every metric, every patient's silent scream he had ignored.

Ty sat in the small therapy room, hands folded, eyes attentive. He spoke softly, articulating feelings he hadn't dared face. The craving was still there... a reminder of how easily control could be lost, but it no longer defined him. Presence, empathy, and intervention were his new anchors.

His mother sat beside him, holding his hand, a lifeline finally reaching through the chaos. The past weeks had left scars, but the foundation for recovery was forming.

Outside the clinic, the world carried on, unaware of the silent victories happening in this small room. One child, one family, one conscience reclaiming space from the machine.

Vivian Roth and her executives convened a crisis meeting. Minor dips in metrics had sparked alarms. Whistleblowers' reports hinted at human damage. Public relations risk. Liability exposure.

Roth's voice was cold, precise. "Adjust the systems. Retrain physicians. Ensure metrics are restored. And... monitor intervention programs. If human error is inevitable, at least contain it."

The empire remained unshaken, but cracks were forming. Human intervention had disrupted the machine. For the first time, the consequences of greed, control, and indifference were visible... not just in spreadsheets, but in lives.

Marcus filed detailed reports documenting the effects of the intervention. He reached out to families, coordinated therapy, and slowly began dismantling the chain of control he had once helped maintain. Kelly continued to monitor, educate, and advocate for patients whose lives were quietly at risk.

Their work was painstaking, imperfect, slow but it mattered. Numbers would recover, metrics would stabilize, but human lives, once disrupted, needed more than charts. They needed care, accountability, and presence.

Marcus sat alone after a long day, staring at a blank screen. The numbers were no longer his refuge. They were a reminder of what had been lost and what could still be saved.

Ty had begun to smile again, tentatively, cautiously. Other patients had started therapy. Families had regained some semblance of cohesion. The machine still hummed, corporate greed still thrived, but intervention proved one undeniable truth: human accountability could push back against even the most entrenched system.

Marcus whispered to himself, tired but resolute: "Numbers don't cry... but people do. And if we ignore them, those tears will never stop."

The Reckoning of Roth Global

The boardroom of Roth Global gleamed with polished glass and chrome, a cathedral to precision, control, and profit. Vivian Roth sat at the head of the table, face unreadable, eyes sharp, scanning reports that had arrived that morning.

The numbers were off. Slightly, yes but enough to indicate disruption, deviation, and exposure. More concerning, internal whistleblowers had compiled testimonies: families' cries, teenagers' spiraling health reports, and documentation of emotional dependence.

For the first time, Roth could feel the machinery she had built begin to falter.

Executives shifted uncomfortably. Liam Ward, ever composed, spoke first. "Metrics are dipping due to coordinated intervention by field clinicians. Families are reporting anomalies. Certain patients are no longer following standard protocol. We have a compliance problem."

Vivian's lips pressed into a thin line. "And the human error reports?"

"Substantiated," Ward replied. "There is evidence that certain physicians, Kelly and Hale specifically, have been acting against standard procedures, guiding patients away from prescribed dependencies."

The silence that followed was heavier than any number. Roth's empire had never faced defiance in the human element before. The spreadsheets were clean, the metrics predictable... until now.

An email thread, leaked anonymously, circulated to journalists. Families began speaking to local media, documenting the manipulation, the dependence, the human toll. The story was explosive: a corporate cartel masquerading as healthcare, exploiting dependency for profit.

Roth's control was slipping. The empire she had meticulously built could no longer contain the human chaos that her machine had generated.

Marcus and Kelly had anticipated this. They had prepared reports, testimony, patient records, and therapy documentation. They had anticipated the exposure not as revenge, but as a chance to stop the machine before more lives were irreparably damaged.

Marcus watched the news coverage as families told their stories. Numbers, once so sterile and commanding, were now screaming the consequences of corporate neglect. Kelly's notebook, once filled with discreet observations, had become a weapon of accountability.

Ty, sitting in therapy, absorbed the reports cautiously. His world was quiet but fragile, the corporate machinery exposed, but the effects of prior dependency lingering in memory and habit. Yet, he smiled again... tentatively, cautiously because he had learned that human intervention could disrupt even the most powerful systems.

The intervention had saved him, not numbers, not compliance, not spreadsheets, but human care and moral courage.

Vivian Roth stood before her board, unyielding but cornered. The reports were public. Media scrutiny was relentless. Families were filing complaints, regulatory agencies were opening investigations, and internal compliance officers were compiling internal accountability reports.

She spoke, voice calm, practiced, but sharp as a scalpel: "We will cooperate. We will audit. We will restructure. But let it be clear. This organization remains committed to its objectives. Deviations will not be tolerated."

Her empire was shaken, but she remained in control, at least publicly. Internally, cracks had formed, and those cracks could widen with the continued courage of people like Marcus and Kelly.

Marcus sat alone, reviewing patient files. The empire was faltering, but recovery was far from complete. Children like Ty were on a slow, deliberate path back to stability, while families continued to heal. He realized the reckoning was not just for Roth Global. It was for everyone complicit in allowing dependency to flourish unchecked.

Kelly placed a hand on his shoulder. "We did what we could. We stopped the machine, even if only in part. Now, it's about healing, accountability, and vigilance."

Marcus nodded. The human cost had been immense. The numbers, for once, had screamed louder than ever but it was the courage to act that had begun to change the course of lives.

Outside, media cameras focused on Roth Global's headquarters. Inside, executives whispered, strategized, and recalculated. The empire had survived exposure, but only just. Public pressure, whistleblowers, and moral accountability had forced the first cracks.

Marcus and Kelly prepared their next moves. Ty and other patients continued their slow path to recovery. The reckoning had begun, but the story was far from over. The machine had faltered, and the human element had proven its strength but how many lives could still be salvaged?

Redemption and Rebuilding

The sun rose over the city like a tentative promise. Wet streets glimmered in gold and silver, reflecting a world quietly moving forward. Inside a small clinic, Ty Brooks sat upright, fingers tracing the edge of the therapy desk. He inhaled deeply, the tremor in his hands almost gone. He wasn't "fixed," not entirely but he was present, aware, human in a way the pills had tried to erase.

Marcus Hale watched from across the room, notebook in hand, recording progress. This was different from spreadsheets, from metrics, from sterile dashboards. These were human lives in motion... messy, imperfect, and real.

Ty's eyes met his mother's across the room. She smiled, tentative but warm, a bridge rebuilt after weeks of silence and fear. Words weren't enough, but presence was. He took a deep breath, steadying himself.

"I... I think I can do this," Ty whispered.

His mother nodded. "We'll do it together."

For the first time in weeks, Ty's world felt like it belonged to him, not to a machine, a system, or a spreadsheet. Recovery wasn't linear, but it was possible.

Marcus reviewed files from other patients, noticing small victories: improved behavior, better family interactions, reduced dependency signals. He felt a cautious pride.

Kelly placed a hand on his shoulder. "We've started something, Marcus. Not everything will be perfect, but lives have changed because we intervened. That counts."

He nodded, eyes lingering on Ty in the therapy room. "It's more than numbers now. More than charts. We're finally seeing the human element win."

Together, they began coordinating broader recovery programs: therapy sessions, family workshops, community outreach. Every intervention was a small rebellion against the system that had exploited vulnerability.

Across town, Ty's family held dinner together. Conversations were awkward, laughter hesitant, but it existed. Small victories... the rebuilding of trust, communication, and understanding. They acknowledged the damage, yet they also celebrated survival and resilience.

For Ty, these moments were as important as any therapy session. They were tangible reminders that life could be more than pills, metrics, and silent despair.

Vivian Roth and her executives faced regulatory investigations, media scrutiny, and public accountability. The empire had survived, but not unscathed. Policies were revised, oversight strengthened, and human consequences could no longer be ignored... even within a corporation built on efficiency, greed, and metrics.

Roth remained strategic, calm, calculating but the cracks were permanent. Systems designed to exploit had been forced to acknowledge morality, accountability, and the human cost of their actions.

Marcus walked through the clinic at the end of the day, observing children interacting, families learning, healing slowly but surely. The weight on his shoulders had lessened, replaced by purpose. He had contributed to the system's oversight and harm but now he could help rebuild, guide, and protect.

Kelly followed, eyes scanning the activity, noting progress. "We can't undo everything," she said softly. "But we can save the next generation. And that matters."

Marcus smiled faintly, feeling a sense of hard-earned redemption. "Yes," he whispered. "It does."

Ty walked outside, feeling sunlight on his face. He wasn't cured. He wasn't completely safe from past dependency, but he was aware, resilient, and supported. Every step was deliberate, every breath a reclaiming of life.

He glanced back at the clinic, where Marcus and Kelly oversaw the slow, ongoing recovery of others. He knew the world wasn't perfect, that the corporate machine still hummed somewhere above but he had survived, and that survival mattered.

The story of addiction, corporate greed, and human exploitation had left scars on children, families, and even those complicit in the system. But intervention, presence, and courage had begun to tip the balance. Human lives had been prioritized, and in the wake of reckoning, redemption was possible.

Marcus closed his notebook. Kelly smiled beside him. Ty and other children continued their journey. Outside, the city moved forward, indifferent yet unknowingly transformed by those who had dared to intervene.

Humanity had prevailed, not perfectly, not completely, but persistently. The numbers might never cry, but people could act. And in that action, lives were rebuilt, hope was restored, and innocence, though fragile, could rise again.

"Mirror mirror"

When Your Opinion Matters Most Of All

Mirror, mirror on the wall. Why do people only see themselves in pieces? They call it "conversation," but really it's confession through contradiction. You speak your truth, they call it attitude. You ask a question, they call it disrespect. You hold up a mirror, they swear you threw a stone. See, some people don't want dialogue. They want dominance disguised as discussion.

They don't hear your words, they hear the threat of awakening. Because the moment you question their comfort, you become the enemy of their illusion. They'll call you "negative" just because you won't nod along. They'll say you're "always complaining" because your silence doesn't serve their script. But you're not whining. You're witnessing.

You're not argumentative. You're awake. And when you start seeing the cracks in the wall, they'll tell you to stop staring. But you can't unsee the truth once it calls your name. Because every time you look in the mirror, you're reminded: the reflection isn't the problem. It's the denial staring back.

The Mirror Speaks

You stand there again. Same mirror. Same wall. But something feels different this time like the reflection is tired of pretending, too. The silence breaks first. Then the mirror says, "Why do you only come here to defend yourself?" You freeze. Because you don't know if it's talking about them or you. "Why do you argue to be right," it whispers, "when you could speak to be understood?" You stare deeper.

The reflection doesn't blink. It doesn't flatter. It doesn't lie, "You call them toxic," it says, "but what about your need to prove them wrong? You call them blind, but what about your pride in being the one who sees?" Your heart thuds.

The mirror continues... soft, but slicing through the noise like glass breaking in slow motion. "Everyone wants to be the truth-teller," it says. "Few can handle being the truth-seeker." Because truth-seeking means seeing all of it not just what fits your side of the story. You want to turn away. You want to say, "I'm not the problem." But the mirror doesn't move. It just waits. Patient. Unforgiving. "Maybe you both are," it says. "And maybe that's where the healing begins." Then silence again. Just you and a reflection that refuses to let you hide behind your own righteousness.

Reflections Of The Unhealed

The next time you stand before the mirror, you don't come to argue. You come to listen. The light hits differently, warmer, but still revealing. You notice how many versions of you have stood in this same place trying to prove a point instead of finding peace. The mirror speaks again: "Every argument you've ever had wasn't about right or wrong. It was about recognition. You wanted to be seen, but they only saw themselves."

You nod slowly. Because that's the truth. Half the world isn't even fighting you. They're fighting their own reflection through you. "People defend their delusion," the mirror continues, "because it's all they know.

You become the enemy not because you're wrong but because you make them feel exposed." You remember all the times you tried to speak clarity into confusion and were met with accusations instead of understanding. They called you dramatic, bitter, difficult as if your awareness was a weapon instead of a warning.

But now you see it: their reactions were never about you. They were about the storm, they've been pretending it wasn't there. "Humans don't argue to connect," the mirror says. "They argue to protect. And the louder they defend, the more fragile their truth must be." You ask quietly, "So what am I protecting?" The reflection doesn't hesitate. "Your pain," it says. "The part of you that still needs to be right because once upon a time, no one listened when you were wronged."

You exhale. And for the first time, you don't feel like the enemy. You just feel... seen. The mirror softens, almost kind now: "once you understand that everyone's opinion is just a projection of their own reflection, you stop needing to convince them and start healing yourself." And in that moment, you realize the mirror was never judging you. It was waiting for you to see beyond it.

When The Mirror Wears A Face

You meet someone. Their smile feels like clarity. Their eyes feel like peace. You tell yourself, "This one is different." But give it time. Because sooner or later, love becomes a mirror too. At first, the reflection is gentle. They reflect back the parts of you you like. The confidence. The charm. The way you care. But then the shadows surface.

Old triggers dressed in new affection. Sudden silences that sound like rejection. Small arguments that feel way too big. And the mirror whispers: "Now let's see if you've really learned." You realize you're not fighting them. You're fighting every person whoever made you feel unheard. And they're not fighting you.

They're fighting every ghost whoever made them feel unseen. That's why love feels like war sometimes. It's two wounds trying to hold hands. You start to notice the patterns: how you raise your voice when you feel ignored. How they shut down when they feel attacked. How both of you are just protecting the same soft place inside that neither of you learned to name. The mirror inside you says: "Peace isn't found in winning the argument. It's found in understanding the wound." So you breathe before you speak.

You listen before you defend. You stop trying to change them and start trying to see them. That's when it shifts. The conversation slows down. The silence becomes safer. The reflection softens. Because love doesn't ask for perfection. It asks for awareness. And once you can see your reflection without flinching, you can love theirs without fear. You finally understand that every relationship is a mirror offering two choices: to project or to reflect. To repeat or to heal. And this time, you choose healing.

The Evolution Of Love

Love changes when you do. It stops being a battlefield and starts becoming a sanctuary. You no longer chase what validates you. You attract what aligns with you. You no longer beg to be seen. You invite those who already can. The mirror that once shouted truth now whispers balance. Because you've learned: love doesn't fix what's broken. It honors what's human.

The evolved kind of love feels different. It's quiet. It's patient. It's safe. There's no scoreboard, no emotional tug-of-war. You don't keep tabs on who apologized last or who gave more. You just give because you want to. Not from fear of loss, but from the freedom of abundance. You've outgrown the need to win. Now you want to understand. You've outgrown the fantasy of perfect harmony. Now you respect the rhythm of repair. Because real love doesn't mean never arguing. It means never forgetting that you're on the same side.

You speak differently now. You listen slower. You forgive faster. Not because you've become naïve, but because peace feels better than proof. You realize that evolved love isn't about finding your "other half." It's about meeting another whole soul and building something sacred between you. It's two people who've met their own reflections, faced their shadows, and still choose light not because it's easy, but because it's true. You stop saying, "I need you to complete me."

You start saying, "I honor the way you mirror me." And that's when you understand that love isn't the opposite of pain. It's the evolution of it. It's what happens when two healed hearts stop surviving together and start creating together. No longer mirror and reflection but partners in evolution.

The Language Of Evolved Love

Evolved love doesn't shout. It listens. It doesn't compete to be heard. It creates space for understanding. Because when you've healed, you realize: communication isn't about winning the argument. It's about protecting the connection. You learn to speak in tones that don't bruise the spirit. You start to choose words that builds, not breaks.

When love evolves, silence stops being a punishment. It becomes a reflection. A pause. A breath before the truth. The language of evolved love is made of things unseen: • patience that holds instead of controls. • apologies that come without excuses. • boundaries spoken with kindness, not threat. • honesty offered as intimacy, not ammunition. You stop saying, "I'm right, you're wrong." You start saying, "I hear you. Here's what I feel." You no longer weaponize vulnerability. You welcome it. Because now you know vulnerability isn't weakness.

It's the bridge where real connection begins. Evolved love sounds like this: "I was triggered not by you, but by what this reminded me of." "I need a moment, not distance." "I'm listening, not waiting to respond." It feels like this: calm energy even in conflict. Safety even in silence. Soft eyes even in disagreement. This is not the love you learned. It's the love you remembered. The kind that existed before pain taught you to defend.

Before pride taught you to perform. Before, survival taught you to shut down. Now you speak love fluently not through grand gestures, but through emotional fluency. Because when love evolves, you don't fall into it. You rise into it. Consciously. Gently. Together. And maybe that's the new vow: not "forever," but "authentic." Not "never hurt me," but "let's heal honestly." Because evolved love isn't about avoiding conflict. It's about evolving through it, hand in hand, with hearts that choose growth over ego.

"How Could You? I Trusted You."

She didn't whisper it. She spit it. How. Could. You. The words didn't echo off the walls, they hit them like fists. Her own voice startled her low, cracked, trembling but steady enough to carry the weight of every time she'd ever been lied to. "I trusted you, motherfucker." Her phone sat on the kitchen counter, screen lit up, still open to that nothing-ass message: "going to bed early. Talk tomorrow." Fourteen words. Fourteen lies. Fourteen reasons for her chest to tighten like a vice. He wasn't doing anything wrong or maybe he was.

That's the part that drives a woman insane. When it looks like something, but you can't prove it. When the picture on the screen tells one story, and your gut screams another. When every silence sounds like another woman breathing.

She poured another drink. Straight. She didn't need ice. She needed answers. Her name was Rayna, 52 years old, and she'd survived men who promised forever but only meant "until they got bored." She'd survived the marriage that chewed her down to an apology, the boyfriend who swore he was loyal while deleting texts at 2 a.m., and the pastor who told her to "pray about it" when she said she couldn't sleep through the sound of her own anxiety.

And now, Marcus, the younger one, the one who smiled like god made him special was out here playing cool like he didn't know what that silence did to her. Every woman like Rayna knows that silence. It's not peace.

It's suspicion. It's your nervous system on fire, your logic drowned under emotion, your body reliving every ghost that ever lied to you. Because when a woman has been broken by life, trust becomes hallucination. You think you're seeing the truth, but really, you're seeing your fears dressed up in new faces. Still, Rayna believed him once.

He held her face in his hands and said, "You're safe with me." And she wanted so badly to believe him, she gave him everything she never gave anyone else her raw, unfiltered self. That's the danger of healed women who ain't all the way healed: they look calm, but they bleed privately.

They forgive publicly, but they never forget the map of where the knife went in. "you said you'd never make me question myself," she whispered now, softer. "You said I could trust you." Her hands trembled, not from the liquor but from the rage that comes after humiliation. That moment when you realize... you knew better.

You saw the signs, but you wanted to believe in something good for once. And now, here she was again fighting ghosts, shadowboxing with illusions, trying to separate reality from her own mind's betrayal. Because the truth was this: he didn't even have to lie. She'd already built the lie herself. She filled in every gap his silence left. That's how the mind punishes you after heartbreak. It doesn't wait for proof. It invents it.

The Evidence She Invented

The mind has a sound. It's not words. It's rhythm: tap-tap-tap, the pulse of suspicion that starts soft and turns into thunder. That's how it begins for Rayna. A simple sound: the click of her phone not lighting up. Silence, then the faint hum of the refrigerator. That's the language her fear speaks in small, domestic noises that stretch into proof of betrayal.

She scrolls their messages again. "Goodnight." That one word echoes like a slamming door. Her trauma turns vowels into verdicts. He didn't use an emoji. He used to use an emoji. That means he's done. It's not logic; it's the phonology of panic. Every syllable is dissected. Every pause is a paragraph. Her chest tightens. Memory bleeds into the present tense.

Cognitive Loop 1: Pattern Recognition Gone Rogue

The human brain is a pattern-machine. When you've been lied to enough, it learns to hunt for deceit even in kindness. Neuroscientists call it hypervigilance. A survival reflex that refuses to retire. But Rayna doesn't know that term; she just knows the feeling. It's like standing in emotional crossfire, ducking bullets that aren't there. Her nervous system is still in yesterday's war.

She tells herself she's "just paying attention." But attention has turned into obsession. She scrolls, zooms, replays, analyzes every action a desperate prayer to the god of certainty. "If I can prove he's lying," she whispers, "then I won't be crazy." That's the cruel trick of trauma thinking: it convinces you that pain equals accuracy.

Cognitive Loop 2: The Narrative Reflex

The psyche hates blank space, so it fills silence with story.

In psychology, it's called confabulation. The brain creating meaning where none exists to preserve emotional coherence.

Rayna builds her plot carefully:

- He didn't text back → He's with someone.
- he's online but not replying → He's deleting messages.
- he said he was tired → That's code for "I'm somewhere I shouldn't be."

Every leap feels rational in her body because anxiety speaks the body's native tongue, adrenaline. She paces the floor, heart syncing with the rhythm of her suspicion.

To her, imagination doesn't feel like fiction; it feels like intuition.

Cognitive Loop 3: The Mirror Illusion

At 1 a.m., she stares at her reflection. "Why do I always pick men who do this to me?" That's when the distortion deepens. She doesn't see Marcus anymore. She sees them: the ex who cheated, the father who left, the friend who swore loyalty then disappeared. Trauma overlays faces like translucent film. Reality becomes collage.

Neuroscience calls it emotional imprinting past experiences hijacking present perception. Spiritually, it feels like déjà vu in hell. "he's doing it again." "No," whispers a faint sane voice. "he's not." "Then why does it feel the same?" Because feelings aren't facts. They're flashbacks. Marcus's reality: across town, Marcus is half-asleep on his brother's couch, phone dead, dreaming of her. He's not perfect, but he's consistent.

He believes love is shown in patterns of peace, not performance. He doesn't know that silence to him equals abandonment to her. In the morning, he'll bring her coffee, unaware that overnight she's built a courtroom in her mind with him on trial and every ex serving as witness.

Cognitive Loop 4: Emotional Logic

By 3 a.m. Rayna's body is exhausted, but her mind refuses to surrender. It needs closure even if it must invent it. She drafts an invisible closing argument: "Your honor, exhibit a: tone shift. Exhibit b: late replies. Exhibit c: intuition." Verdict: guilty until proven perfect. This is the phonology of fear. Its vocabulary is repetition, its grammar is assumption, its punctuation is panic.

Every anxious thought ends with an exclamation mark. Morning after: the sun rises like an interrogation light. Her eyes burn. She hasn't slept. When his knock comes three gentle taps. She feels both relief and rage. He stands there holding coffee and her favorite pastry.

She stares as if it's evidence of a crime. "You think this fixes everything?" She snaps. "Everything?" He repeats softly. "What happened while I was gone?" She can't answer because she doesn't know how to explain the invisible war she fought alone. A war between neurons and memories.

Between logic and the ghosts of men who lied. He sets the coffee down, watching her quietly. "You keep fighting me," he says, "but I'm not your past." Her throat closes. Because part of her knows he's right and that knowledge is unbearable. To accept it would mean she's been hurting herself with her own imagination.

And that kind of self-awareness feels like dying. Psychological note (narrator voice): people don't cling to illusions because they want to suffer. They cling because certainty feels safer than confusion, even when certainty is false.

Rayna would rather be right and heartbroken than admit she might be wrong and safe. That's how trauma holds love hostage: it forces the present to pay rent for the past. It mistakes safety for danger and confusion for intuition.

She doesn't apologize. She just says, almost to herself: "It's hard to believe in peace when every calm moment once came before a storm." He nods. "Then maybe this time," he says, "the calm is the love." And for the first time in years, she feels both fear and possibility sharing the same heartbeat.

The Silence That Screams

Silence should feel safe. But for Rayna, silence is a ghost with perfect timing. Every quiet space reminds her of waiting... waiting for the call that never came, the apology that never arrived, the man who said "I'll be right back" and never was.

So when Marcus grows quiet not distant, just still. She feels the same chill crawling up her spine. Her body says: it's happening again. He doesn't have to do anything wrong. All he has to do is pause, and her nervous system starts rehearsing old tragedies.

The Body's Language

Psychologists call it somatic memory. The way the body remembers pain even when the mind wants to forget. To Rayna, stillness means danger. Calm means an incoming storm. Her body is fluent in heartbreak, but illiterate in peace. So when Marcus stops talking to breathe, her subconscious hears abandonment. "Why'd you get quiet?" She asks, "I'm just thinking," he says. "About what?" "About how beautiful you look when you're mad." She laughs, but it's hollow. Her laughter hides the fear that if she lets her guard down, he'll disappear like the others.

The Inheritance Of Distrust

This isn't just heartbreak. It's an inheritance. Her mother taught her that men who smile too easily are hiding something. Her aunt taught her that being a woman means preparing to be disappointed. Her own life taught her that love is temporary... a favor you earn, not a gift you keep.

So even when Marcus shows up every time, her mind keeps receipts from men who didn't. Trauma is thrifty. It never wastes a single scar. "You think I don't see what's happening?" She says, "You think I'm naive?" "No," he replies gently. "I think you're protecting yourself from someone who isn't here anymore." That sentence lands like thunder behind her ribs. Because he's right but her pain doesn't care. Her pain only knows survival.

The Psychology Of Self-Sabotage

There's a scientific name for what she's doing: confirmation bias. The brain searches for evidence that supports its fear even if it has to twist reality to find it. It's like looking for monsters under the bed when the monster lives in the mirror. Because once you've been betrayed enough, you start betraying yourself first just to feel in control of the loss.

That's Rayna's cycle:

Preemptive heartbreak.

Self-sabotage disguised as self-protection.

And a man standing there arms open trying not to take her wounds personally.

Marcus' Test

Marcus has his own history quiet, disciplined, and private. He's not used to having his every silence dissected. But he's patient, because he knows healing isn't linear —it's cyclical. So instead of arguing, he does something radical. He doesn't defend himself. He stays calm.

He looks her in the eye and says, "I don't want to win against your fears. I want to walk through them with you." And that's the first time she realizes —he's not her opponent. He's her mirror, reflecting both the light and the damage.

When Peace Feels Like Punishment

But here's the problem with peace: it feels foreign to those who've lived in chaos too long. Rayna mistakes his stability for indifference, his stillness for distance, his patience for lack of passion. Because in her old world, love was loud —yelling, crying, breaking, making up.

The silence now feels like abandonment's twin. Her brain whispers, he's getting bored. Her body tenses like an alarm clock that never stops ringing. But deep down, something in her is starting to shift —a small rebellion against her own narrative.

Internal Monologue — The Shift

Maybe he's not leaving. Maybe I just don't know what staying looks like. Maybe love isn't supposed to sound like proof. That realization doesn't bring peace —it brings panic. Because if she's been wrong about this... what else has she been wrong about?

Healing isn't a light switch —it's a rewiring. And in this moment, her heart sparks for the first time in years —not because of what he said, but because he didn't leave when she accused him.

The Night That Changed Everything

That night, she sits on the edge of the bed, watching him sleep. She studies the calm rise and fall of his chest —the kind of peace that used to scare her. She whispers to herself, "he's not them." Then softer: "I'm not her anymore, either." For the first time, her body doesn't fight the quiet. It surrenders to it —the same silence that used to scream now starts to hum. Psychological reflection: love doesn't heal trauma by promising never to hurt you.

It heals by staying when the storm of your past tries to make you push it away. By refusing to become the villain your fear keeps auditioning for. Marcus didn't fix Rayna. He mirrored her brokenness back to her until she saw herself clearly. That's not romance. That's recovery.

The Anatomy Of Safety

Safety.

A word that sounds simple until you've lived without it. For most people, safety is a locked door or a warm hug. For Rayna, it's a foreign language—one she's been trying to learn with a broken tongue. Because when you've lived in survival mode too long, peace doesn't feel peaceful. It feels suspicious.

The Addiction To Chaos

Every toxic relationship she ever survived came with a soundtrack — arguments, apologies, long nights of begging and proving and crying. It taught her one rule: if it doesn't hurt, it isn't real. So when Marcus shows up calm, steady, unshaken —her nervous system starts panicking.

"Why are you so quiet?"

"Because I'm listening."

"To what?"

"to how loud your fear is."

He says it softly, not as a jab, but a truth. Her body tenses, ready for war. But there's no explosion. Just silence. And his eyes, still there. Still steady. It's disarming —how peace can feel like a threat when you're addicted to adrenaline. Her therapist once said, "You can't detox from chaos until you stop mistaking it for love." But Rayna doesn't want detox —she wants control. Chaos gave her that. Peace doesn't.

The Physiology Of Peace

Peace has a heartbeat —slow, steady, patient. It moves differently than pain. Pain screams; peace hums. Pain accelerates; peace grounds. Marcus has learned her body's language before she even speaks.

He knows the way her shoulders stiffen when she's bracing for disappointment. He knows the way she laughs when she's really afraid. He knows that sometimes silence is her body saying, "Please don't make me hope again." So he doesn't talk her out of fear. He just sits with it. That's what safety looks like —not perfection, but presence.

The Mirror Moment

That night, she stands in the bathroom staring at her reflection. Her face looks tired —not just from lack of sleep, but from carrying the weight of old stories. She whispers to the mirror: "Why do I keep waiting for someone to hurt me?"

The mirror doesn't answer, but her reflection shifts. She looks softer —sad, but aware. For the first time, she realizes: it's not the men that scare me anymore. It's believing I deserve something gentle. That's the hardest truth of healing —learning you were built for more than survival.

The Science Of Softness

Trauma scientists call it neuroplasticity —the brain's ability to rewire after years of fear. But in real life, it's slower than science makes it sound. It's learning to unclench your jaw when someone says "I love you." It's learning to accept compliments without looking for hidden motives.

It's trusting that someone's consistency isn't a setup for betrayal. Marcus becomes her new pattern —predictable in the best way. His love isn't fireworks; it's sunrise. The kind of light that doesn't ask to be noticed —it just shows up every day.

When She Finally Exhales

Weeks pass. The tension in her voice starts to fade. The paranoia quiets. Her mind, once a crime scene, begins to feel like home again. One morning, she wakes up to him cooking breakfast. Music low, sunlight spilling through the blinds. No drama. No doubt. Just breathe.

And it hits her —this is what healing sounds like: the hum of bacon in a pan, the steady rhythm of his foot tapping to a song, and her own heart, no longer racing, but keeping time.

She sits there watching him, eyes wet but peaceful. "You're really not going anywhere, are you?" She says quietly. He smiles, doesn't turn around. "Not unless you ask me to." Her throat tightens. Because that's the thing —she's finally learning that love doesn't cage you. It waits at the door until you feel safe enough to let it in.

The New Rule

Before him, her rule was "never trust silence." Now it's "not every quiet is abandonment." Safety doesn't mean nothing bad will ever happen again. It means when fear knocks, there's someone beside you who won't let it in alone. Rayna still has moments —flashbacks, doubts, days she's triggered by ghosts. But Marcus doesn't rescue her; he reminds her.

"You don't need saving anymore," he tells her. "You just need space to believe you're safe." And that's the anatomy of it —safety isn't a feeling someone gives you. It's a muscle you rebuild, one heartbeat at a time. That night, she sleeps without checking his phone. Without inventing stories. Without armor. And for the first time in her life, peace doesn't feel like danger. It feels like home.

The Conflicted Mind (The Withdrawal From Chaos)

Healing doesn't always feel like healing. Sometimes it feels like nothing. No adrenaline. No high. No drama to prove the love is real. Just... quiet. That's the problem with peace —it doesn't flood the brain with dopamine like survival did. It doesn't give her the same rush she got from the rollercoaster of old love. It feels empty, like standing in the middle of calm waters and wondering where the waves went. Her therapist called it emotional withdrawal. But to Rayna, it feels like loneliness in disguise.

The Split-Brain

The human brain is an argument that never ends. One side craves safety. The other side misses chaos. The left hemisphere whispers logic: "he's consistent. He's kind. You're finally safe." The right hemisphere hums with memory: "But remember how alive you felt when you were fighting? When it hurt? When it burned?"

It's a tug-of-war between biology and biography —between what her body remembers and what her heart desires. Every time Marcus chooses calm, she feels unseen. Every time he refuses to fight, she feels unloved. It's twisted —but it's honest. Because sometimes the pain you escaped becomes the only language you understand.

The Fear Of Peace

Peace feels like silence. Silence feels like distance. Distance feels like danger. Danger feels like home. That's the unconscious loop of the conflicted mind. So when Marcus spends the afternoon reading instead of hovering, she starts to spiral. Her mind invents meaning: "he's bored," "he's tired of me," "he's just waiting for a reason to go."

She tests him —small, sharp comments meant to provoke a reaction. Old habits. Unspoken fear dressed as attitude. He looks up from the book, calm as ever. "You looking for a fight or reassurance?" That hits. Because she doesn't know the difference yet.

The Psychology Of Relapse

Trauma recovery isn't linear —it's circular. You revisit the same emotional places, but each time you arrive with more awareness. That's progress disguised as repetition. Rayna starts craving the chemical chaos again —the highs, the breakdowns, the makeups that feel like resurrection. Because peace doesn't offer that rush, it offers stability —and stability is quiet. To a healed mind, that's heaven. To a healing mind, that's hell, "it's too calm," she says one night. "That's the point," he answers. "It feels like something's missing."

"Maybe it's just the noise you used to call love." Her chest tightens. She knows he's right. But her emotions don't care. Her body still wants its fix —the storm, the argument, the apology that makes her feel chosen again.

The Crash

She picks a fight. Small at first —about dishes, timing, tone. But the moment his voice stays level, she turns the volume up. "Say something! Do something!" She yells, "I'm not your enemy," he replies. "Then stop being so calm!" And there it is —the confession her pride was protecting. She doesn't want calm. She wants proof.

Proof that she's worth fighting for. Proof that she still matters enough to make someone lose control. Marcus finally steps forward, close enough for her to see the softness in his eyes. "You want passion, but what you really want is reassurance. You've mistaken chaos for connection." She freezes. Because no one ever said it that plain before.

The Inner War

That night, when he leaves her space to cool off, she sits on the floor, knees to chest. The silence feels deafening again —but this time she hears something new beneath it: her own breathing. She realizes she's been living like an addict —not for a person, but for intensity. Her trauma fed her dopamine like poison disguised as honey.

And now she's sober —shaking, sweating, scared. This is what withdrawal from chaos feels like: a craving for the pain that made you feel alive. "What if love is supposed to be boring?" She whispers to herself. But her heart answers quietly, "What if boring is just another word for peace?"

The Revelation

When Marcus returns, she doesn't apologize. She just says, "It's hard to want peace when pain was the only proof I ever had." He nods, sits beside her, doesn't speak. That silence again. But this time it doesn't scream —it breathes. He wraps his arm around her shoulders. Not to fix. Not to lecture. Just to anchor her back to the moment. "I know you're scared," he says softly. "But your heart's learning a new language.

Don't quit before it becomes fluent." She exhales —a long, trembling sound. It's the sound of surrender, not defeat. Healing doesn't erase the addiction to chaos overnight. It teaches you to stop answering when it calls. And the conflicted mind? It's not a curse —it's the bridge between survival and freedom. Rayna isn't healed. But for the first time, she's not mistaking her triggers for truth. And that's where real peace begins.

When The Echo Talks Back

Healing has a sound. So does relapse. But the most dangerous sound of all is the echo —the voice that sounds like you, but speaks from your pain. It starts one night while Rayna is scrolling. A message slides in from a familiar name. A ghost in digital form.

Her ex —the one who taught her how to confuse chaos for love. "Hey, stranger... just checking on you." Her chest tightens. Not from love. From memory. From the echo of old validation calling her name like a siren.

The Ghost Of The High

The conflicted mind is tricky. Even after you detox from chaos, part of you still craves the thrill. Not because you want the pain —but because pain was predictable, and peace feels too quiet to trust. She stares at the message. Her thumb hovers. She can hear her old self whisper: just one reply. You owe him nothing —but closure.

But closure is never the goal. It's the trap. She doesn't reply. Not yet. But she feels the temptation —that low vibration of nostalgia, the lie that says, you miss him. She doesn't miss him. She misses who she thought she was when she survived him.

When Memory Masquerades As Desire

That's how the echo works —it doesn't shout. It seduces. It uses your own memories as bait. Remember the way he looked at you? Remember how alive it felt when you fought? Remember how good the making up was? Every memory plays like a highlight reel —no volume, just visuals. Her brain edits out the parts where she cried herself numb. That's the deceit of nostalgia: it turns pain into poetry. Meanwhile, Marcus is in the kitchen, humming, unaware of the war in her phone.

The Science Of Triggered Peace

When she first met Marcus, peace felt strange. Now peace feels sacred —but fragile. One notification can shake her foundation. Her body remembers chaos like a lover's scent. That's the biology of trauma —the nervous system doesn't forget its favorite drug.

It doesn't care that the ex lied. It only remembers how alive it felt to chase and collapse and resurrect. That's not love —that's chemistry dressed in heartbreak.

The Echo Speaks

Later that night, she's alone. Phone screen glowing like temptation in the dark. She reads the message again. Then another one appears: "You ever think about us?" And this time, she hears it differently. It's not his voice — it's her echo talking through him. The echo says: You still need to prove you were enough.

The echo says: you still owe the past a reaction. The echo says: You'll never be fully loved without the fire. But the new Rayna —the one Marcus has been teaching how to breathe—leans back and whispers out loud: "You don't get to narrate my peace anymore." For the first time, the echo talks back —and she answers it.

The Test

Marcus walks in quietly. He doesn't ask, doesn't pry. He just feels the tension in the room. "You okay?" "Yeah," she says softly. "Just... deleting something I should've deleted a long time ago." He doesn't ask what it was. He just nods —trusting her evolution.

That trust lands deeper than any reassurance ever could. Her phone screen goes black. So does the chapter of her life that thrived on confusion. But the silence that follows? It's not empty this time. It's cleansing.

When The Past Realizes You're Not Coming Back

That night, the ex texts one more time: "You really done with me?" She doesn't respond. Not out of anger. Out of growth. Because the moment she realized she didn't need to respond —that's when she knew the healing had worked. The echo tries again, whispering doubt. But this time, her peace speaks louder. Her new silence isn't weakness —it's authority.

The Conversation With Herself

In bed later, Marcus asleep beside her, she whispers to herself: "You don't have to rehearse old roles to feel relevant." "You don't have to be broken to be desired." "You don't have to answer everything that calls you by your wounds."

Her old self might've called that cowardice. Her healed self knows it's power. The echo fades. The silence hums. And for once, her heart and her mind agree. The most powerful sound in a healed woman's life is not her laughter, not her love, not even her rage.

It's the quiet after she chooses not to return to what once destroyed her. That's when peace stops being fragile —and becomes her foundation.

Nobody Appreciates Me

There's a silence that follows survival —a kind that doesn't echo, doesn't soothe, just exists. That's where Rayna's been living lately —in the aftermath of endurance. She survived the storm. But nobody clapped when she made it out.

The Cost Of Strength

People say, "You're so strong." But they don't mean it as praise —they mean it as permission. Permission to pile more on her back. Permission to ignore her pain because she "can handle it." She's tired of being congratulated for carrying what broke her. Her strength was never a gift — it was a scar that learned how to walk.

The Invisible Labor Of Healing

She looks around her house one morning —dishes clean, laundry folded, Marcus asleep peacefully —and realizes that everyone benefits from her healing, but nobody notices how heavy it is to keep it going. They see the calm. They don't see the war it takes to stay calm.

Every breath she takes costs her a battle with herself —a choice to not react the old way, to not spiral when she feels unseen, to not raise her voice when silence could say more. Healing, she thinks, is the most unappreciated job in the world.

The Mind That Can't Rest

That night, she sits in bed scrolling through memories —old photos, texts, journals —looking for something she can't name. Not closure. Not nostalgia. Just proof that she existed before all this strength. Her mind loops through every time she was blamed for her own pain. Every time she forgave too fast, loved too hard, stayed too long.

Every time, people took her peace as passive and her silence as stupidity. She whispers under her breath, "Nobody appreciates what it costs to stay kind in a world that keeps trying to make you cold." And that's the moment the truth hits —she's not angry at the people who hurt her anymore. She's angry that healing still feels like begging for permission to rest.

The Man Who Sees Her

Marcus senses it —the quiet edge in her voice. He doesn't try to fix it. He just sits beside her. "You okay?" He asks softly. "No," she says. "I'm just... tired of surviving." He nods. Doesn't argue. Doesn't make it about him. That's the difference between love and ego —love listens. Ego lectures.

After a long silence, he says, "You don't have to keep proving you're strong for me." And something cracks inside her. Because that's what she's been doing —performing healed, performing peace, performing gratitude —all because she didn't want to be a burden anymore, but that's what trauma does —it teaches you that being loved comes with a price tag called performance.

The Unspoken Wound

Rayna leans back, tears finally falling, and admits the sentence she's never said out loud before: "nobody appreciates the version of me that's still learning how to be okay." Marcus takes her hand. "Then let me appreciate her. The unpolished version. The one that still flinches but shows up anyway." And for a split second —she believes him. Not fully. Not forever. But enough. Enough to exhale.

The Psychology Of Unrecognized Pain

The truth is, people who've had to survive everyone and everything learn how to equate appreciation with safety. If they're not seen, they don't feel safe. If they're not thanked, they feel disposable. If they're not understood, they spiral into isolation.

That's how the mind weaponizes old wounds —by convincing you that invisibility is rejection, when sometimes, it's just peace being quiet. But when you've lived too long in fight-or-flight, peace feels like abandonment. So Rayna sits with that contradiction —peaceful life, chaotic mind. Loved woman, lonely heart. Healing body, haunted soul.

The Turn

Later that night, Marcus asleep again, Rayna walks into the mirror and studies her reflection. Her eyes look tired, but not hopeless. Her lips tremble, but they still curve into something soft —almost forgiveness. "Maybe," she says quietly to herself, "the reason nobody appreciates me... is that I've been showing up for them instead of me." That's the shift. That's the beginning of something new. Not revenge. Not validation. Just reclamation. Every survivor reaches a point where appreciation doesn't heal —alignment does, where applause means less than inner peace.

Where survival stops being the goal and becomes the origin story. Rayna finally exhales. Not the sigh of exhaustion —the sigh of release. Because for the first time, she understands: being unappreciated doesn't mean being unloved. It just means she's finally learning to love herself without the audience.

The Mirror's Confession

The mirror doesn't lie. But it doesn't tell the whole truth either. It shows you what you've allowed yourself to see, and hides what you refuse to face. Rayna stands in front of it at midnight, the room quiet except for the hum of the city outside. She stares at herself —every line, every shadow, every scar she's tried to hide. The survival woman stares back, arms folded across her chest, guarding the wounds she's carried for decades. "Who are you?" She whispers.

And suddenly, the mirror answers —not in words, but in memory. Flashbacks of every fight she survived, every betrayal she endured, every night she cried herself awake. Every time she chose survival over surrender, strength over softness. I am all of it, the mirror seems to say. I am you. And you've carried me alone.

The Mask Of Survival

For so long, she's worn a mask: a mask of strength. A mask of calm. A mask that smiled when it hurt, spoke when it silenced, and moved forward when she wanted to stop. The confession is simple and terrifying: "I've been pretending. Pretending I'm okay. Pretending peace is safe. Pretending love doesn't scare me." Her own reflection flinches. Because pretending kept her alive —but pretending kept her heart caged.

The Whisper Of Fear

Every confession has a cost. Rayna feels it now —the fear that admitting weakness will make her invisible, that vulnerability will be punished, that love will leave again. But the mirror presses closer: "You survived everything. What else is left to fear?" Her knees buckle. Her hands tremble. Her voice cracks: "I... I don't know how to be the real me." The mirror answers with its quiet clarity: "The real you has always been here. You just refused to see her."

The Unmasking

Rayna reaches up, touches her reflection. For the first time, she doesn't see the survival mask. She sees a woman who laughed through the tears, loved through the betrayals, and kept going even when nobody appreciated her. Every scar, every bruise, every sleepless night becomes a confession — a testimony: "I was afraid. I was angry. I was broken.

I was unappreciated. I survived anyway. I loved anyway." Tears stream down her face. Not just for herself, but for the girl she left behind, the version of her who thought love meant war, the version who would have given up if someone had truly seen her. "I forgive you," she whispers. "I forgive me."

The Psychology Of Revelation

The mirror doesn't just reflect the body —it reflects the soul. And the soul doesn't heal by hiding scars. It heals by naming them. By confessing them. By unmasking the fear that has held love hostage. Rayna's confessions are loud and private: "I don't need to prove my strength anymore.

I don't need chaos to feel alive. I don't need to chase validation that doesn't exist. I am enough. I am worthy. I am safe." The words vibrate in her chest, settle in her bones. It's both terrifying and liberating —the first real exhale she's taken in years.

The Shift

The mirror no longer intimidates her. It supports her. It's no longer a judge —it's a witness. And that witness sees her fully, without masks, without excuses, without pretense. She finally understands: healing isn't about finding someone to validate you. It's about finding yourself. Loving yourself. Confessing to yourself. And surviving without apology.

Rayna turns away from the mirror. She doesn't see scars or shadows anymore —she sees light and depth, resilience and softness, brokenness and power, all at once. She whispers softly: "I am no longer the girl who survived everyone and everything. I am the woman who survived herself." And for the first time, she smiles —not a mask, not for anyone else, not as armor—just a smile born of truth, of freedom, of self-acknowledgment.

The Peace Test

Peace isn't quiet. Peace is hard. It demands work. Courage. Surrender. Rayna thought she had learned how to exhale. But peace isn't something you take. It's something you prove —to yourself, to others, to history. And today, her peace would be tested.

The Shadows Of Trauma

Marcus stands at the kitchen counter, chopping vegetables, humming. A simple act. Routine. Life. But for Rayna, every mundane moment is a battlefield. Because peace feels suspicious when you've survived chaos your whole life, she watches him, the rhythm of his hands, the calm steadiness.

"I don't deserve this," she thinks. "I don't deserve him. I don't deserve myself." She remembers the exes, the betrayals, the nights spent questioning every word, every gesture. She remembers the voice in her head —the echo—that whispers: it will never last. It's too quiet. He's waiting to leave.

The Weight Of Recognition

Marcus doesn't notice her stare. Or maybe he does, and he simply doesn't flinch. That's part of his own healing —he's survived his own storms. But he has scars too, deep ones, invisible ones, and he carries them like a secret prayer. They are two people broken, two people learning, two people afraid to trust peace yet craving it more than chaos.

Rayna realizes something: "he's been loving me all along. Even when I was at my worst, even when I accused him, even when I withdrew... he stayed." And the truth hits —Marcus has been showing love the only way he knew how: steady, unshakable, patient. His love isn't loud. It's consistent. His love doesn't demand proof. His love survives silence.

The Mirror Of Mutual Healing

Sitting down beside him, Rayna reaches for his hand. "You... You've been loving me through all of this," she says quietly. He looks at her —eyes soft but honest— "I've been trying. But you have to understand, I've been surviving my own storms too." There it is —the unspoken truth. He's not perfect.

He has his own demons, his own scars, his own nights of doubt. He's just further along in the journey, with tools she's only beginning to learn. And in that moment, the weight of her fear begins to lift —because loving him doesn't mean denying herself. It means meeting him where he is, and allowing herself to be met.

The Sacrifice Of Control

Finding peace requires letting go. Letting go of control. Letting go of the need to predict, anticipate, and preempt betrayal. Rayna exhales. For the first time in a long time, she allows herself to trust love without testing it. "I'm scared," she admits. "I know," he replies. "I'm scared too."

The honesty between them doesn't fracture; it cements. Their fears are no longer weapons. Their vulnerabilities are mirrors, reflecting courage back at each other.

The Trial Of Peace

The day brings challenges. A minor argument about schedules, a triggering comment from a friend, a fleeting panic about being abandoned.

Old Rayna would have spiraled. She would have lashed out, retreated, or questioned love itself. New Rayna hesitates. Breathes. Pauses. She allows Marcus to respond without judgment. She allows herself to feel without fleeing. Every choice is a small victory:

- a breath instead of a reaction
- a conversation instead of a silent accusation
- trust instead of fear

This is the test. This is how you prove peace is earned not by chaos, not by survival, but by showing up fully, even when afraid.

The Recognition Of Growth

That evening, they sit on the porch, watching the sky turn copper and violet. Marcus reaches over, intertwines fingers with hers. "We're both haunted," he says. "But look at us. Still standing." She leans into him, feeling the warmth, the steadiness.

"I've been afraid my scars would push you away." "Your scars aren't a problem," he says. "They're proof. Proof that you're still here. Proof that you can love yourself. Proof that I can love you." She realizes that finding peace isn't just about letting go of the past.

It's about accepting the present fully. It's about seeing the person beside you... broken, healed, human and deciding to stay anyway. Finding peace isn't a single moment.

It's a thousand choices layered into days, into breaths, into conversations. It's learning to love without expecting chaos to confirm it. It's choosing to trust love when your nervous system screams otherwise. Rayna closes her eyes, resting against Marcus. For the first time, she feels the quiet hum of alignment between two souls.

Two flawed, scarred, human hearts, learning that healing together doesn't erase pain. It transforms it. "I think," she whispers, "I'm finally ready to be loved without testing it." "And I'm ready to love you without asking for permission," he replies. And in the space between them, peace takes root.

The Heart Learns Its Language

Love isn't learned in classrooms. It isn't written in books. It is felt, tested, survived, and nurtured. Rayna had learned to survive everything. Marcus had learned to survive himself. Now, together, they were learning to thrive.

The New Rhythm

Morning comes with coffee, quiet chatter, the mundane turning sacred. Rayna notices the small things. Marcus humming while making the bed, the way he remembers the exact way she likes her tea, the pause in his eyes when he listens fully. "You're really paying attention," she says, almost in disbelief. "Always," he replies. "You deserve to be heard.

Not corrected. Not fixed. Just heard." It's a language she hasn't understood until now, the language of love spoken in calm tones, consistent actions, and respect for her boundaries.

The Shadows Still Linger

But love doesn't erase the past. It doesn't make trauma vanish. Marcus has shadows too... fears, insecurities, memories of being hurt, of being abandoned. Sometimes his patience cracks, and his voice hardens. Sometimes she misinterprets his quiet as judgment.

They still trigger each other, but differently now. Instead of spiraling into chaos, they pause. They speak. They clarify. They ask instead of assuming. They level up together, not against each other.

The Psychology Of Dual Healing

Psychologists call this co-regulation: two nervous systems learning to stabilize each other. Rayna feels her panic rise. Marcus notices. He doesn't react with frustration or defense. He breathes with her. "It's okay," he says softly.

"We're learning the same language." And that phrase simple, grounding becomes a lifeline. Love is no longer about proving worth. It's about meeting halfway, lifting each other, and honoring the process.

The Lesson Of Vulnerability

That night, she shares a secret she's never told anyone: "Sometimes I feel guilty for being scared even now... for needing reassurance after everything I've survived." He doesn't flinch. He doesn't lecture. He simply replies: "I feel the same. But we're learning to stay present, not perfect."

It's a new kind of intimacy. One built not on perfection, but authenticity. They are unpolished, scared, human and choosing to love anyway.

Leveling Up

They start practicing small rituals:

- morning check-ins about feelings
- evenings spent sharing gratitude
- nights where triggers are spoken aloud, not acted on
- silent touches, hand squeezes, small notes left for each other

Each act isn't grand. But each act rewires their brains. Slowly, steadily, together. They are learning that love isn't a rescue. It's a partnership. It's growth. It's leveling up without leaving each other behind.

The Revelation

Rayna realizes: I am not defined by the trauma I survived. I am defined by the love I allow myself to receive. By the trust I allow myself to give. By the courage I have to stand in my own light and still reach for another's. Marcus smiles, sensing the shift. His own heart has mirrored hers.Strengthened by her courage, softened by her vulnerability. Two flawed hearts. Two scarred souls. Two people choosing to level up together instead of letting the past dictate their present.

The heart has a language older than words. It speaks in consistency, patience, attention, and respect. It answers fear with presence. It builds trust with action. Rayna's heart had learned it slowly. Marcus's heart had taught it gently. Together, they are fluent. And for the first time, the future doesn't feel like something to survive. It feels like something to live.

Full Circle

The past doesn't knock politely. It doesn't announce itself. It whispers, it echoes, it waits. Testing the foundation you've worked so hard to build. Rayna feels it in the quiet moments: a flash of memory, a familiar doubt, a shadowed feeling of not enough. But now, the echoes don't control her. Now, she answers.

The Return Of The Echo

A message arrives from someone she once trusted... a past lover, a ghost of old chaos. It reads: "You really think you're done with the past?" She holds the phone, breath trembling. Old Rayna would have spiraled. Old Rayna would have argued, explained, chased, and justified. But the new Rayna doesn't reply. Instead, she turns to Marcus.

"Do you see this?" She asks. "I do," he replies, "but it doesn't need your energy. It can't touch what we've built." And suddenly, she understands: healing isn't about erasing the past. It's about reclaiming your present.

The Test Of Trust

Later, a disagreement arises small, mundane, nothing life-threatening. Old Rayna would have erupted, consumed by fear and old survival instincts. Instead, they pause. They talk. They listen. They navigate the storm together, not against each other.

Marcus admits his own fear: "Sometimes I'm scared I'll repeat my old mistakes." Rayna takes his hand, recognizing her own truth in his words: "Sometimes I'm scared too. But we're not our pasts. We're our choices." Two scarred hearts, finally learning the language of mutual grace.

The Power Of Mutual Healing

They sit on the porch as the sun sets. The silence isn't empty. It's heavy with understanding. Rayna realizes something: the love I needed all along wasn't about being saved. It was about being seen. It was about finding someone willing to show up, even with their own wounds.

Marcus leans over and whispers: "I see you, completely. The broken, the scared, the resilient... all of you." For the first time, she doesn't flinch from love. For the first time, love doesn't ask her to perform, prove, or fight. It simply exists... steady, unwavering, patient.

The Symbolism Of A Full Circle

A full circle isn't returning to the beginning. It's standing where you once fell, recognizing every scar, every lesson, every misstep, and knowing that it led you to this moment. They laugh quietly at a memory that would have once ruined a day. They share a touch that speaks louder than apologies ever could. They look at each other, two people who survived everything now choosing to thrive together. "We're here," Rayna says softly.

"Yes," Marcus replies. "And we're staying." The revelation of the connection their love isn't perfect. Their scars aren't gone. But they have learned something more profound: healing doesn't mean being unbroken. Love doesn't mean being flawless.

Peace doesn't mean fear disappears. It means choosing each other in spite of it all. It means leveling up together. It means knowing the past has shaped you, but doesn't define you. As night falls, Rayna rests her head on Marcus's shoulder.

She breathes in the life they've built, quiet but alive. She smiles, not as a mask, not as armor, not as a survivor performing strength but as a woman who has found the courage to live fully in love, with herself and another. Full circle isn't an ending. It's a beginning. A declaration that the past will echo, but it will no longer dictate the present. And in that space, peace doesn't whisper. It sings.

5

The Beginning of Us

I wasn't supposed to fall in love that summer. Mama told me boys were a distraction. Daddy just shook his head whenever I stayed on the phone too long. But I was seventeen, and my heart wanted what my house never gave me—someone to see me. Someone to choose me. His name was Tyrone Carter, but everybody called him Ty.

He had that smile that made you forget your own name for a second. The kind of smile that felt like sunlight after too many cloudy days. And when he looked at me? I swear it felt like God himself pressed pause on the whole world. Shayla said he was trouble. She always said that.

"Naomi, he's fine, yeah. But fine don't pay bills, and fine don't keep promises." I laughed her off, like I always did. Shayla had this hard way about her, like she'd already lived three lives in one. Me? I still believed in love songs and butterflies.

The first time Ty held my hand, it was at the basketball court after his game. Sweat still clung to him, and I didn't even care. His palm was warm, rough but steady. He pulled me close like I belonged there, like I'd always belonged there.

"You my girl now," he whispered. Just like that. No question. A statement. And my heart, foolish and hungry, believed every word. At home, Mama was too tired to notice me floating around the kitchen, smiling at nothing.

Daddy barely looked up from his paper. It was like I lived in a house where silence was louder than voices. So when Ty talked, even when he teased, even when he made fun of my little braids coming loose—I clung to it. Because finally, somebody saw me.

The First Betrayal – Seeds of Distrust

Somebody Saw Me

Mama said boys only wanted one thing. Daddy said nothing at all. And me? I wanted everything—late-night calls, hand-holding at the park, someone who looked at me like I mattered. That's what Ty did. At least in the beginning. He had that smile—the one that made me feel like the world finally noticed me.

He said, "You my girl now," like it wasn't a question. And my heart, too hungry to argue, believed him. At home, nobody cared why I was smiling at nothing. Mama was too tired, Daddy too silent. So when Ty talked—even when he teased—I clung to his words like they were gospel. Finally, somebody saw me.

But here's the thing about being seen: sometimes people don't see you. They see what they want from you. They see your loneliness, your hunger, your ache to be chosen. And Ty? He saw all of that in me before I even understood it in myself. I didn't know it then, but the night he called me "his girl," he was planting something in me. A seed. And seeds don't just grow flowers. They grow weeds, too. The summer I met Ty, I was seventeen, but inside I felt both younger and older than that.

Younger, because I still believed in the kind of love you see in music videos, where the boy fights for the girl, no matter what. Older, because I'd already grown used to living in a house where silence was louder than words. Mama worked double shifts at the hospital. When she came home, her body moved like it was made of bricks.

She didn't ask about my day. She asked if I did the dishes. Daddy worked too, but when he wasn't working, he was on the porch with his beer, staring into the street like he was waiting for someone to come back who never would. So when Ty looked at me like I was worth looking at, it didn't just feel good. It felt necessary.

Ty's world was nothing like mine. He had a crew—always laughing, always loud, always moving in a way that made people clear space for them. I didn't belong there, not really, but the moment he laced his fingers through mine, I felt like I had been upgraded. Like the whole block knew: Naomi finally mattered. Shayla, my best friend since middle school, saw it different. "Girl, he trouble. The kind of fine that come with consequences."

I rolled my eyes. "Not everybody a villain, Shay." She smirked. "Not everybody, no. But Ty Carter? Please." I hated that she said it with certainty, like she'd read the last page of a book I was only just starting. The first time Ty kissed me, it was at the basketball court.

His friends were clowning, music blasting from somebody's speaker. The sky was spilling orange and pink, and my heart was a runaway train. He leaned in, quick, sure, like he'd done it a thousand times before. When his lips met mine, I felt like I'd stepped into the song I'd been waiting my whole life to hear. But afterward—after the chorus faded—he pulled back and smirked. "You mine now. Don't forget that." It wasn't romantic. It wasn't tender. It was a claim. And I, desperate to be claimed, nodded without question.

That night, lying in bed, staring at the ceiling fan spinning slow, I thought about how different his voice sounded from my father's silence. How his eyes burned in ways Mama's never did when she looked at me. And in my hunger, I told myself this was love. But deep down, buried under all the butterflies and teenage dreams, something small whispered: Be careful. Love shouldn't feel like ownership. I ignored it. I always ignored it. Because finally—finally—somebody saw me.

Red Flags Don't Always Look Red

Ty liked to show me off. We'd walk down the block, his hand heavy on my waist like he was announcing something to the whole world. "This mine," his eyes said. Sometimes he'd whisper it out loud, low enough for only me to hear. At first, I thought it was sweet. Who doesn't want to be chosen like that? But sweetness can turn sticky real fast. The first time it happened, we were at the corner store.

Some boy from school held the door open for me. Just polite, nothing else. I said, "Thank you." Ty's face shifted. His jaw locked, his arm around me tightened. "What you say thank you to him for?" he asked as we walked inside. I blinked, confused. "Because... he held the door?" Ty shook his head, low chuckle in his throat that didn't sound like laughter. "Naomi, you don't owe every dude your smile.

Don't give 'em nothing." I didn't know what to say. He wasn't yelling, but his words hung in the air like a warning. Later that night, on the phone, I told Shayla. She snorted. "Girl, that's jealousy. First sign." I tried to defend him. "No, it's just... he likes me. He don't want nobody else looking at me." Shayla sighed so loud, I could hear the shake of her head through the line. "Naomi, listen to yourself.

Since when is liking somebody the same thing as controlling them?" I wanted to argue. I wanted to tell her she didn't get it, that Ty made me feel special in a way nobody ever had. But the truth was, a small part of me knew she was right. I just wasn't ready to hear it. Because being wanted—being claimed—felt better than being invisible.

Home didn't make it easier. Mama came home one night, dropped her bag, kicked her shoes off like her feet were on fire. She heated up leftovers, barely spoke. Daddy sat on the couch, TV glowing in his face, not saying a word. I wanted to tell them about Ty.

I wanted to say, Somebody loves me. Somebody picked me. But looking at them, I swallowed the words. How could I talk about love in a house where nobody touched, nobody smiled, nobody asked how the other one was doing? So I went upstairs, dialed Ty's number, and let his voice fill the silence.

One Friday, he picked me up after school. His car smelled like cologne and fast food. Music blasting, windows down, his crew laughing in the back. We stopped at the park. He pulled me close, hand tight on my thigh. "Don't wear that skirt around nobody but me," he muttered. I looked down at my outfit—just a plain denim skirt, nothing crazy. "What's wrong with it?" I asked. "Too many eyes out here.

Don't matter if you don't see it—they do. And I don't like it." The way he said it made my stomach twist. Half of me wanted to argue. The other half wanted to please him, keep him happy, keep him choosing me. So I tugged at the hem and said, "Okay." And the smile that spread across his face made me forget the unease in my chest—for a while. That night, lying in bed, I thought about Mama again.

How she worked herself into the ground but never complained. How Daddy stayed but barely spoke. Maybe this was just what love looked like—swallowing your words, bending yourself smaller, keeping the peace. Maybe I was just learning the rules early.

The First Crack

I should've known the moment it happened that summer would change me forever. It was a Thursday—hot, sticky, the kind of heat that made your skin feel like it was sticking to itself. Ty and I were sitting on the curb outside my house, sharing a soda, his arm lazily draped around my shoulders. I felt like the world was ours. Then I saw her. Her laugh—high, loud, like she was auditioning for a spot in the sky. She walked past us, and Ty's head turned, his eyes following every step. I froze.

"Who's that?" I asked, trying to keep my voice light. "Who?" he said, smirking. "The girl... you just looked at." He rolled his eyes and laughed, brushing my hand off his arm. "Naomi, she's nothing. Just some girl from school. Don't worry about her."

But I worried. I wanted to believe him. I wanted to believe he wouldn't do anything, wouldn't even feel anything for her. But my stomach twisted, like a fist had clenched itself inside. "Nothing?" I pressed. "You looked..." My words faltered, embarrassed even for feeling them. "Naomi." He leaned closer, brushing a strand of hair from my face.

"You my girl. You hear me? Nobody else matters." I nodded. My throat tight. My heart wanted to scream, but I swallowed. I wanted to believe him. I always wanted to believe him. That night, I lay in bed, staring at the ceiling, wondering if I was imagining things. Maybe I had seen too much, worried too much.

Maybe it really was nothing. I grabbed my journal, the one I never let anyone touch, and wrote: *He says I'm his girl. Why do I feel like I'm not enough?* It was the first time I ever questioned myself because of someone else. Because of love. The next day, Shayla called. Her voice was sharp, like she could see the storm I was trying to hide from.

"You saw it, didn't you?" she asked. "I... I don't know what you mean," I mumbled. "Naomi, he's already looking at someone else. You didn't notice?" I did notice. But I hated myself for noticing. I hated the thought that maybe my stomach knew more than my heart did.

"Shayla, it's nothing. He told me I'm his girl," I said, trying to sound confident. "You're seventeen. That's all you are right now. Don't let him twist you before you even know what love is." I hung up before I could argue. I loved him. I needed him. And I knew... deep down... that maybe she was right. Over the next few days, Ty's "nothing" turned into attention again—his texts, his teasing, little favors, kisses on my forehead that made me melt. Each time, I forgot the girl I saw him looking at on Thursday.

Each time, I blamed myself for thinking I'd seen too much. It was the first crack. The first real split in my heart. And the worst part? I didn't pull away. I clung harder. Because love, when it's new and thrilling, makes you forget that cracks exist. It makes you forget that people are not always what they seem. It makes you believe you can fix someone else's heart with your own.

Whispered Warnings

I should have listened. I really should have. But I didn't. Shayla and the girls cornered me one Saturday after school, sitting cross-legged on the worn carpet in her tiny living room. The air smelled like popcorn and nail polish.

They looked at me like I had lost my mind. "Naomi," Shayla said, her eyes sharp, cutting through me like a knife, "he's playing you. You know that, right?" I shook my head, fingers twisting the hem of my shirt. "He's not. He wouldn't do that. I… I trust him." Vanessa, a girl from our math class who always seemed older than her sixteen years, leaned forward. "Naomi, you're seventeen. He's nineteen.

You think he's in love with you? Or does he just like being needed?" I felt my throat tighten. My chest, like it was trying to squeeze out of my ribcage. "He loves me," I whispered, almost to myself. Shayla rolled her eyes. "He loves being loved. That's not the same thing." I wanted to argue. I wanted to tell them I knew him.

That he had said he was mine, and that I felt it in my bones. I wanted to scream that nobody else understood. But a small, quiet part of me—the part that stayed up at night listening to the silence in my house—wondered if they were right. Maybe he wasn't who I thought he was. Maybe. Ty called that night.

"Where you at?" he asked, voice low, smooth. "At home," I said, clutching the phone like it was the only thing keeping me steady. "I been thinking 'bout you all day," he said, and I felt my chest swell. "You my girl, Naomi. Don't listen to what them girls say." I closed my eyes and let it wash over me. Let it drown out Shayla's warnings.

Let it drown out that small, stubborn voice inside me that whispered, he's not yours. He can't be trusted. "I won't," I said softly, almost a prayer. The next week, little things started slipping into my days. Ty would cancel plans at the last minute but act like it was no big deal.

He'd flirt in front of me with other girls and laugh it off like it was a joke. When I got upset, he'd do something small—brush my hair back, kiss my hand, whisper my name—and I'd forgive him. Every. Single. Time.

It was like walking on a floor made of glass. Every step could cut me, but the pain came slowly, and the pleasure felt too good to notice the bleeding. Shayla didn't stop trying. "You better wake up, Naomi," she said during lunch one day, poking me in the arm with her French manicure.

"One day you gonna look up and see he been lying the whole time, and you'll be too deep to pull out." "I'm not deep," I said, forcing a laugh. "I can handle it." Her eyes softened. "I hope so. I really do. But some people don't know how to love right. Some people—" she stopped herself, shaking her head, "—some people just don't see you. Not really." I looked down at my tray, chewing my fries slowly.

Maybe she was right. Maybe she wasn't. But for that moment, I closed my eyes and pictured Ty's smile. The way he made me feel like I mattered. Like finally, somebody saw me. And just like that, I chose him again.

Silent Homes, Loud Hearts

Home was supposed to be safe. It wasn't. Mama came in late, her hair pulled back tight, her shoes kicking against the tile as she dumped her bag on the counter. "Dinner's in the microwave," she mumbled, eyes already back on her phone. Daddy sat in his chair, hands on his knees, staring at the TV like it was the only thing keeping him alive.

He didn't look at me. Didn't ask about my day. Didn't ask if I had done my homework or eaten lunch. So I didn't say a word. I didn't need to. Ty, on the other hand, made me feel alive. He called me in the middle of the night sometimes, just to hear me laugh.

He held my hand tight when we walked past a group of boys who tried to talk to me. He kissed me like he was claiming me, like I was the most important thing in the world. And in that moment, home didn't matter. Family didn't matter. Only he mattered. I wanted to tell my parents. I wanted to shout, "Somebody loves me! Somebody picked me!" But what would they say? Mama would sigh, tired and distracted. Daddy would shrug and turn back to the TV. I already knew the answer: nothing.

So I went to my room and dialed Ty's number instead. It was easy to forget that love could hurt when Ty was around. He had this way of making every ordinary moment feel electric. Sitting on the curb, sharing a soda, listening to music blasting from his beat-up car—they were simple things, but with him, they felt monumental. And yet... small cracks were forming. The other day, he'd snapped at me because I smiled at a boy in class.

The week before, he flirted with another girl right in front of me, then laughed it off like it was nothing. Each time, I forgave him. Each time, he kissed my hand or whispered my name, and I forgot the sting.

I wondered if this is what love was supposed to feel like: confusing, thrilling, painful, and impossible to let go of. I thought about Shayla's warnings. "Naomi, you're seventeen. He's nineteen. You don't need to let him rewrite your heart." I loved her for saying it. I hated her for saying it.

And still, I ignored her. Because Ty made me feel alive in a way my family never had. When I lay in bed at night, the ceiling fan spinning above me, I could hear the silence of the house like a drumbeat. Silent. Empty. Lonely. And then Ty's voice would come over the phone, soft, protective, claiming me.

Finally—finally—I was seen. But being seen didn't make the silence at home disappear. It didn't make me less hungry for attention, less desperate for affection. It only made me cling harder, trust harder, and forgive faster. Because I needed him. And for the first time, I realized—I would do almost anything to keep him.

Betrayal, First Taste

I should have seen it coming. But I didn't. Ty called me that Friday like nothing had happened. His voice was smooth, like honey over broken glass. "Hey, baby," he said. My chest tightened. "What's up?" "Nothing," I mumbled, trying to sound casual.

But the nothing didn't matter. What mattered was what I saw later. I was walking past the corner store, thinking about picking up a soda, when I saw him. Not alone. Not harmless. But laughing with her.

The girl from school. The one I'd seen him looking at weeks ago. Laughing like she owned his attention, like I didn't exist. And my stomach dropped like a stone in a well. I wanted to scream. I wanted to run over there and rip the happiness out of her hands.

But I didn't. Instead, I watched, frozen. When I finally saw him later that night, my chest felt like it had been carved open. "You... what's going on?"

I demanded, voice shaking, heart hammering. Ty smirked, that infuriating smirk that used to make me melt. "What do you mean?" "The girl. At the store. Laughing. You were... you were..." "Naomi," he said, calm, soft, patronizing.

"You're imagining things. You always do. You see threats where there ain't none." And just like that, the stone in my chest turned into molten fire. I wanted to throw something at him. I wanted to scream so loud that the night swallowed me whole. But instead, I swallowed it. "Maybe I am," I whispered, feeling my own sanity slip through my fingers. The rage started quietly at first.

A fire behind my eyes, burning my chest every time he smiled, every time he reached for my hand, every time he whispered, You're mine. I hated him for the way he made me doubt myself. I hated myself for loving him anyway. I hated the way my own heart betrayed me, clinging to his words like they were lifelines. He didn't cheat in front of me again—not exactly.

But he left traces. Little glances. Texts I wasn't supposed to see. Comments to friends that made me doubt myself. And every time I confronted him, he twisted it, smoothed it over, made me feel guilty for questioning him.

I was learning the first lesson in manipulation: when someone controls the story, they control your reality. That night, alone in my room, I ripped open my journal like it was a lifeboat. *I hate him. I hate me. I hate that I want him.*

Tears blurred the words, anger shaking my hand as I wrote. Rage and hurt intertwined. How could someone you loved make you feel so small, so insane, so powerless? And yet... the next time he called, I answered. Because love—or what I thought was love—had me in its grip. And I was starting to understand. Not fully. Not yet. But enough to feel the fire.

The Pull of Comfort

It should have been easy. To walk away. To slam the door and never look back. But it wasn't. Ty's voice was the first thing I heard when I got home that Friday night. Soft, low, like he was reading my thoughts before I even had them. "Naomi... you okay?" I wanted to scream at him. I wanted to hurl every word of rage I had.

But instead, my fingers gripped the phone like it was a lifeline. "I'm fine," I whispered. The lie was thin. I could feel it cracking under my chest. He knew I wasn't fine. And that was the cruelest part. Ty showed up outside my house twenty minutes later, leaning against his car, looking impossibly calm, impossibly effortless.

The sun glinted off the windshield like it had chosen to spotlight him, and I hated it. I hated him. I hated that I wanted him. "Get in," he said. I hesitated. My stomach twisted, warning bells screaming.

But then I saw that smile—the one that had made me feel seen, wanted, alive. And my body moved before my brain could stop it. I got in. The drive was quiet at first. Just the hum of the tires on asphalt, the wind through the windows, music low, almost like it was sneaking into my ears without permission.

"Why'd you ignore me today?" he finally asked, his hand brushing mine. "I... I was mad," I said, more truthful than I realized. "Good," he said, smiling. "I like it when you get mad. Makes it real. Shows you care." I blinked. "Care? You're the one—" "I know," he interrupted gently. "I messed up. I shouldn't have laughed with her. I shouldn't have made you feel small. I'm sorry. You know I'm sorry."

And just like that, my chest unclenched. My heart, still raw from betrayal, began to forgive him again. That's how it worked. Pain, then pleasure. Rage, then comfort. Every apology, every small act of kindness, every whispered promise pulled me back in. Every time, I forgot the fire burning behind my eyes. Every time, I convinced myself I was strong enough to handle it. But I wasn't. I wanted to hate him.

I wanted to burn every memory of him like the gasoline fire I imagined in my dreams. And yet... when he held my hand, traced my jaw with his thumb, whispered my name, I melted. I told myself it was love. I told myself that being chosen, even imperfectly, was better than being invisible.

But deep down, my gut, the one part of me that had started to see through his manipulation, screamed, *Run. Run now before it's too late.* I didn't. Home felt colder than ever that night. Mama was asleep on the couch, exhausted. Daddy was in his chair, silent, the TV flickering across his face.

I went to my room, climbed into bed, and clutched my pillow like a shield. Ty called ten minutes later. I answered. Because comfort—even toxic comfort—was better than the silence at home. And I needed him.

Fractured Trust

It all hit me at once. The texts I wasn't supposed to see. The lies he told me with a smile. The way he made me feel insane for trusting my own eyes, my own gut. I wanted to scream, to throw the phone across the room.

I wanted to burn the memory of every kiss, every soft word, every "you're mine" that had wrapped me in chains. Ty had become a storm I couldn't escape, and I was drowning in it. I confronted him, voice trembling with rage I couldn't contain. "Why, Ty? Why are you like this? You say I'm yours, but you do everything to prove I'm nothing."

He leaned back, smirk curling at the corner of his lips. "Naomi... baby, you overreact. You think everything's a test? You think I'm the villain?" "I'm not imagining this!" I shouted. "I see what you do!" He shrugged, calm, practiced. "Then maybe it's you, Naomi. Maybe you're the problem. Maybe you see threats where there are none.

You're insecure. That's all it is." My fists clenched. I wanted to hit him. I wanted to make him feel the fire inside me. But I didn't. Because a small, broken piece of me still hoped he'd change. That night, I couldn't sleep.

I lay in the dark, replaying every lie, every excuse, every soft word that had pulled me back in. And for the first time, I saw it clearly: I wasn't crazy. I wasn't overreacting. He was manipulating me. And I hated him. I hated myself. I hated that I loved him.

Breaking Point

It was over the phone. "I can't do this anymore, Ty. I'm done," I whispered. He laughed softly, almost tenderly, like I was the one making a mistake. "Naomi... you'll be back. You always come back." "No," I said, shaking, tears burning my cheeks. "Not this time." I hung up. The weeks that followed were hell.

I hated myself for feeling empty without him. I hated that part of me still longed for the warmth of his touch. But slowly, painfully, I began to reclaim myself. I spent nights writing in my journal, pouring out rage, grief, and betrayal. I called Shayla, cried on her shoulder, let her remind me I was stronger than I felt. I stopped calling Ty.

Blocked his number. Removed him from my social media. It wasn't easy. Every memory screamed at me. But I realized something crucial: I didn't need someone to see me to matter. I already mattered.

Seeds of Distrust

By the time school started again, I had changed. Hardened, maybe. Wiser, certainly. I walked past the places Ty used to hang out without looking back. I laughed with friends without waiting for his call. I focused on myself. Mama noticed, eventually. "You're different," she said one evening, handing me a plate of food.

"Yes," I replied softly, and meant it. I wasn't the same naïve girl who had fallen for the charm of a boy who could never love me right. But I was better. Stronger. Smarter. And I had my voice back. For the first time, I realized something: the fire Ty had left behind wasn't just destruction. It was a seed.

A seed of awareness. A seed of strength. A seed that would make me impossible to manipulate again. I was hurt. I was angry. I was scared. But I was free. And I would never let anyone see me and claim me like that again.

The Cage

It started small. "Don't wear that dress," Marcus said one night as Jade got ready. She laughed, thinking it was a joke. "Why not? It's just dinner."

His smile was sharp, controlled. "Because it's for me. Not for them." She rolled her eyes but changed anyway.

The next week, he questioned why she was out so late with her girlfriends. The week after that, he showed up at her job unannounced, his arm heavy around her waist, marking territory. At first, it felt protective.

Then it felt suffocating. Her friends noticed before she did. "Girl, he's isolating you," Shayla warned (yes—the same Shayla who had warned Naomi back in Book 1, now older, wiser, watching Jade slip into the same trap). "He's controlling your clothes, your time, your people. That's not love."

Jade shook her head, though her chest tightened. "It's just how he is. He's intense. He loves hard." But late at night, when she stared at the ceiling fan spinning shadows across the room, she wondered if she was in love—or in a cage.

The Mask Slips

The lipstick stain hadn't been enough to convince her. The late nights at the office hadn't either. But when she found the messages on his phone, she couldn't deny it anymore. *Baby, last night was amazing. When can I see you again? Don't tell your girl.* Her heart plummeted, breaking clean in two. When she confronted him, she expected rage.

Instead, she got laughter. "You went through my phone?" Marcus asked, shaking his head. "That's crazy. You're crazy." "Crazy? Marcus, the proof is right here!" she shouted, shoving the phone toward him. He leaned back on the couch, calm, infuriatingly calm. "Those texts don't mean anything.

You're reading too much into it. You're insecure, Jade. Always looking for something to be mad about." Tears blurred her vision, but rage burned through them. "You're cheating on me!" Marcus leaned in close, his voice soft, deadly. "I'm not cheating.

But even if I was—who else is gonna love you like I do?" The words cut deeper than the betrayal itself. Because part of her feared he was right.

The Spiral

From that moment, nothing made sense. She hated him. She loved him. She couldn't breathe without him. Marcus tightened the grip. Flowers when she threatened to leave. Silence when she asked for answers. Kisses when she cried. Control when she tried to resist. Her friends' voices grew fainter. Her own voice disappeared under his.

One night, she caught her reflection in the mirror and barely recognized herself. Hollow eyes. Forced smile. A woman unraveling in the name of love. But still, she stayed. Because leaving meant facing the emptiness Marcus had filled. Leaving meant admitting she'd chosen chaos over peace, and now peace felt foreign.

The Other Woman

Jade wasn't looking for proof anymore. But proof found her. It started with a late-night call Marcus "accidentally" left his phone unattended for. A name she didn't recognize flashed across the screen: Nia. She answered before she could stop herself. "Marcus?" the voice purred. "Last night was perfect. I can still feel you." Jade's stomach lurched.

Her hand trembled, but her voice came out cold. "This is Jade. Who the hell are you?" The silence on the other end stretched too long. Finally, a laugh—low, mocking. "So you're the girlfriend. Cute." Click. Jade stood frozen, the phone hot in her hand, her chest heaving like the air had been knocked out of her.

Everything inside her screamed to deny it. But she couldn't unhear the truth. Marcus wasn't just cheating. He had a whole other woman who knew about her. And the way she laughed... like Jade was the fool.

Fire in the Veins

When Marcus came home, Jade was waiting. The phone sat on the table like evidence in a courtroom. Her eyes were sharp, blazing with fury. "Who's Nia?" she demanded. He sighed, tossed his keys down. "Jade, you trippin' again—" "No!" she screamed, her voice shaking the walls. "Don't you dare gaslight me this time!" She called. I heard her.

S"he laughed at me, Marcus. Laughed. Like I'm some kind of joke." Marcus's mask slipped for the first time. His jaw clenched. His eyes narrowed. "Maybe you are a joke," he spat, stepping closer.

"Always snooping, always accusing. You push me into other women's arms. You ever think about that?" The words sliced through her like knives. She wanted to crumble, to let the shame swallow her.

But something inside her snapped instead. "I'm done," she said, her voice low, steady, dangerous. He laughed, but it sounded forced. "You ain't goin' nowhere." And for the first time, Jade didn't believe him.

The Leaving

The night she left, rain pounded the streets like the sky was screaming with her. She packed a single bag. Not everything—just enough to walk away with her sanity. Marcus followed her to the door, his voice alternating between begging and threatening.

"You really gon' leave me? After everything I've done for you?" "You ain't nothing without me, Jade. Nothing!" "Please... don't go. I'll change. I swear." But she didn't look back.

Her hands shook as she closed the door, but her feet carried her forward. Every step was heavy with grief, rage, betrayal—yet laced with the faintest whisper of freedom. For the first time, Jade heard her own heartbeat louder than his voice. And she knew: leaving Marcus wasn't the end. It was the beginning.

Crossing Paths

Jade showed up at Shayla's door with her hair wet from rain, mascara smeared like war paint. She clutched a duffel bag, eyes swollen, voice flat. "Can I stay?" Shayla didn't ask questions. She just stepped aside.

On the couch, Naomi sat scrolling her phone, legs curled up, looking almost peaceful—until her eyes lifted and locked with Jade's. They didn't know each other. But in that split second, Jade saw it—the tired eyes, the hollow smile, the way her body sagged like it had been carrying invisible chains.

"You left him," Naomi said. Her voice wasn't soft. It was sharp, certain. Jade froze, bag still in her hand. "How do you know?" Naomi leaned back, lips curling into something bitter. "Because men like Ty and Marcus? They don't let go. And women like us—we don't leave unless we're dying inside."

The words sliced Jade open. She dropped her bag, sat hard on the couch, and the tears came hot and violent. Naomi didn't comfort her. She just watched, a silent witness. And maybe that was worse—because Naomi's silence said: I already know your story. I've lived it.

Stories in the Dark

They stayed up until 3 a.m., trading nightmares like kids swapping candy. Naomi spoke of Ty's vanishing acts, his half-truths and full lies, the way he dangled affection like a carrot. "He'd disappear for three days," Naomi said, voice flat, eyes far away. "Then come back with a smile and a story. And I believed him. Every time. Like a fool." Jade nodded, wiping her face with the back of her hand.

"Marcus wasn't a ghost. He was a jailer. Wanted me dressed the way he liked, wanted me home when he said. And when I caught him cheating, you know what he told me?"

Naomi arched a brow. "What?" "That it was my fault." Jade's voice cracked, rage mixing with shame. "Said I pushed him to it. Said no one else would put up with me." Naomi's mouth twisted into something dark.

"Ty said the same shit. Like they got the same damn script." Shayla, leaning against the kitchen counter, finally spoke. "Because they do got the same script. Men like that don't love you—they feed off you. Off your silence, your doubt, your need to fix them." Jade's hands balled into fists. "I hate him. I hate myself for letting him—" Her voice broke. Naomi leaned closer, her whisper almost venom. "Don't you dare hate yourself.

Save that hate for him. Let it burn." The room went still, heavy with the weight of rage unspoken. Two women, bound not by friendship but by the toxic fingerprints left on their hearts. And both of them knew: Ty and Marcus weren't finished. Not by a long shot.

Old Ghosts

Jade's phone wouldn't stop buzzing. At first, she ignored it. Turned it face-down. Tried to focus on the TV as Naomi flipped through channels. But Marcus's name lit up again and again. MARCUS CALLING... MARCUS CALLING...

She knew she should block him. Knew answering was like lighting a match in a room full of gas. But the sound of his voice echoed in her head: *Who else gonna love you like me?* Her hand hovered over the phone. Naomi's sharp voice cut through. "Don't." Jade jerked, guilty. "I wasn't—" "Yes, you were." Naomi didn't even look at her.

"That's how it starts. One answer. One 'let me hear him out.' Next thing you know, you're right back in the cage." Jade bit her lip, fighting tears. But her silence was already an answer. Across the room, Naomi's phone buzzed.

Her heart stopped. Ty: Miss me? She slammed the phone face-down on the table, pulse racing. Her stomach twisted with disgust and longing all at once. “Shit,” Naomi whispered. Shayla’s voice came from the kitchen, sharp as glass.

“See? Both of y’all about to fall for the same tricks. Different men, same poison.” Naomi and Jade shared a look. Shame. Hunger. Rage. Because the ghosts weren’t ghosts. They were still alive, still circling. And the women weren’t ready to stop answering.

The Knock at the Door

It happened on a Thursday night. Rain beat the windows. The apartment smelled like wine and takeout. And then—BANG. BANG. BANG. Shayla jumped. “Who the hell—” But Jade already knew. Her stomach dropped. “Open up, Jade!” Marcus’s voice roared through the door, full of rage and possession. “I know you in there!” Jade froze, eyes wide, heart pounding so hard she thought she’d faint. Naomi stood, anger flaring.

“You told him where you were?” Jade shook her head, tears spilling. “I don’t know how—he just—” Marcus slammed his fist against the door again, harder. The sound rattled the walls. “You think you can just leave me? After everything I did for you? You ungrateful bitch!” Jade’s breath came in shallow gasps.

Her whole body trembled. Naomi stepped between her and the door, voice low and fierce. “Don’t you dare open it.” Then, almost as if the universe was laughing, Naomi’s phone lit up again. Ty: Outside. Come down. Her knees buckled. She pressed a hand to her chest, eyes darting to the door. Two men. Two monsters. Both waiting outside like wolves. The women looked at each other. Naomi’s jaw tightened. “They came hunting.” Shayla grabbed a baseball bat from the corner.

“Then let ‘em learn—this ain’t the same women they broke.” The banging grew louder. The phones buzzed. The air crackled with fear and fury. And for the first time, Naomi and Jade realized: this wasn't about love anymore. It was war.

Back to the Fire

Naomi's heels clicked against wet pavement as she ran to Ty's car, rain plastering her hair to her face. He was waiting, engine humming, smile sweet and poisonous. "Damn, baby," he said, leaning over to open the door. "You look even better when you mad." Naomi slid inside, heart pounding. "Why are you here?"

Ty smirked. "Because you still mine. No matter what story you tell yourself." His words coiled around her spine. She wanted to slap him, scream at him—but instead, her lips trembled with a whisper. "I hate you." Ty leaned close, breath warm against her ear. "Good. Hate means you still feel me." Her body betrayed her.

The tears that slipped out weren't just grief—they were hunger. The sick, twisted hunger of wanting the very man who destroyed her. And Ty knew it.

The Breaking Point

Back in Shayla's apartment, Jade sat on the floor, hand bleeding, heart still hammering from Marcus's invasion. Shayla wrapped her hand in a dish towel, muttering curses under her breath. "He's gonna come back. Men like that don't lose easy." Jade's voice cracked.

"I almost let him take me again." Shayla grabbed her chin, forcing her to look up. "Almost don't matter. You're still here." Jade swallowed hard. For the first time, she felt something shift inside her—not strength, not yet, but defiance. Meanwhile, Naomi was spiraling deeper.

Ty drove her to his apartment. His cologne, his voice, his touch—they were the same poison wrapped in velvet. "You think Jade and Shayla know you like I do?" he whispered as he kissed her neck. "They don't know the real you. Only I do." Her body trembled.

Her heart screamed no, but her skin betrayed her. Because trauma bonds don't break clean. They rip you apart, piece by piece, until you don't know what's yours and what's his. By the time dawn broke, Naomi wasn't just back with Ty. She was back in chains.

Silence and Survival

The next morning told two different stories. In Shayla's apartment, Jade sat at the kitchen table, sipping bitter coffee with her bandaged hand. She was exhausted, shattered—but alive. And for the first time, she didn't feel Marcus's voice in her head. Only her own.

At Ty's place, Naomi stared at her reflection in the bathroom mirror. Mascara smeared, hickeys on her neck, shame burning her chest. She whispered to her reflection, "I said I'd never come back." Her reflection didn't answer. Behind her, Ty called out, lazy and smug.

"Baby, make us some breakfast." Naomi's eyes filled with tears. She pressed a hand to the glass, as if begging the woman in the mirror to rescue her. But the silence screamed louder than her voice.

6

Swipe Culture at Fifty

The Hook-Up Era

Jordan Rivers sat in his home office, laptop open, glass of bourbon sweating in his hand. Fifty-two, and still feeling like he was walking a tightrope between experience and impulse. He'd been through relationships, heartbreaks, and mistakes enough to know better, yet temptation had a way of finding him even now.

Maya Thompson, his partner of four years, was in the kitchen, humming while organizing dinner. She looked effortless at fifty—poised, confident, but there was a tension in her eyes that Jordan knew too well. Trust had been fragile between them ever since they got serious, especially in the age of social media, DMs, and the constant pull of attention.

Then there was KJ—Jordan's old friend turned relentless reminder of youth and lust. Fifty-four, charismatic, always smiling like he owned the room. KJ had this irritating way of testing boundaries, whispering temptation in subtle, dangerous ways. He had no filter, and the damn guy knew it.

Jordan scrolled through his feed, trying not to notice the flirtatious comments and suggestive DMs that had flooded his inbox. Every notification felt like a little trap, a siren song for someone who knew better but couldn't fully ignore the pull.

"You okay over there?" Maya's voice snapped him out of his thoughts.

"Yeah... just thinking," he muttered, setting the glass down. Thinking about the number of times digital attention had almost destroyed relationships he'd cared about, thinking about how temptation could sneak in even when you were supposed to be mature enough to recognize it.

Maya walked over, resting her hand on his shoulder. "You've been on that damn phone for twenty minutes. Who's sliding into your DMs now?"

Jordan gave a weak laugh. "No one... just notifications." He wasn't lying. There was no one significant—just attention from strangers, some harmless, some not. But the temptation wasn't about them; it was about the ego boost, the thrill, the confirmation that even after fifty years on this planet, he could still matter.

"Look," Maya said softly, "we've been through this. I get it. But this... this scrolling, this checking—it's like a test you're taking every damn day."

Jordan nodded. She was right. Real love wasn't about validation from strangers. But the digital world had a way of making even experienced men doubt themselves.

That's when KJ called, the voice on the other end breezy, casual, dangerous. "Jordan! Man, we gotta hit the new rooftop lounge tonight. You're not letting a little social media crap ruin your fun, are you?"

Jordan's stomach tightened. He didn't need the party. He didn't need the distractions. But the pull was there, subtle and insistent—the part of him that wanted to feel young, desirable, and reckless.

"I... I don't know, KJ. Maya and I have plans," Jordan said, trying to sound firm.

KJ laughed. "Come on, man. You're fifty-two, not dead. Live a little. Remember who you are. Don't let the damn DMs make you paranoid."

Jordan hung up and sat back, heart pounding. That was the thing about temptation—it wasn't about youth anymore. It was about ego, curiosity, and remembering the thrills of the past. Some old habits didn't die—they just got quieter, sneakier, harder to resist.

Maya watched him, arms crossed. "You can't hide behind your age, Jordan. Temptation doesn't care if you've got gray hair and a mortgage. It'll hit you right where it hurts."

He exhaled, knowing she was right. The hook-up era wasn't just for the young. It had evolved, grown more subtle, more invasive. And it didn't matter if you were fifty-two—you still had to fight for loyalty, for trust, for love that mattered.

Jordan turned off the laptop, finally deciding. The world could tempt him all it wanted, but his life, his love, and his peace were worth protecting.

But he knew one thing: the fight wasn't going to be easy.

Digital Desire

Jordan sat in the quiet of his study, phone buzzing again. Fifty-two, and still feeling like he was fighting a war he never enlisted for: attention, validation, and the subtle seduction of digital desire.

It wasn't the same as in his twenties. There were no reckless nights or foolish hookups—but there was curiosity, ego, and the small thrill of being noticed. A comment here, a DM there, and suddenly the mind wandered to places it shouldn't.

Ava Collins' name flashed on the screen. Forty-eight, sophisticated, sharp as hell, and dangerously aware of how to pull on someone's ego. Jordan hadn't sought her attention, but somehow, her messages found him. Subtle, flattering, teasing. "Still got it, Jordan? Bet you've got some stories to tell."

Maya was in the next room, humming as she worked on dinner. She trusted him—or at least she wanted to—but this digital landscape made even trust shaky. Every notification could be a distraction, a temptation, or worse, the start of a betrayal.

Jordan stared at the screen, heart racing. Part of him wanted to reply, just a little, just to see where it went. Another part of him, the part that had survived decades of heartbreak, whispered: Don't. Don't even think about it.

KJ had texted earlier, a casual "You up for tonight?" laced with nostalgia and challenge. Jordan knew what KJ represented: the pull of youth, lust, and ego wrapped in charm. KJ didn't care about loyalty. He cared about fun, excitement, and proving that age didn't mean restraint.

Jordan's thumb hovered over Ava's message. One reply could spiral him into a game he didn't want to play, one where attention and validation replaced connection. One reply could undo everything he had worked to protect.

He put the phone down and exhaled. That's the thing about digital desire—it was subtle, invasive, and persistent. It didn't care about years, wisdom, or loyalty. It thrived on curiosity, ego, and the gaps where trust wavered.

Maya walked in, a knowing look in her eyes. "You okay?"

He nodded, even though he wasn't. "Yeah... just... thinking."

She sighed, sitting next to him. "This... this scrolling, these messages, it's a test. And it's relentless. I've seen it eat relationships alive."

"I know," he admitted. "It's like... it's not about the people messaging me. It's about what it makes me feel. Validation. Attention. Reminders that I'm still... relevant."

"And it's poison," she said bluntly. "It's tempting you to forget what matters. Don't let it. Don't let strangers or memories or curiosity destroy what we have."

Jordan nodded, the weight of her words settling. He had faced heartbreak, mistakes, and misjudgments in his life. This digital temptation felt like a new battlefield—a place where loyalty and desire collided, where ego whispered louder than reason.

The night settled around them. Notifications kept coming, but Jordan had made a choice. He would fight the pull, focus on the real love sitting next to him, and remember that attention from strangers—even subtle, flattering attention—was no replacement for intimacy, trust, and the years of commitment he had built with Maya..

Love or Leverage

Jordan Rivers leaned back in his leather chair, the hum of the ceiling fan cutting through the silence of his study. Fifty-two, experienced, yet the game of love still felt like a battlefield. He'd learned over decades that relationships weren't just about connection—they were about power, trust, and how easily those things could be manipulated.

KJ's latest text popped up: "Man, life's too short. Don't let anyone tie you down."

Jordan frowned. It wasn't the words; it was the subtext. KJ always framed temptation as freedom. Fun. Adventure. But Jordan knew the truth: every flirtation, every subtle distraction, every online comment had the potential to weaken what he and Maya had built over the years.

Maya entered the room, setting her tea on the desk. She looked at him, eyes narrowing slightly. "KJ still bothering you?"

Jordan shook his head. "It's not him... it's just..." He trailed off, realizing that decades of experience had taught him to spot the danger in subtlety. KJ didn't need to be aggressive. He didn't need to overtly flirt. A smile, a casual comment, a memory of the past—suddenly the ground under your feet felt shaky.

"That's exactly the problem," Maya said. "It's always subtle. That's how people test boundaries, Jordan. They see how far they can push before you break, before you give in."

Jordan swallowed hard. Love wasn't just about connection anymore—it was strategy. Every interaction, every decision, every glance could be leveraged. Someone who wanted what he had—Maya, the stability, the history—could try to take it subtly, patiently, over time.

And then there was Ava. Forty-eight, digitally savvy, alluring. Her presence was almost ghostlike, appearing in the form of messages and posts that reminded Jordan he could still be desired, still be the man others noticed. It wasn't a threat in the obvious way, but it was a test: would he let ego and curiosity outweigh loyalty?

He rubbed his temples. "It's exhausting," he admitted. "It's like... love isn't just about us. It's about defending us against everyone else, even people who don't know the rules of our relationship."

Maya reached for his hand. "It's because it matters. The more you care, the more others want to disrupt it. The more solid what you have, the more tempting it becomes for someone else to try and take it. That's reality at fifty-two, Jordan. Not some high school fantasy."

Jordan nodded, heart pounding with both fear and resolve. He'd seen marriages crumble over things far less subtle. He'd seen friendships exploited for personal gain. He knew that love at this age required vigilance, courage, and an unwillingness to let others play with your emotions.

"Then what do we do?" he asked.

Maya's eyes softened. "We choose each other. Every damn day. We show up fully, honestly, and protect what we've built. We don't let ego, temptation, or strangers' attention dictate our choices."

Jordan exhaled, feeling the weight of decades pressing on him. Love wasn't just about desire or intimacy anymore—it was about strategy, awareness, and resilience. And at fifty-two, he was learning that the hardest battles weren't with strangers or temptation—they were with the parts of himself that wanted to take shortcuts, that wanted to feel the thrill instead of honoring the bond he had with Maya.

Outside, the city lights flickered, indifferent to human struggles. But inside, Jordan made a silent vow: he wouldn't let leverage or temptation ruin what mattered most. The game had changed, and so had he.

He was older. Wiser. And he was done losing to illusions.

Temptation at Every Swipe

Jordan sat back in his recliner, phone in hand, the dim glow reflecting off the lines of experience on his face. Fifty-two, and yet the pull of temptation still lurked like a shadow. Social media had a way of sneaking in where life and loyalty lived—quiet, relentless, and subtle.

He scrolled without purpose, though purpose was exactly what he was avoiding. Likes, comments, messages—each pinged a whisper of validation he didn't need but craved. Ava's latest message: "You still think about the old days?"

The words were innocent on the surface, but the intent wasn't. Fifty-two years of life had taught Jordan that curiosity could be dangerous. It could turn a fleeting thought into an obsession. And he was still human. Still flawed. Still tempted.

Maya's voice called from the kitchen. "Jordan, dinner's ready!"

He put the phone down, heart thumping. She didn't need to see the little swirl of chaos inside him—the way a simple text could make him question loyalty, desire, and satisfaction all at once.

KJ called again later, voice booming over the speakerphone like he was twenty-five instead of fifty-four. "Man, you can't tell me you're letting a damn notification dictate your night. Come out with me!"

Jordan laughed, but it wasn't real. "KJ, I told you—I've got responsibilities. And Maya..." He trailed off, knowing KJ's idea of fun wasn't built for long-term relationships.

"That's exactly why you need it!" KJ said, undeterred. "The thrill. The ego boost. You think you're too old for a little temptation? Bullshit. Temptation doesn't care about your age!"

Jordan hung up and stared at the ceiling. KJ was right in a way he hated: temptation didn't care. It didn't check IDs. It didn't respect marriages, relationships, or years of commitment. It only existed to test boundaries—and he was being tested constantly.

Maya walked in, holding two glasses of wine. She leaned against the doorway, eyes sharp. "You're fighting it again, aren't you?"

Jordan shook his head. "I'm not... it's just—these little messages, calls... it's relentless. Even at our age, it doesn't stop. And part of me wants to see where it goes, just for the ego hit."

Her gaze softened but didn't waver. "That's the trap, Jordan. The pull isn't about them. It's about you—your insecurities, your curiosity, your need to feel... desirable. You think it's harmless. But temptation at fifty-two isn't harmless. It can break decades of trust in a heartbeat."

He took a deep breath, setting the phone aside. "I know. I just... I forget sometimes. That even after all these years, I still have to choose. Every day."

Maya crossed the room, sitting beside him. "And that's why we survive. We don't ignore temptation; we face it. We acknowledge it, and then we choose what matters. Us. Trust. Love. Real connection."

Jordan nodded, heart pounding but steadying. He wasn't naive. He knew temptation would return—constant, patient, cunning. Every notification, every comment, every DM could be a test. But for the first time in a long time, he felt capable of resisting, of choosing what mattered over what felt good for a fleeting moment.

The digital world might never stop trying to pull him in, but Jordan finally understood the truth: the fight wasn't against others. It was against the part of himself that could be swayed by attention, ego, or curiosity. And he was ready to win.

Trust Issues Reloaded

Jordan sat in his study, the quiet heavier than the hum of the city outside. Fifty-two, and he'd thought he knew himself. He'd survived heartbreaks, betrayals, and the subtle manipulations of life. Yet here he was, feeling the gnawing tension of trust issues that refused to die.

It wasn't just about Maya anymore—or even the digital temptations that kept cropping up. It was about him. His past, his insecurities, and the realization that decades of life hadn't fully immunized him against doubt.

Maya had noticed the way he hesitated before picking up calls or replying to messages. She'd noticed the tiny pauses, the subtle questions in his eyes, the defensive tone creeping into conversations. And she hadn't said much, but Jordan knew: she saw everything.

Then came KJ, that persistent reminder that boundaries were fragile, even at fifty-four. "You know, man, life's too damn short to sweat every little thing," he'd said over the phone the night before. But Jordan didn't see it as wisdom—he saw it as a challenge. KJ thrived on testing people, on reminding them that loyalty was a choice, and temptation was relentless.

Jordan exhaled, running a hand over his gray-streaked hair. Trust was complicated at this age. It wasn't just a feeling—it was history, experience, and scars rolled into one. Every relationship came with baggage. Every new connection carried the weight of everything you'd endured before.

Maya entered the room, her eyes soft but piercing. "Jordan... talk to me," she said gently. "You've been distant. I can feel it. And I don't need you to explain every damn thought, but I need honesty. That's what trust is."

He nodded, swallowing hard. "It's just... sometimes I feel like I'm fighting ghosts. Every message, every call, every little thing online—it's like it's testing us. Testing me. And part of me wonders... am I strong enough to keep choosing what matters?"

Maya came closer, resting her hand on his shoulder. "Trust isn't about being perfect. It's about showing up. Even when it's messy. Even when temptation is there, and even when your past makes you second-guess yourself. We've built something real, Jordan. And real isn't flawless—it's deliberate. It's patient. It's honest."

He looked into her eyes and felt the weight of the years settle. She was right. Love at fifty-two wasn't about the thrill of the chase. It was about resilience. About choosing each other even when the world—online or offline—was pushing for doubt, distraction, and ego.

Ava's messages, KJ's calls, the constant buzz of social media—they were distractions. Tools of temptation. But Jordan realized something crucial: the real battle wasn't outside. It was inside him. The part that wanted validation. The part that wanted excitement over stability. The part that feared vulnerability.

He took Maya's hand. "I know. I'll do better. Not because it's easy, but because it matters."

She smiled, a quiet, steady smile that carried decades of love, patience, and understanding. "That's all I need, Jordan. Presence. Honesty. Commitment."

In that moment, the trust issues didn't vanish—but they shifted. They became challenges, not curses. Obstacles to navigate, not walls to tear them apart. And Jordan, for the first time in a long time, felt capable of facing them head-on.

Because at fifty-two, he understood something he hadn't in his younger years: trust wasn't a given. It was a daily choice. And he was ready to make that choice every damn day.

The Illusion of Choice

Jordan sat on his porch, the cool night air brushing against his face. Fifty-two years old and yet, somehow, the world still felt full of options—some real, some dangerous illusions. Social media had a way of making even seasoned adults feel like life was a buffet of endless choices. Every notification, every comment, every DM whispered: you could have more, be more, experience more.

He took a sip of his bourbon and thought about Ava Collins, forty-eight, digitally polished and effortlessly alluring. Her messages weren't aggressive, just perfectly placed nudges that made him question satisfaction and loyalty. The temptation wasn't in lust anymore—it was in curiosity, ego, and the seductive idea that he could still reinvent himself at fifty-two.

Maya appeared in the doorway, arms crossed, eyes sharp. "You're thinking about her again, aren't you?"

Jordan exhaled, knowing she could read him like an open book. "It's not... I mean, yes, I'm aware. But it's not like I want anything to happen. It's just... the options. Sometimes it feels like the world is testing me."

Maya shook her head. "No, Jordan. It's not testing you. It's deceiving you. This illusion of choice—this endless parade of attention—is designed to make you doubt what you already have. And it's dangerous, especially at our age. You've built a life. You've built us. Don't let a ghost of temptation make you forget that."

He leaned back, rubbing his face. "It's hard sometimes, though. I mean... fifty-two, and I still feel like I have to prove something—to myself, to the world."

"Prove what?" Maya asked softly, coming closer. "That you can be tempted? That you can chase attention? That you're still... relevant?"

Jordan didn't answer immediately. She was right. The pull of perceived freedom—the idea that he could swipe, reply, explore, indulge in curiosity—was intoxicating. And yet, beneath it all, he knew it was hollow. Options didn't equal fulfillment. Attention didn't equal intimacy. And digital temptation didn't equal real connection.

KJ called earlier that evening, voice booming, teasing: "Man, don't tell me you're letting a few notifications make you feel trapped! You're fifty-two. You've got the world at your fingertips!"

Jordan had laughed, but now he realized the truth: the world wasn't at his fingertips. It was a mirage. Freedom was an illusion when it came at the cost of loyalty, intimacy, and years of commitment.

Maya touched his arm, grounding him. "You have choices every day. The choice is whether you honor what matters or chase fleeting thrills. That's it. The rest is smoke and mirrors."

Jordan nodded, heart steadying. He looked out at the city lights, realizing the lesson had been there all along. The pull of social media, of digital validation, of temptation—it wasn't real freedom. It was an illusion, carefully constructed to distract him from what truly mattered.

And for the first time in years, he felt clarity. Fifty-two, experienced, and still tempted—but now aware. The choices weren't infinite. They were deliberate. And he would choose loyalty, love, and truth.

The Cost of Attention

Jordan Rivers leaned back in his chair, scrolling through his feed again. Fifty-two, and still, the pull of attention—likes, comments, messages—gnawed at him in ways he hadn't expected. It wasn't about lust anymore. It was about relevance, ego, and the quiet voice that whispered: you're still noticed, you still matter.

But attention came at a cost. The kind that didn't show up in numbers or notifications. The kind that eroded intimacy, trust, and the quiet satisfaction of real connection.

Maya watched him from the doorway, arms crossed. "You know this isn't healthy, right?" she said, her voice calm but firm.

Jordan sighed. "I know. But it's hard. It feels... validating. Even at fifty-two, I want to feel like I matter. That someone sees me."

Maya stepped closer. "You do matter, Jordan. You always have. But what you're chasing isn't attention—it's a distraction. A substitute for the real work of connection. That's the cost, and it's steep. Every moment you spend looking for approval online is a moment you're not investing in us."

Jordan nodded, heart heavy. She was right. The pull of digital attention wasn't malicious—it was seductive. It didn't scream betrayal. It whispered, it caressed, it lulled you into thinking you were just harmlessly curious. And that was what made it so dangerous.

KJ had called earlier, full of energy and bravado. "Man, you're fifty-two and acting like a teenager! Don't tell me a few DMs are enough to make you second-guess yourself!"

Jordan had laughed, but inside, the tension remained. KJ thrived on the thrill of ego validation, and Jordan couldn't escape the subtle pressure. It wasn't just about him. It was about what the attention represented: youth, desirability, excitement. Things he had to reconcile with the reality of his age and responsibilities.

Ava's messages lingered, too. Forty-eight, articulate, enticing—but harmless, if he ignored them. And he could ignore them, mostly. The fight wasn't external—it was inside him, the need to feel desired, alive, and relevant.

Maya reached for his hand. "You know the truth, Jordan. Attention online is cheap. Approval is fleeting. It doesn't build connection, it doesn't deepen love, and it sure as hell doesn't earn trust."

Jordan squeezed her hand, feeling the weight of years, mistakes, and lessons. He'd chased attention before—he'd learned what it cost him. And yet, even with decades of experience, the pull never fully disappeared.

But this time, he understood the stakes. He couldn't afford to chase illusions. Every like, every DM, every whisper of digital temptation had a price. And he wasn't willing to pay it—not for ego, not for validation, not at fifty-two.

The lights of the city blinked outside his window, indifferent to human struggles. But inside, Jordan felt something shift: clarity, focus, and resolve. Attention had a cost, but he was finally willing to pay it in the currency that mattered—presence, loyalty, and love with Maya.

The Mask of Perfection

Jordan Rivers stared at his reflection in the mirror, gray streaks in his hair, lines around his eyes, and hands slightly weathered. Fifty-two years had left marks—proof of experience, mistakes, and triumphs. But it wasn't the physical signs that worried him tonight. It was the mask he felt he wore for the world.

Social media, friends, even colleagues—everyone seemed to be performing. Posting perfect meals, flawless vacations, and curated smiles. It was exhausting, and at this age, the pressure didn't lessen—it just took on new forms. The mask of perfection was subtle, but relentless.

Maya entered the room, watching him quietly. "You've been staring at that mirror a long time," she said, voice soft but knowing.

"I'm thinking," he replied, exhaling. "About how everyone's pretending. On their feeds, in their lives... acting like everything's perfect, like their marriages, careers, and even bodies are flawless. And here we are, just... existing."

Maya came closer. "That's the illusion. Perfection isn't real, Jordan. People want you to think it's real because it makes them feel better about themselves. But behind every perfect post, there's doubt, temptation, mistakes, and regrets. The mask doesn't protect anyone—it isolates them."

Jordan nodded slowly. At fifty-two, he'd learned that truth. Life wasn't about perfection. It was about authenticity—messy, complicated, and often uncomfortable. The mask of perfection could fool strangers online, but it could never fool the people who mattered most.

KJ had posted another photo earlier, a casual image of his 'perfect night out,' a grin plastered on his face. Jordan scrolled past without liking it. The temptation to compare, to feel envy, was subtle but persistent. But he recognized it for what it was—a trap.

Ava's messages, too, carried the unspoken weight of performance. She was charming, sophisticated, alluring—but Jordan knew that behind every carefully worded compliment, every teasing question, was the potential to disrupt trust. The mask of perfection wasn't just online; it was in people's intentions, in the expectations they placed on him, on Maya, on everything they had built.

Maya rested her hand on his arm. "We don't need masks. We've spent too long hiding behind them already. We're not perfect. We're us. That's what matters."

Jordan exhaled, feeling a weight lift. She was right. The mask of perfection—tempting as it was—had no power over them if they chose authenticity over illusion. At fifty-two, he knew that the real challenge wasn't avoiding temptation or distractions. It was seeing people, including himself, clearly, flaws and all, and choosing love anyway.

He met Maya's eyes, and for the first time that evening, he felt something steadier than desire, than doubt, than ego. He felt connection. He felt real.

The world could keep its masks, its illusions, and its curated perfection. Jordan and Maya would keep their honesty, their laughter, their trust. That was enough. That was more than enough.

Real Love vs. Digital Illusions

Jordan Rivers sat on the balcony, the city lights stretching out like a web of endless distraction. Fifty-two years old, and yet, some days, it felt like the digital world was designed to make him doubt everything he had built.

Maya was inside, laughing softly on a call with her sister. The sound made him smile, grounding him. Real love wasn't always loud or flashy—it was steady, persistent, and patient. But temptation? Temptation whispered through notifications, DMs, and carefully curated feeds, promising thrills, ego boosts, and the illusion of connection.

Ava Collins' messages had arrived again. Forty-eight, precise, teasing, and just enough to pull at Jordan's curiosity. "You've changed, haven't you? Do you ever wonder what life could've been?"

The words were harmless—or so they seemed. But Jordan knew better. Fifty-two had taught him that harmlessness was a lie. Curiosity could turn into obsession; nostalgia could become temptation. And the digital world thrived on that sliver of vulnerability.

KJ had texted earlier, a casual "Man, you're killing me, staying home again. Live a little!" Jordan laughed quietly, knowing that KJ's idea of living was chaos, ego, and temptation without consequence. And he wasn't twenty-five anymore. He had responsibilities, commitments, and a love that mattered.

Maya walked out to the balcony, her hand brushing against his. "You're thinking about them again," she said softly.

Jordan shook his head. "It's not them. It's... what they represent. The attention, the curiosity, the reminder that I can still be noticed, still be desired."

"And it's fake," Maya said, voice steady. "All of it. Likes, comments, messages—they don't build connection, intimacy, or trust. They're illusions. Real love... what we have... isn't flashy. It doesn't need validation. It survives because it's grounded in honesty, history, and care."

Jordan exhaled, feeling the weight of decades pressing down. Real love had been tested, bruised, and stretched. It wasn't perfect, and it wasn't always easy. But it endured. It didn't get swept away by a notification, a DM, or a digital flirtation.

He looked at Maya, eyes steady. "You're right. I don't need this crap to feel alive. I've got something real. Something worth protecting."

She smiled, leaning into him. "And that's the difference. Real love requires choice. Attention online? That's just smoke. Nothing lasts there. But what we've built... that's ours. That's the legacy of love that's survived time, temptation, and ego."

Jordan nodded, feeling a clarity he hadn't felt in years. Digital illusions could wait. Notifications could blink endlessly. But real love—messy, flawed, and unfiltered—was sitting right here, steady, patient, and enduring.

And at fifty-two, he finally understood the truth: illusions might tempt, but love that mattered would always win.

7

The Masks We Are Taught to Wear

THE PERFORMANCE

The Masks We Are Taught to Wear

The First Script

People think performance starts on stage. They think it starts when the lights come up and the crowd hushes. But the real performance starts way earlier—in your mother's arms, in your father's shadow, in a crib where you learned crying only works until people get tired of hearing you.

We're born honest. Then the world teaches us that honesty is dangerous.

Before I could form a full sentence, I learned the first rule: *"Be good."*

Good didn't mean real. Good didn't mean truthful. Good meant quiet, obedient, predictable. Good meant shrinking so adults could expand. Good meant swallowing questions because adults didn't want to explain why they were wrong.

I remember being told, "Smile for the family." It didn't matter if I was tired. It didn't matter if my stomach was twisted. It didn't matter if the room felt like a trap. Smile. Sit up straight. Don't embarrass us.

Children become performers long before they know what a lie is. We learn facial expressions like choreography. We learn responses like scripted lines. We learn to play whatever character keeps us safe.

Parents love the version of you that makes their life easier.

Schools sharpen the act. Teachers reward the quiet kids, not the curious ones. "Use inside voices." "Don't question authority." "Don't speak unless called on."

They say they're preparing you for life. Really, they're preparing you for performance.

Then the church steps in—where God apparently only loves you if you're polite, where everyone pretends they aren't sinning even though their hearts are twisted up in the same darkness you're drowning in, where you learn to sit, stand, kneel, smile, confess, and pretend.

Every adult tells you to "just be yourself," then punishes you the moment you try.

So you learn the mask. You adjust it with every room you walk into. You polish it so it doesn't crack under pressure. You protect it like it's your real face, because at some point, you forget the difference.

And by the time you're grown?

You're not living. You're performing. And you don't even remember who taught you the script.

The Family Audience

Family is the first crowd you ever perform for, and the last one you stop performing for. They raised you, fed you, clothed you—and somehow still trained you to hide every part of yourself that made them uncomfortable.

People talk about family like it's sacred, like the bloodline is holy, untouchable, automatically loving. But the truth? Family is where most of the damage is done. Not always out of cruelty—sometimes out of fear, sometimes out of tradition, sometimes out of their own unhealed wounds, bleeding onto you before you even know what bleeding means.

Family expects roles, not honesty.

Maybe you were the smart one, the child they bragged about to strangers but never actually listened to. Maybe you were the responsible one, the one raising the younger kids while the adults were too drunk, too angry, too distracted, too broken. Maybe you were the quiet one, the child who learned early that silence keeps the peace—and peace, no matter how fake, was better than another night of shouting.

Or maybe you became the strong one, the one who had no room to cry because everyone else needed you to be solid, like your feelings didn't exist, like your tears would make them collapse.

Families don't ask who you are. They tell you who to be.

And once they decide your role, you can't break character.

If you dare step out of it—if the quiet one suddenly speaks up, if the strong one finally breaks, if the responsible one says "no," if the smart one stops performing excellence—the whole family system panics.

Because your performance kept their dysfunction balanced. Your mask maintained their illusion of stability.

I remember sitting at the dinner table one night, everyone eating in silence except the clinking forks, like a room full of strangers who shared a last name but not a life.

That's when it hit me: every single person at that table was acting.

My mother—playing the role of "fine," even though her eyes were hollowed out from years of carrying secrets. My father—playing "provider," even though he was emotionally bankrupt. My siblings—playing "normal," each one hiding their own private storm.

And me?

I played whatever character they needed that day.

Sometimes the peacekeeper. Sometimes the ghost. Sometimes the one who pretended everything was okay so we didn't have to talk about the things eating us alive.

Families don't want the truth. They want consistency. They want the version of you that keeps the machine running, even if the machine is grinding you down to dust.

You learn to adjust your tone. Your expression. Your attitude. Your whole identity.

You become fluent in the emotional weather of a household that never asked if you were cold or burning.

And when you finally realize that the family you love never learned to love the real you—only the role you played—that realization hits harder than any heartbreak adulthood will ever deliver.

Because you can break up with a lover.

But how do you break up with a version of yourself your family won't let you stop being?

The Job Mask

There's a special kind of performance that happens at work—a polished, sanitized version of yourself that clocks in even when your soul is dragging behind you.

The job is a stage with no curtains, no breaks, no room for the truth. Just fluorescent lights, polite lies, and people pretending they aren't slowly dying inside.

You walk through the doors, and the mask snaps into place automatically. Like muscle memory. Like survival.

"Good morning." Even when you barely slept. Even when your chest feels like a collapsed building.

"How are you?" Fine. Always fine. Because the workplace isn't designed for real human beings. It's designed for productivity machines wearing human skin.

Everybody's playing a part.

The coworkers smiling through stretched nerves, pretending they didn't cry in their car before walking in. The supervisors acting like leaders while fighting their own battles with insecurity and incompetence. The boss performing confidence—voice firm, eyes steady—but you can feel the desperation bleeding through, the panic of someone who knows the whole system is one mistake away from falling apart.

The job mask is heavy. But the scariest part? It's expected.

Companies love the buzzwords: "authenticity," "team culture," "work-life balance."

But if you walked in and told the truth—"I'm struggling," "I'm burnt out," "I feel invisible," "I'm drowning"—they'd label you "unprofessional."

Because professionalism is just another word for performance.

At work, you don't speak your mind. You adjust your tone to be "non-threatening." You hide your exhaustion behind emails with fake enthusiasm. You choke down your creativity because suggestions challenge the hierarchy. You shrink your personality to fit the mold of "appropriate," which really means: don't make anybody uncomfortable with your humanity.

The lunchroom is the saddest theatre of all—smiles that don't reach the eyes, small talk that feels like chewing cardboard, everyone pretending they actually care about the weather so they don't accidentally say what's really on their mind.

And every day, you watch people break in slow motion.

That coworker who used to laugh loud now laughs only with their mouth, never their eyes. That manager who used to have passion now checks the clock more than they check their own pulse. That new hire who walked in bright and hopeful now walks with the gray resignation of someone who understands this place will eat them alive if they let it.

You start to realize something sharp.

The workplace doesn't just teach you how to perform. It teaches you how to disappear.

It demands your time, your focus, your emotional labor, your weekends, your peace. It rewards the mask but punishes the truth behind it.

And no matter how much you give—no matter how well you perform—you're replaceable.

A number. A name on a badge. A body filling a seat. A signature at the bottom of a form.

But here's the twist.

You learn so much about people at work—not because they're honest, but because performance reveals more than truth ever will.

The coworker who jokes all day is hiding depression. The one who overachieves is running from childhood expectations they could never meet. The quiet one is holding a storm behind their ribs nobody notices. The boss who micromanages is terrified of being exposed.

Everybody's acting. Everybody's tired. Everybody's pretending they're okay.

Including you.

You leave the building and your shoulders drop. Your breath deepens. Your face relaxes into something that might actually be your own.

But you know something the world never admits.

The job mask doesn't fall off when you clock out.

It follows you home. It follows you into your relationships. It follows you into your dreams.

Because once you learn how to perform, it becomes second nature.

And forgetting the performance—that's the real work.

The Lover Mask

Love is supposed to be the one place you can exhale, the one room where you can peel off every layer and stand there in your raw, unedited truth—but most people never experience that. Not really.

Most people date in disguise. They fall in love while half-performing, half-hiding, half-hoping the other person won't notice the pieces they keep tucked away.

Dating is two strangers walking toward each other holding masks behind their backs, both praying the other person won't ask to see what's underneath too soon.

At the beginning, you're performing possibility. You're selling potential. You're curating your personality like a storefront display. You want to be chosen, so you bend yourself into the shape you think they want.

You laugh at jokes you don't actually like. You pretend not to notice the small red flags because honesty this early feels like sabotage. You hide your anxieties, your triggers, your trauma—because nobody wants to lead with the truth. The truth feels like a burden. The truth feels like too much.

But the real performance comes later—when the honeymoon haze clears, when comfort settles in like thick dust, when you start to know each other too well and not well enough at the same time.

The lover mask is crafted specifically for intimacy: "Don't be too emotional." "Don't be too distant." "Don't be too needy." "Don't be too indifferent." "Don't expect too much." "Don't reveal too much." "Don't ask for more than they're willing to give."

You contort yourself into a shape they'll stay for. A shape they'll choose. A shape they won't abandon.

Because that's the secret fear behind every love story—the fear of being left standing alone with your truth showing.

Relationships become negotiations of comfort zones: who will speak first, who will apologize first, who will carry the emotional load, who will shrink to keep the peace, who will pretend they aren't hurt, who will pretend they're fine with "less," who will pretend this is enough.

People don't date each other. They date each other's performances.

You say, "I'm okay," when your heart is heavy. You say, "It's fine," when it's not. You say, "I understand," when you actually feel unseen.

Sometimes the relationship lasts years before you realize you've never shown your real face.

And even worse—they've never shown you theirs.

Love becomes a duet of half-truths, two people editing themselves in real time to keep the illusion alive. Because if either one of you drops the mask, everything might fall apart.

Then there's the other side—the private performance, the one you do alone.

Pretending you're not bothered. Pretending their distance doesn't sting. Pretending their coldness doesn't trigger old wounds. Pretending you don't notice the slow shift, the cracking foundation, the emotional leaks they refuse to acknowledge.

You practice monologues in the shower that you never say aloud. You rewrite arguments in your head so they don't explode in real life. You shrink yourself so your truth doesn't overwhelm them.

And intimacy—the real kind, the soul-level kind—becomes rarer than oxygen.

The cruel irony? You end up lonely right next to someone. Lonely in shared beds. Lonely in long relationships. Lonely in households filled with the sound of two hearts beating out of sync.

Because the lover mask doesn't exist to create connection. It exists to avoid conflict. To avoid rejection. To avoid the terrifying risk of being fully seen.

But the truth eventually demands space. It pushes through the cracks. It claws its way out. It shows itself in arguments, in silence, in withdrawal, in resentment, in the soft ache you feel every night before sleep—the ache of knowing you've never been fully loved because you've never been fully known.

And that's the tragedy of modern love: everybody wants real. Nobody wants to risk it.

The Social Media Persona

Social media turned the whole world into a stage and everyone into actors, desperately auditioning for attention, validation, and relevance.

You log in, and instantly you feel it—the pressure to present, to perform, to polish yourself until you shine so bright nobody can see the cracks underneath.

It's not just an app. It's a marketplace of masks.

People aren't sharing their lives. They're selling versions of themselves curated down to the pixel.

You take a picture, but the picture isn't enough. You adjust the angle. Then you adjust your face. Then you adjust your body. Then you adjust your story—because the truth feels too raw, too messy, too human.

You delete the photo and retake it twelve times because you want to look "natural," which in today's world means unnaturally perfect with no signs of struggle.

You post the smiling photo—not the one from earlier where your eyes were swollen from crying. You caption it something harmless, something cute, something inspirational enough to distract people from the fact that you haven't slept in days and your heart feels like a clenched fist.

People double-tap the lie and scroll away.

And you learn a hard truth: it's not authenticity people reward—it's performance.

Scroll long enough and it becomes obvious.

Everyone is pretending.

The couple posting vacation pictures? They fought the whole trip and slept back-to-back every night.

The girl writing long, confident captions about self-love and growth? She breaks down when the notifications stop.

The influencer bragging about success? Drowning in debt, living off brand deals and borrowed confidence.

The man recording motivational videos? Hates his life offline.

The "happy" family posting matching outfits? They argue in the car before smiling on cue.

Everyone edits their truth until it's palatable. Everyone hides their pain until it's unrecognizable. Everyone posts the highlight reel and buries the director's cut.

And you—you try to keep up. You try to stay relevant. You try to look stable even when your world is bending under you like weak metal.

You compare yourself to strangers you don't even know. You measure your worth in likes, your beauty in comments, your relevance in shares.

You start performing not just for others—but for yourself. You start believing the fake version of your life is better than the real one. You start chasing the mask instead of fixing the wounds beneath it.

Social media doesn't just shape perception—it distorts identity.

You filter your face, then start hating the unfiltered version. You pose your body, then start disliking your real posture. You post positivity, then feel guilty for your sadness. You compare your behind-the-scenes to everyone else's final draft.

You become addicted not to connection—but to applause.

And the scariest part? When you log off, the performance doesn't stop. It follows you into real life.

You start acting like your online persona. You start minimizing your pain so you don't disappoint strangers. You start chasing attention because silence feels like failure.

You lose yourself piece by piece, scroll by scroll, post by post.

Until one day you look in the mirror and realize the person staring back looks exactly like your profile picture—perfect, hollow, edited, incomplete.

A masterpiece of performance.

A stranger wearing your face.

The Doctor, The Teacher, The Therapist

There are performances we choose, and then there are performances forced on us by the systems built long before we were born.

The doctor's office. The classroom. The therapy room.

Places that should feel safe, but somehow demand even more acting than the world outside.

Because these are the places where you're supposed to tell the truth—yet these are the places where you learn to lie the cleanest.

THE DOCTOR MASK

You're sitting in that cold, sterile room, and instantly you feel small. Not physically—spiritually. Like your whole existence is under a microscope, held by someone who doesn't know you but gets to define you in twenty minutes.

You tell the doctor what hurts, but you don't tell them everything. You trim the truth to make it tidy, because vulnerability in a medical room feels like exposing your guts on a silver tray.

Doctors say, "Tell me what's wrong." But their faces tell you, "Tell me the quick version."

So you downplay the pain. You minimize the fear. You hide the mental breakdown brewing under your ribs. You don't say you're lonely, or angry, or exhausted from carrying so much without breaking.

Because the doctor isn't just diagnosing your body—they're evaluating your credibility. And you don't want to be labeled "dramatic," or "overreacting," or "non-compliant."

So you put on the medical mask: polite, calm, articulate—the version of yourself who deserves care.

The version who won't be dismissed.

The version society takes seriously.

It is a performance of survival.

THE TEACHER MASK

School was the first institution to teach you how to shrink.

You didn't show the real you in class—you showed the "acceptable" you. The one who didn't disrupt. The one who hid confusion because raising your hand to ask a question felt like announcing you were behind.

You learned to look attentive even when your mind drifted into storms no one could see.

Teachers say, "Be yourself." But they grade compliance. They reward silence. They love the neat answers that match the neat boxes they were trained to fit you into.

You learned early that the real world doesn't want to know how smart you are—it wants to know how obedient you can pretend to be.

And that performance follows you into adulthood. Every boardroom is just a bigger classroom. Every boss is just a louder teacher. Every task is just another assignment graded by people who don't know your story.

THE THERAPIST MASK

Of all the masks you wear, this one is the most ironic—the one place designed for honesty is the place where people hide the most.

You sit across from someone trained to understand you, but you still edit your pain like an essay. You offer pieces, not the whole picture. You give them the trauma you can articulate, not the chaos you can't.

You're afraid of being judged. Afraid of being pitied. Afraid of sounding crazy. Afraid of unlocking something you aren't prepared to feel.

So you perform your trauma in a version that's easier to discuss.

You cry, but not too much. You talk, but not too deep. You reveal, but not too raw.

The therapist asks, "How does that make you feel?" And you give the answer that sounds smart, insightful, controlled—even though your real answer is a messy roar of emotions you've never named.

You're in the one room where you could finally drop the act, but the performance is so ingrained you don't even realize you're doing it.

Trauma teaches you to protect yourself. Therapy asks you to unlearn the shield. That's the hardest performance to break.

THE SYSTEMS THAT WANT YOUR MASK MORE THAN YOUR TRUTH

Doctors want you compliant. Teachers want you manageable. Therapists want you open—but only in ways that fit their framework.

And you're stuck between these worlds, trying to be honest while also trying to be accepted, understood, believed.

You realize something heartbreaking: every system in society teaches you to perform. Almost none teach you how to be human.

The doctor wants your symptoms, not your story. The teacher wants your work ethic, not your chaos. The therapist wants your vulnerability, but filtered.

So you learn to walk in and out of these rooms, switching masks like costumes—polished, practiced, perfected.

And you wonder—if all these places require a performance, where does the real you get to breathe?

The Break in the Script

There comes a moment—quiet at first, like a soft tearing sound inside your chest—when the performance you've been carrying your whole life finally starts to crack.

It doesn't happen all at once. It begins in small betrayals of the mask.

You forget to smile at someone. You snap when you usually swallow it. You tell a truth you weren't supposed to say out loud. You stop pretending you're okay for a split second—and the world looks at you like you malfunctioned.

Because people get used to your mask. They expect it. They depend on it. They rely on the role you've rehearsed so well they forgot it wasn't the real you.

The break in the script always starts as a feeling: a pressure in your chest, a heaviness behind your eyes, a voice in your head whispering, *"I can't do this anymore."*

But you don't quit right away. You try to force the performance back together. You tape it. You patch it. You tighten the edges. You try to behave. Try to go along. Try to keep the peace.

But the script you've lived by—the one written by family, by society, by trauma, by fear—stops fitting.

It's like trying to squeeze into clothes that belonged to an old version of you that no longer exists.

The unraveling hits every part of your life at once.

The job—

You start slipping.

You forget to answer emails with fake enthusiasm. You stop caring about office politics. You show up late. You look around the room and realize you don't respect half the people controlling your paycheck. You've outgrown the role, but the job won't let you leave the stage gracefully.

The relationship—

The cracks become visible.

You stop cushioning your words. You stop saying "it's fine." You stop pretending their bare minimum is enough. You stop pretending the love you're receiving matches the love you're giving.

Your silence turns into sighs. Your sighs turn into distance. Your distance turns into arguments. Your arguments turn into truths you buried years ago finally clawing their way out.

Social media—

The mask glitches.

You post less. You care less about the likes. You scroll through the lies and feel nothing but exhaustion. You start deleting photos that no longer match the person you're slowly becoming.

Family—

They feel the shift immediately.

You're not playing your assigned role, and it scares them. They think you're changing, but really, you're returning to who you were meant to be before the world taught you to hide.

When you stop performing, families call it rebellion. Co-workers call it attitude. Partners call it selfishness. Society calls it ungrateful.

But you know what it really is.

The beginning of honesty.

The break in the script is both terrifying and liberating. It feels like losing control and gaining clarity at the exact same time.

You start noticing how much of your life has been lived in rooms that suffocate you. You start noticing how often you said "yes" when your soul was screaming "no." You start noticing how many people love your mask more than they ever loved you.

And there's a moment—a quiet, brutal moment—when you sit alone and realize:

The performance isn't protecting you anymore.

It's killing you.

That's when the break becomes a rupture. That's when the mask slips completely. That's when the script collapses.

And that's when everything around you—every relationship, every routine, every identity you thought was permanent—starts to shift.

Because once you taste the beginning of your truth, you can never fully go back to your lie.

The Great Unmasking

The moment the mask falls isn't loud. It isn't dramatic. It's not some movie scene where you stand on a table and scream your truth while everyone gasps and clutches their chest.

No. The unmasking is much quieter than that—but far more violent.

It begins with a stillness in your spirit, a kind of internal refusal. You wake up one morning and your soul simply says, *"I'm done."*

Done pretending. Done performing. Done bending. Done swallowing. Done shaping yourself into something palatable for people who never deserved the real version of you in the first place.

The great unmasking doesn't look like liberation at first. It looks like chaos.

Because the truth is disruptive. The truth is inconvenient. The truth costs. And when you finally let it out, the world around you reacts like you lit a match in a room soaked in gasoline.

The job feels it first.

You stop sugarcoating. You stop overextending. You stop hiding the exhaustion under "No worries!" You start saying things like, *"I don't have the bandwidth for that." "That's not my responsibility." "I'm not staying late."*

And people look at you like you've grown a second head. Because they weren't in love with you—they were in love with your compliance.

Lose the compliance, and suddenly you're "difficult," "cold," "changed."

But the truth is, you're finally becoming who you were before the world convinced you that honesty makes you unlikable.

The relationship feels it next.

You stop walking on eggshells. You stop buffering their insecurities. You stop pretending the love is balanced when you've been carrying both sides of the relationship on your back.

You stop watering dead plants, stop romanticizing potential, stop performing loyalty to someone who only loved the edited version of you.

Your truth leaks into the conversations. Your boundaries sharpen. Your voice grows a spine.

And suddenly, your partner has a problem.

Not with your truth—but with the fact that they can't control the narrative anymore.

Family feels it the hardest.

Because family builds entire identities on the roles they assigned you. Once you break character, their whole script collapses.

They say things like, *"You're not yourself." "You've changed." "Why are you acting like this?" "What happened to the old you?"*

Not realizing you're finally acting like yourself for the first time in your life.

The great unmasking threatens them because your honesty exposes their denial. Your boundaries expose their manipulation. Your growth exposes their stagnation.

They loved the mask. The real you? They have to learn how to meet that person—and some never will.

And then there's you—standing in the middle of the wreckage.

Because make no mistake: the unmasking is messy. It breaks things. It breaks relationships, routines, patterns, illusions.

It breaks the version of you that survived on silence.

But beneath all that breaking is something new—something raw, wild, frightening, and real.

You feel emotions you used to numb. You say things you used to bury. You allow yourself to want things you once pretended you didn't need.

You become alive in ways that feel wrong at first—because performing became your normal and honesty feels like rebellion.

The world won't celebrate your unmasking. They'll call it attitude, ego, arrogance, selfishness.

They'll call it everything except what it is: healing.

Because healing isn't gentle. Healing disrupts the arrangements everyone built around your pain. Healing makes you unpredictable to people who preferred you broken.

And once you start speaking your truth, you see the world with new eyes—sharper, clearer, less forgiving.

You realize how many people benefited from the version of you that never said "no." You realize how many situations you tolerated out of fear. You realize how long you lived with your wings folded, your mouth closed, your heart dimmed.

The great unmasking is terrifying, unstable, and lonely—but it is the doorway to every version of yourself you were always meant to become.

And once you step through it?

There is no going back.

The Collapse of the Roles

Before the unmasking comes the collapse. Not outside—inside.

It's the moment when every role you've ever played starts to feel like a costume soaked in gasoline, itching, burning, too tight to tolerate for even one more day.

The perfect worker. The forgiving partner. The reliable child. The strong friend. The drama-free sibling. The well-behaved adult. The always-smiling public version of you.

All of it begins to crack.

Not because you're becoming worse—but because you're finally refusing to be fake.

The job collapses first.

You're sitting in some pointless meeting, listening to someone with half your competence explain something with twice the confidence, and the realization hits: *I don't care anymore. At all.*

Not in a lazy way. Not in a rebellious way. In a truthful way.

Your soul is no longer willing to auction itself off for a paycheck, a title, or a nod of approval.

You stop pretending that mediocrity is brilliance, that disrespect is "just leadership," that burnout is "a busy season."

And the second they sense your spirit pulling away, they panic.

Because they didn't hire a person—they hired a role. And the role is dissolving.

The partner feels the shift too.

You stop cushioning your truths. You stop minimizing your needs. You stop pouring emotion into a relationship built on your silence.

Suddenly the arguments aren't about the dishes, the timing, the tone.

They're about the fact that the version of you they could manipulate, guilt-trip, or sweet-talk into submission is gone.

They say you're distant. Cold. Different.

No. You're unedited.

And people who fell in love with your edited self will always fear the director's-cut version.

Friendships get exposed next.

The ones who only call when they need something. The ones who love you traumatized because it keeps you small. The ones who melt away when you start healing, because healed you has boundaries—and boundaries feel like betrayal to people who depended on your lack of them.

When you stop playing your role, they stop knowing what to do with you.

Some drift. Some argue. Some attack.

But the real ones? They lean in closer. They ask real questions. They grow with you.

Your unmasking becomes the sorting mechanism they never expected.

Family feels it the most violently.

Because family doesn't see you as a person; they see you as a position.

The peacemaker. The quiet one. The responsible one. The black sheep. The strong one. The one who never complains.

They don't realize those roles were carved out of your survival.

So when you stop playing along, they swear something is wrong with you.

"You're acting funny."

"You're so distant."

"You're ungrateful."

"You're disrespectful."

Translation: *You're no longer easy for us to control.*

Family expects you to shrink forever, to swallow forever, to keep the mask glued on even when it suffocates you.

But a mask that stops serving its purpose starts slipping. And once it slips, the truth pours out like floodwater.

Then comes the moment—the breaking point.

You look around at the life you built on top of these collapsing roles and realize:

This wasn't a life. It was a performance with the lights always on and the audience never satisfied.

The applause was never real. The approval was conditional. The love was transactional. The loyalty was built on lies.

And once you see the stage for what it is—a prison with spotlights—you can't unsee it.

You can't go back. You can't un-know. You can't un-feel.

Everything falls apart so that who you really are can fall into place.

The collapse isn't a failure.

It's a release. A dismantling. A demolition.

The destruction of every identity that was built to keep you safe but ended up keeping you small.

You lose people. You lose comfort. You lose illusions.

But what you gain?

Yourself.

And that scares the world—because the real you doesn't fit inside the roles they built to contain you.

The real you is too honest, too awake, too aware.

The collapse is not the end.

It's the threshold.

Step over it, and nothing will ever be the same.

The World Reacts to Your Awakening

When you start waking up, the world doesn't clap for you. It flinches.

People don't celebrate your clarity—they feel threatened by it. Because your awakening exposes every place they're still asleep.

Your honesty reveals their denial. Your boundaries reveal their entitlement. Your growth reveals their stagnation. Your confidence reveals their insecurity.

Awakening makes you a mirror—and most people don't like mirrors. Not the honest ones.

The First Reaction: Silence

Not the peaceful kind. The suspicious kind.

People who once called you every day go quiet. People who demanded your time suddenly "give you space." People who relied on your emotional labor stop showing up because they can feel the shift in your energy, even if you haven't said a word.

Your silence used to be compliance. Now it's power. And they don't know what to do with that.

The Second Reaction: Confusion

They start studying you like you're an object that malfunctioned.

"Why are you acting different?"

"What's gotten into you?"

"You're not yourself."

They can't comprehend that the version of you they were familiar with was the lie—and this you is the truth.

They're confused because they mistook your suffering for your personality. They thought your exhaustion was who you were. They thought your people-pleasing was your nature. They thought your silence meant you agreed.

Now they're confused because you found your voice and stopped apologizing for existing.

The Third Reaction: Anger

This is the reaction that always arrives when you stop playing the role they prefer.

People don't get angry because you changed. They get angry because your change inconveniences them.

Anger comes from the partner who can't control the narrative anymore, the parent who can't guilt you into obedience, the friend who can't drain you for comfort, the coworker who can't dump their workload on you, the sibling who can't treat you like the family scapegoat, the boss who can't manipulate you into silence.

Your awakening interrupts their benefits, their comfort, their illusion of power.

So they get loud. They get dramatic. They get disrespectful.

Because they can feel their access to you slipping.

The Fourth Reaction: Projection

When people can't control you, they rewrite the story.

You become "the problem," "the arrogant one," "the unappreciative one," "the distant one," "the selfish one."

They project their discomfort onto you so they don't have to confront the truth about themselves.

They don't see your awakening as growth. They see it as betrayal.

Because they only valued you when you were convenient.

The Fifth Reaction: Distance

The ones who can't handle the real you start backing up.

Not because they want to—but because your evolution exposes their refusal to evolve.

Your new boundaries create space. Your honesty creates separation. Your strength removes the weak links. Your purpose filters the people who were only meant for your past self.

This loss hurts. But it's clean.

It's the kind of pain that makes space for the right people to step forward.

The Final Reaction: Respect

This one comes later—sometimes months, sometimes years.

Once the dust clears, the same people who judged your awakening watch you from a distance and see your peace, your growth, your stability, your power, your confidence, your boundaries, your self-respect.

They begin to realize you weren't acting out—you were rising up.

The world eventually respects what it can no longer manipulate.

But the point of awakening isn't to earn their respect.

It's to finally respect yourself.

Because when you awaken, you become dangerous—not in a violent way, but in a liberated way.

Dangerous to people who depended on your silence. Dangerous to systems built on your obedience. Dangerous to roles that required your suffering. Dangerous to illusions that kept you small.

Awakening is disruptive by design. It is meant to shake the world around you until everything that doesn't align falls away.

And what remains?

You. Unfiltered. Unafraid. Unmasked.

The person you were always meant to be once the performance ended.

The Rebel You Didn't Know You Were Becoming

Awakening doesn't just change your life—it changes your posture in the world. You stop moving like someone begging for permission and start moving like someone carrying truth under their skin.

You become a quiet kind of rebel. Not with signs, not with protests, but with a shift so subtle that only people who depended on your weakness feel threatened.

This is about that shift—the moment you stop living like a guest in your own life and start acting like the owner.

The First Sign: You Say "No" Without Explaining

For years, your "no" came with a paragraph. A justification. A soft apology. A polite performance designed to make other people comfortable.

Awakening changes that.

Your "no" becomes a complete sentence. Sharp. Unapologetic. Solid.

And people react like you just flipped a table over. They hear "no" as violence because they only knew you when "yes" was survival.

But the rebel in you is done sacrificing your life for someone else's convenience.

The Second Sign: You Stop Overperforming

You no longer overextend, overexplain, overcompensate, overwork, over-apologize, over-give, overstay, over-fix, over-caretake, or over-silence yourself.

You stop being the dependable one, the one who holds everything together even when you're falling apart inside.

Instead, you give exactly what you choose to give—not an ounce more.

People call it selfish. You call it self-preservation. The rebel in you knows the difference.

The Third Sign: You Don't Entertain Nonsense

You don't argue with liars. You don't debate with manipulators. You don't explain yourself to people who are committed to misunderstanding you. You don't fight for a seat at a table you don't even want to eat at.

You've outgrown the drama they're still addicted to.

Your peace becomes your protest.

The Fourth Sign: You Start Telling the Truth, Even When Your Voice Shakes

Awakening turns whispers into declarations. The truth you used to lock inside your chest begins to roam freely.

You stop editing yourself to make others feel comfortable.

You say what needs to be said: "I don't trust you." "This relationship drains me." "I'm not happy here." "You hurt me." "I deserve more." "This isn't love—it's habit." "I'm done pretending."

Your honesty doesn't make you cruel—it makes you free. And freedom has always scared the people who benefit from your chains.

The Fifth Sign: You Become Immune to Their Version of You

When people lose access to the old you, they create a story about the new you.

"She thinks she's better." "He's acting strange." "They're too sensitive." "They've changed."

Yes. You changed. You outgrew the script they wrote for you. And now they can't cast you in their low-budget drama anymore.

You no longer react to the labels. You no longer shrink to fit the narrative. You no longer audition for acceptance.

You know who you are—and that is the most rebellious thing you've ever done.

The Sixth Sign: You Choose Yourself Without Feeling Guilty

This is the moment the transformation becomes irreversible.

You start choosing your rest, your peace, your sanity, your voice, your truth, your boundaries, your needs, your dreams, your emotional safety.

And you stop apologizing for prioritizing your life over their expectations.

Choosing yourself isn't abandonment—it's alignment. It's a reunion with the version of you that was buried under performance, silence, and survival.

The rebel in you knows that loving yourself is the loudest rebellion of all.

The Final Sign: The Future No Longer Scares You

Because now, you're building a future that actually belongs to you.

A life without the masks. A path without the roles. A version of you that doesn't need to hide.

You don't know exactly where you're going—but for the first time, it doesn't feel scary.

It feels powerful. It feels possible. It feels like freedom.

The rebel in you isn't destructive. It's resurrective.

They thought you were falling apart. But really?

You were falling into yourself.

The Emotional Whiplash of Becoming Real

Becoming real is not a peaceful process. It's emotional whiplash—your spirit accelerating forward while your old life yanks you backward with everything it has.

Awakening feels like progress one day and regression the next. Clarity in the morning, breakdowns at night. Strength in your chest, grief in your throat.

Healing is not a straight line—it's a demolition site.

The Grief You Didn't Expect

You think waking up will feel good. Like a sunrise. Like fresh air. Like freedom.

And sometimes it does. But mostly? It feels like mourning.

Because when you stop performing, you lose versions of yourself you lived in for years.

You grieve the old you—even the parts that hurt you. Even the roles that suffocated you. Even the illusions that kept you safe.

Growth feels like death because something inside is dying. The fake self. The survival self. The self who dimmed their light just to keep the peace.

Awakening is birth and funeral at the same time.

The Guilt Hits Hardest at Night

In the daytime, you're strong. Clear. Focused. Your boundaries feel justified. Your voice feels earned.

But at night? The guilt creeps in like smoke under the door.

Did I do too much? Was I too harsh? Should I have stayed quiet? What if I was wrong? What if I'm the problem?

This guilt isn't truth. It's old programming. It's the ghost of the obedient version of you trying to reclaim its power.

Your past self is crying because it knows you're outgrowing it.

The Fear of Being Alone

When you stop performing, people leave. Or drift. Or reveal who they really were when you weren't bending for them.

This creates a loneliness that feels like punishment—but it's actually protection.

Your spirit is decluttering your life even when your heart doesn't consent.

You fear being alone because for the first time, you're spending time with the real you—and you're not used to her yet.

But the more time you spend there, the more you realize you're not lonely—you're becoming whole.

The Rage You Buried Starts Speaking

Oh, the rage. The anger. The heat that rises through your ribs and makes your hands shake.

For years, you swallowed words that should've been spoken. You held peace you didn't owe anyone. You accepted treatment you should've rejected.

That rage isn't wrong. It's data.

It's your spirit saying: "I deserved better." "I was mistreated." "I am not the villain here." "I will not tolerate that again."

This rage burns the bridges that should've collapsed years ago.

The Confusion Between Healing and Isolation

You start canceling plans, pulling back, going inward, choosing solitude over noise.

People assume you're pushing them away. But really, you're pulling yourself together.

Healing requires isolation the same way a wound requires rest. The same way an injured limb needs stillness. The same way a broken bone needs time.

You're not hiding. You're regenerating.

But it feels confusing because healing looks like disappearing.

The Unexpected Peace After the Storm

Then one random day—maybe in the car, maybe in the shower, maybe walking into work—you notice something.

You're not scared anymore. You're not ashamed anymore. You're not shrinking anymore. You're not pretending anymore.

The chaos settles. The fog lifts. The guilt quiets down. The anger finds direction.

And for the first time, you feel something unfamiliar but beautiful.

Peace that wasn't earned through suffering. Peace that wasn't negotiated. Peace that wasn't a reward for obedience.

Peace just because you exist.

The New You Doesn't Ask for Permission

This is the real transformation.

Your decisions become yours. Your voice becomes clear. Your needs become priority. Your identity becomes grounded. Your energy becomes expensive. Your truth becomes non-negotiable.

You no longer beg for love, chase validation, or manage other people's comfort at the expense of your own sanity.

Your life becomes intentional. Your choices become aligned. Your spirit becomes sovereign.

This is the emotional whiplash of becoming real: pain, clarity, guilt, relief, loss, power, fear, freedom.

You don't just change—you resurrect.

The Reckoning With Your Past Selves

There comes a point in every awakening where the present version of you has to sit across the table from every version you used to be.

No distractions. No excuses. No masks. Just you and the ghosts of who you were when survival was your only strategy.

This is the reckoning—the confrontation you didn't know you needed until the silence made it unavoidable.

The Self Who Stayed Silent

They show up first.

The you who swallowed the truth because speaking it meant conflict. The you who let disrespect slide because you were taught that being liked mattered more than being safe. The you who apologized for things that weren't your fault. The you who played small because shrinking made you less of a target.

This version sits across from you, eyes tired, voice thin, hands shaking from all the words they never said.

You want to judge them. You want to yell, *"How could you let them treat us like that?"*

But then the truth hits.

They didn't fail you. They protected you with the only tools they had.

Silence was their shield. Obedience was their armor. Disappearing was their strategy. Enduring was their only option.

You owe this version of yourself not anger—but gratitude.

They kept you alive long enough for the awakened you to finally arrive.

The Self Who Performed

This one sits with their back too straight, smiling too big, talking too fast.

The one who was always "fine." Always "handling it." Always the strong one, the reliable one, the one who never broke—because breaking was forbidden.

This version is exhausted. You can see it in their eyes, the way they tremble from holding up the world with bones that were never meant to carry that weight.

You want to tell them, *"You didn't have to work that hard."*

But they look back at you and whisper, *"I thought I did. I thought no one would love the real me."*

And there it is—the wound beneath the performance. The belief that your real self was too much, not enough, or unlovable.

You don't judge this version either. You honor them.

They survived what the real you would've never endured.

The Self Who Loved the Wrong People

This version enters quietly. Heavy. Older than their age. Carrying heartbreak like a second skin.

They loved people who didn't love them back. They forgave people who didn't deserve access. They waited on people who never showed up. They stayed loyal to people who fed off their softness.

This version sits across from you and avoids eye contact because they're ashamed.

You reach for their hand.

"You did the best you could with the heart you had."

And just like that, their shame dissolves.

Because loving deeply was never the mistake. The mistake was believing you had to suffer to be worthy.

That belief is what you leave behind.

The Self Who Broke

This one is the hardest to face.

The version of you who hit the floor. Who couldn't pretend anymore. Who screamed into pillows, punched walls, shook with rage, cried until their chest hurt, and wondered if life would ever feel safe again.

The broken you who thought the pain would swallow them whole.

You sit in front of this version and see the truth.

They weren't weak. They were honest.

They were the first version who stopped performing. The first version who refused to suffer in silence. The first version who let the collapse happen instead of holding it all together.

They weren't breaking.

They were opening.

And because they opened, the new you could be born.

The Self You Are Becoming

Finally, the future version of you steps into the room.

Not perfect. Not healed all the way. But whole. Clear-eyed. Unbothered. Rooted. Unapologetic.

Their presence is calm but powerful—the kind of energy you once mistook for arrogance but now understand is self-respect.

This version of you doesn't flinch. Doesn't beg. Doesn't bend. Doesn't dim.

They look at you and say:

"I am proud of you. Every version of you. The loud ones, the quiet ones, the broken ones, the ones who kept going even when you had nothing left."

You realize then that awakening isn't about becoming someone new. It's about gathering every scattered version of yourself and saying:

"You are all allowed here."

This is the reckoning—the merging, the acceptance, the integration of every self you've ever had to be.

And after this moment, you walk forward lighter, clearer, and more whole than you have ever been.

The Day You Finally Break the Generational Script

Every family has a script. Unspoken, inherited, rehearsed. Passed down like an heirloom nobody asked for but everyone is expected to carry.

Be quiet. Be strong. Be loyal. Be forgiving. Be blind. Be numb. Be available. Be small.

Families don't hand you the script—they perform it until you learn your lines. And you learn them well. Too well.

But awakening forces you to look at this script with new eyes. Eyes that can finally see how much of your life was never truly yours.

This is the moment you stop reciting the lines and decide to rewrite the whole damn play.

The Family Rules You Never Voted For

You realize the script was built out of trauma, fear, silence, shame, avoidance, image, control, and denial.

The rules weren't chosen—they were inherited.

Your mother didn't speak up because her mother was punished when she did. Your father didn't break the pattern because his father normalized destruction. Your aunt swallowed pain because she saw what happened to the women who spoke it aloud. Your uncle kept secrets because secrets kept him safe as a child.

These were never your rules. They were the survival strategies of people who never healed.

And you? You were born into their aftermath.

The Moment You Say "I Don't Accept This Anymore"

Every generational breaker has a moment when they snap.

Sometimes it's a small moment—a disrespectful comment, a gaslighting reaction, a guilt trip disguised as love.

Sometimes it's big—a betrayal, a truth revealed, a line crossed so violently it shatters the whole illusion.

Your moment arrives quietly but with force.

You hear the same old manipulation, but something inside you refuses to shrink this time. You feel the old pressure to play your role, but your spirit—stronger now—pushes back.

You say, either out loud or in your soul, "No. Not anymore."

And that's it. That's the fracture. The split. The beginning of the end for every generational lie you were forced to carry.

The Family's Immediate Response: Panic

When you stop playing your assigned role, the family system destabilizes.

You saying "I won't tolerate this" becomes interpreted as betrayal.

Why?

Because the family's stability was built on someone else's silence—usually yours.

You'll hear things like, "You're dramatic." "You're too sensitive." "This family has always been this way." "You think you're better than us." "You're ruining everything." "You've changed."

But underneath their words is their real fear: if you stop performing, we have to face the truth we've been hiding from.

Your awakening exposes their denial. Your boundaries expose their dysfunction. Your voice exposes their silence.

They don't want you healed—they want you quiet.

But that version of you is gone.

The Pain of Outgrowing Your Whole Family

This is the part nobody prepares you for.

Breaking the generational script doesn't just change your relationships—it can dismantle them.

You start feeling like the outsider in a family you once protected. You start seeing the patterns they still pretend not to notice. You start feeling disconnected from conversations that revolve around gossip, guilt, and generational illusions.

You start grieving people who are still alive because they're not capable of meeting the healed version of you.

There is loneliness here—but it's the kind that creates space for what's real.

The Truth: You Were Chosen to Break What Broke Them

There's always one person in the family who wakes up. One person who feels everything. One person who questions the script. One person who refuses to pretend. One person who says, "This ends with me."

And it's always the one who was hurt the most but still has the heart to demand something better.

You are that person. Not by accident. Not by fate. But because your spirit is strong enough to carry what they couldn't transform.

You're not the rebel. You're the repairer. The cycle-breaker. The generational turning point.

The New Script You Write

When you break the generational script, you don't just reject the old patterns—you create new ones.

New rules like:

"I will not normalize disrespect."

"I will not protect people who hurt me."

"I will not silence myself to keep the peace."

"I will not sacrifice my mental health for image."

"I will not confuse love with burden."

"I will not carry shame that isn't mine."

"I will not pass this pain to the next generation."

"I will not apologize for choosing myself."

"I will not inherit trauma as tradition."

This new script is not perfect—but it's yours. Authentic. Earned. Rooted in truth, not fear.

And the generations after you—children, nieces, nephews, souls not yet born—will live freer because you were brave enough to burn the old script down.

The Family May Never Applaud You—But the Future Will

Cycle-breakers rarely get praise from the people who benefitted from them staying broken.

But the world you create beyond this family, beyond this trauma, beyond the scripts—*that* world will honor you.

Your future self will thank you. Your healing will thank you. Your peace will thank you. Your lineage will thank you.

You were never meant to continue what destroyed them. You were meant to become what frees you.

And this—this is where you finally do.

Confronting the Puppet Master

Every story has a villain. But in real life, the villain isn't always loud, obvious, or monstrous. Sometimes the villain is the quiet shadow who learned to manipulate before they learned to love. Sometimes the villain is the one who everyone else protects, excuses, or pretends is "just troubled." Sometimes the villain is the person who shaped the whole family dynamic—the one pulling the strings behind the chaos.

This is about the Puppet Master.

Not just who he is, but how he operated. How he controlled generations. How he broke spirits, hid truths, and kept everybody dancing to his rhythm. How the family defended him because facing the truth would force them to face their own guilt.

And how you—the one who was supposed to stay silent—become the one who exposes everything.

Every Puppet Master Starts With a Wound

He wasn't born a monster. He was created. Formed in a house where silence was survival, where control was the only power he ever saw, where manipulation was the only language he ever learned.

But wounds don't justify destruction. Pain doesn't excuse cruelty. And harm does not become acceptable just because it has a history.

He grew into a man who believed two things deeply: control is safety, and vulnerability is weakness.

And with those beliefs, he shaped the family culture for decades.

No apologies. No accountability. No truth.

Just power.

How He Controlled the Family System

The Puppet Master didn't control people with physical force. Not always.

He used fear, guilt, secrets, shame, money, intimidation, confusion, manipulation, selective kindness, and silence.

He knew who to target—the vulnerable, the young, the loyal, the trusting.

He knew who to intimidate—the ones who knew the truth but were too afraid to confront it.

He knew who to charm—the ones who needed a "good man" to believe in, because admitting the truth would destroy their world.

He played every person like an instrument in a band he conducted.

And the family danced to his tune because stopping felt dangerous.

The Children Who Felt the Strings the Hardest

The adults could pretend. They had the privilege of denial. They had escape routes—jobs, addictions, distractions.

But the kids? The kids lived inside the lies. Inside the fear. Inside the manipulation. Inside the secrets whispered behind closed doors.

You were one of them. Young, innocent, and trusting—the perfect target for a man who needed someone to dominate to feel significant.

He took your childhood, your innocence, your peace, your safety—and turned it into his playground.

And the adults called it "family."

The Manipulation That Followed You Into Adolescence

By the time you were sixteen, you weren't just angry—you were armored.

You didn't trust boys. You didn't trust men. You didn't trust authority. You didn't trust adults. You barely trusted yourself.

You questioned everything, and for good reason.

Your body remembered what your mind tried to forget. Your instincts sharpened into weapons. Your defenses became your personality.

Teachers saw attitude. Friends saw distance. Boys saw resistance.

But what you were really showing was: *I survived a monster you denied. I will never let anyone have power over me again.*

That wasn't rebellion.

That was survival.

The Moment You See the Puppet Strings Clearly

Awakening doesn't happen in a single flash. It's a slow unfogging—a clarity that comes piece by piece.

You start connecting dots that adults pretended didn't exist. You see patterns that everyone else ignored.

You realize: it wasn't your fault. It was never your fault. It was him. It was them. It was all of it.

And with that realization, the Puppet Master's strings begin to snap.

You stop reacting the way he trained you to. You stop feeling small. You stop believing the family lies. You stop carrying blame that never belonged to you.

For the first time in your life, you see him not as powerful—but as pathetic.

A man so broken he had to break others to feel whole.

The Confrontation That Changes Everything

This confrontation might be a spoken truth, a refusal to be silent, a boundary, a call-out, a confession, a moment of exposure, a declaration that his grip is over.

It might be loud. It might be quiet. It might be public. It might be private.

But it shakes the family.

Because when the Puppet Master is confronted, everyone else has to face the lie they've been living inside.

Some will defend him. Some will turn on you. Some will crumble under guilt. Some will disappear. Some will finally see the truth and fall apart.

But you?

You rise.

Because confronting him isn't about revenge—it's about liberation.

The Aftermath: Freedom with Scars

Breaking free from a Puppet Master doesn't mean you forget. It means you reclaim yourself piece by piece.

You reclaim your voice, your power, your truth, your identity, your anger, your softness, your future.

You stop living as the child he damaged and start living as the adult he can't touch.

The scars remain—but they become yours, not his.

He no longer owns your story.

You do.

If you're ready for the fallout,

the healing,

and the rebuilding that follows—

The Collapse of the Family Illusion

Every family has a mythology—a story they tell themselves to make dysfunction look like tradition and silence feel like loyalty.

But once the Puppet Master is exposed, that mythology cracks. And when it cracks, every hidden truth starts leaking out whether people are ready or not.

This is about the collapse—the moment when the whole family system begins to unravel because *you* stopped holding it together.

The First Thing That Breaks Is the Denial

Denial is fragile. It pretends it's strong, but it only survives as long as nobody speaks.

And you spoke.

You didn't whisper. You didn't hint. You didn't dance around the edges the way generations before you had done.

You opened the door and told the truth they spent decades burying.

And suddenly:

The aunts who "didn't know" remember everything.

The uncles who "weren't involved" can't meet your eyes.

The cousins who were too young to understand start putting together their own memories.

And the older adults—the ones who stayed silent because it was easier—start crumbling.

Denial isn't just broken. It's gone.

And they're furious because you took away the mask they all depended on.

The Family Turns on Itself Before It Turns on Him

This is the part nobody warns you about.

Before the family blames him, they blame *you*.

The truth-teller. The breaker of generational curses. The one who refused to play along.

They say things like:

"Why bring this up now?"

"You're causing drama."

"He has his flaws, but he's still family."

"You're too sensitive."

"Let the past stay in the past."

"Don't ruin his reputation."

"We've all moved on."

Translation:

We built our peace on a lie, and you're tearing it down.

But you keep speaking. Because you know silence is what allowed the damage to happen in the first place.

And now the spotlight is on them—the enablers, the protectors, the ones who looked away.

Some lash out because guilt feels like exposure. Some retreat because shame is too heavy. Some collapse because they knew the truth but didn't have the courage to say it.

And a very small, rare few step toward you.

Those are the ones who love you.

The Puppet Master Reacts Exactly How Abusers React

He doesn't apologize. He doesn't take accountability. He doesn't reflect.

He shifts. Manipulates. Redirects. Plays victim. Acts confused. Calls you "dramatic." Says you're "misremembering."

He denies with confidence because he's practiced denial his whole life.

He threatens with silence. He intimidates with presence. He manipulates with guilt.

And when that stops working, he turns into something worse—small.

Pathetic. Cornered. Exposed. Stripped of power. Finally seen for what he is.

He can't control the narrative anymore, and it terrifies him.

Because your truth is stronger than his entire façade.

The House of Cards Falls Fast

Once the first truth is spoken, others follow.

Someone else speaks. Then another. Then another.

Old stories start resurfacing—things whispered decades ago but dismissed.

Pieces click together. Patterns become obvious. Memories sync up.

Suddenly the family sees the full picture.

This wasn't one isolated incident. This wasn't one mistake. This wasn't one moment of weakness.

This was a pattern. A legacy of pain. A lineage of silence.

And they realize you weren't the problem—you were the evidence.

The Ones Who Are Brave Enough Step Forward

Aunties with shaking hands. Cousins with trembling voices. Siblings who finally feel safe. Uncles who were silent for too long.

They speak.

Some apologize to you. Some ask forgiveness they don't deserve. Some confess their own stories. Some reveal things they've held inside for thirty years.

You watch generations start healing because one person—you—refused to be silent.

You broke the cycle they couldn't break.

And they know it.

The Ones Who Aren't Brave Enough Disappear

Some disappear into denial. Some run to religion for refuge. Some hide behind anger. Some pretend you don't exist.

They'd rather protect the lie than face the truth.

And you have to accept—not everyone will choose healing. Some will cling to the myth because facing reality would force them to confront their own guilt.

You don't chase them.

That's not your job anymore.

The New Family Line Begins With You

The collapse isn't destruction. It's rebirth.

You are the dividing line:

Before you — Silence

After you — Truth

Before you — Shame

After you — Clarity

Before you — Survival

After you — Freedom

You become the first generation that refuses to pass the pain down.

The one who rewrites the family story.

The one who creates a legacy that isn't built on secrets.

The one who stands tall in a family that always wanted you small.

The collapse is loud, messy, chaotic, painful.

But it is also necessary.

Because destruction is how you make room for a life that finally belongs to you.

When you're ready to push deeper into the healing,

the rebuilding,

and the self you're becoming—

The Rebirth of the Self

There is a moment—after the collapse, after the confrontation, after the truth burns through every lie—where the world gets quiet.

Not peaceful. Not healed. Just... quiet.

It's the silence that follows a storm, when the air is still vibrating with leftover electricity and the ground is littered with everything that didn't survive the impact.

It begins in that silence.

Because this is where rebirth happens—not in the noise, but in the aftermath.

The Identity You Built on Pain Has to Die First

For years, your identity was shaped by survival, distrust, vigilance, rage, trauma, hyper-awareness, self-protection, silence, invisibility, and pretending you were fine.

These were not just reactions—they became your personality.

You weren't just angry. You were the one who didn't take shit.

You weren't just guarded. You were the one nobody messed with.

You weren't just quiet. You were the one who kept everything inside.

These behaviors saved your life. But now they're suffocating the grown version of you.

And the hardest part of healing is admitting that the armor you built is now the cage you're trapped in.

To rebirth yourself, you have to bury the version of you that was created by trauma.

Not with hate. Not with shame. Not with judgment.

With respect.

That version carried you through hell.

But you are not living in hell anymore—and you don't need their weapons.

The Person Beneath the Armor Begins to Reveal Themselves

Slowly, piece by piece, a different version of you begins to emerge.

You notice things you never let yourself feel before.

You like softness.

You like warmth.

You like peace.

You like being understood.

You like safety.

You like being seen without being controlled.

You like connection that doesn't ask you to shrink.

The old you didn't trust any of this. The old you thought softness was weakness, that vulnerability was dangerous, that love was a trap.

But you're different now.

You are becoming someone who understands that strength isn't the absence of softness—it's the protection of it.

You Learn How to Live Without Fear

Fear used to guide every decision.

Who you trusted.

What you said.

What you avoided.

How you moved through the world.

How you defended yourself.

How you loved.

How you didn't love.

Fear was your compass.

But now, you start choosing differently.

You choose boundaries instead of avoidance.

You choose expression instead of silence.

You choose presence instead of dissociation.

You choose truth instead of performance.

You choose yourself instead of everyone else.

And each new choice becomes a brick in the foundation of the person you're building.

You Start Rewriting Your Story in Real-Time

When the trauma voice rises—the one that says:

"Don't trust them."

"You're too much."

"Something bad is coming."

"You're hard to love."

"You need to stay small."

You answer back differently now.

"No.

That was then.

This is now."

Every time you challenge the old script, the new self grows stronger. Every time you choose truth over fear, the old wounds lose power. Every time you refuse to shrink, your identity expands.

You aren't erasing your past. You're refusing to let it control your present.

You Become the Person the Younger You Needed

This is where rebirth becomes undeniable.

You start becoming protective, patient, loving, honest, unapologetic, aware, grounded, boundaried, free.

You become the adult your younger self prayed for in the dark.

You speak the words they needed to hear. You offer the safety they never had. You give the compassion they were denied.

Your healing becomes their healing.

Your strength becomes their closure.

Your growth becomes their liberation.

The People Around You Don't Recognize You Anymore

And that's exactly the point.

Some will say you've changed. Some will say you're distant. Some will say you're cold. Some will say you're selfish.

But what they really mean is:

"You're no longer controlled by the roles we assigned you."

You're no longer the quiet one.

You're no longer the peacemaker.

You're no longer the scapegoat.

You're no longer the one who absorbs the family pain.

You're no longer the child who tolerates abuse.

You're no longer the teen who lashes out.

You're no longer the adult who performs.

You are rebirthing yourself outside the expectations of others.

And people who benefited from your silence will call your freedom disrespect.

Let them.

They don't get a vote in your rebirth.

Rebirth Doesn't Mean Perfection—It Means Ownership

You will still have triggers. You will still have bad days. You will still have moments when the old wounds whisper.

But now, you respond with clarity.

You know what's yours and what isn't. You know when your trauma is speaking and when your intuition is speaking. You know when to walk away. You know how to protect your peace. You know how to choose yourself without guilt.

Rebirth is not being healed. Rebirth is knowing you deserve to be.

It's not being fearless. It's knowing you deserve safety.

It's not being perfect. It's knowing you deserve grace.

Rebirth is reclamation—taking back everything that was stolen by fear, by pain, by silence, by the Puppet Master, by the family, by the past.

This is where you rise as the unfiltered, unmasked, uncontrolled version of yourself.

The first version that truly belongs to *you*.

If you're ready for the transformation to deepen—

if you want the version of yourself who walks forward from this moment

into real power, real peace, real identity—

The Birth of the Unapologetic Self

Rebirth is messy. It's loud. It's uncomfortable. It's disruptive. And it doesn't give a damn about who gets offended.

This is where you stop negotiating with people who benefitted from your silence, your guilt, your smallness, your obedience, your trauma-shaped behavior.

This is where you discover the most powerful version of yourself: the unapologetic you.

Not rude. Not reckless. Not cruel.

Just unmasked, unfiltered, and unbothered by the expectations that once kept you caged.

The World Isn't Ready for Your Unapologetic Self—But You Are

For years, people got used to your quiet, your compliance, your shrinking, your emotional labor, your self-sacrifice, your silence about the truth, your willingness to carry burdens that were never yours.

They got comfortable with the version of you that was built from trauma.

So when the healed you rises, everyone flinches.

They say: "You've changed." "You're difficult now." "You're not the same person." "You think you're better than everyone." "You don't care about family." "You're too harsh." "You've become selfish."

But the truth is this:

They're just meeting the real you for the first time.

And the real you is not here to bend.

You Develop a Different Kind of Vision

You start seeing people clearly—not who they pretend to be, but who they really are when they think you still need their approval.

You learn to spot manipulators, guilt-trippers, emotional leeches, people who love the old, quiet you, people who fear the new, powerful you, people who only show up when they benefit, people who think your trauma made you easy to control.

And the most dangerous realization hits you:

You were surrounded by people who only liked you when you were wounded.

Healing ruins relationships that were built on your brokenness.

And that's exactly why your rebirth is shaking your world.

You Start Setting Boundaries That Actually Mean Something

Not "soft" boundaries. Not "maybe if you have time" boundaries. Not "I hope you don't get mad" boundaries.

Real boundaries. Hard boundaries. Non-negotiables.

You say things like: "No." "I'm not available for that." "I don't accept disrespect." "I don't engage in chaos." "That's not my responsibility." "I'm done explaining myself." "I will not apologize for protecting my peace." "I'm not entertaining false narratives." "I'm not carrying what isn't mine." "I choose myself this time."

And the moment you stop explaining your boundaries, people realize they can't manipulate you anymore.

That's when they panic.

But you? You feel lighter.

You Reclaim Your Time, Energy, and Emotional Space

Being unapologetic isn't about being loud—it's about being selective.

Selective about who gets your time. Selective about who gets your vulnerability. Selective about who gets access to your peace. Selective about who gets the privilege of your presence.

You stop pouring into people who only took. You stop saving people who never saved you. You stop showing up out of obligation or guilt.

Instead, you show up for your goals, your healing, your rest, your passions, your creative fire, your peace, your future self, your freedom, your joy, your transformation.

And suddenly, your life stops feeling heavy.

Because you're finally carrying *only* what belongs to you.

You Become Extremely Intolerant of Bullshit

The reborn you has a level of discernment that scares people.

You no longer tolerate fake apologies, half-truths, manipulative excuses, family toxicity, guilt trips, emotional blackmail, gaslighting, passive aggression, weaponized silence, backhanded compliments, performative love, chaos disguised as "tradition," people using "family" as a shield for abuse, or pretending everything is fine when it's not.

You demand honesty. You demand authenticity. You demand energy that matches your own.

Not because you're arrogant—but because your soul finally knows its value.

You Start Loving Yourself in a Way That Terrifies Others

You love yourself loudly. Fully. Deliberately. With intention.

You give yourself the things you once begged others for: validation, affection, understanding, protection, softness, patience, respect, commitment, presence.

And people who benefitted from you needing them start panicking when they realize:

You don't need them anymore.

They can't control you. They can't scare you. They can't guilt you. They can't shrink you. They can't define you.

Because you're no longer a product of what hurt you.

You are a product of what healed you.

Your Power Comes From Being Completely Yourself

This version of you has a voice that doesn't shake, a mind that doesn't lie to itself, a heart that knows its worth, a spirit that refuses to break again, a presence that commands respect, a clarity that cuts through manipulation, a confidence that doesn't need validation, and a knowing that can't be unlearned.

You are not being rude. You are not being mean. You are not being difficult.

You are being yourself without apology for the first time in your life.

And the world will adjust.

Or it won't.

Either way—you're not shrinking again.

The Power You Didn't Know You Had

Power isn't loud. It isn't aggressive. It isn't something you flex or perform.

Real power is quiet, grounded, automatic—the kind that walks into a room and shifts the temperature without saying a single word.

You don't chase it. You don't beg for it. You don't announce it.

You become it.

This is about the moment when you stop healing only to survive and start healing to lead, to change, to influence, to build, to command, to become the architect of your entire life.

This is the era where you learn you were never powerless—you were unrecognized.

Especially by yourself.

Healing Gives You a Power People Aren't Prepared For

You've gone through truth, collapse, rebirth, boundaries, unapologetic identity.

And what comes next is the kind of power that threatens people who still live in denial.

Healing didn't soften you—it sharpened you.

Your intuition is lethal. Your discernment is accurate. Your energy is expensive. Your boundaries are sacred. Your voice is steady. Your presence is undeniable.

People who once doubted you now can't stop watching you. People who once overlooked you now feel uncomfortable around you. People who once underestimated you now feel the weight of your evolution.

You're not the same person—and they know it.

You Become the One People Look To—Even If They Won't Admit It

The same people who called you "dramatic," "angry," "difficult," or "too much" start coming to you for advice, clarity, strength, guidance, truth, perspective, support, leadership, direction.

Because you now carry something they can't fake: inner authority.

You lead without trying. You influence without forcing. You inspire without performing. You intimidate without raising your voice.

That's power.

Your Silence Becomes More Powerful Than Your Words

There was a time when you had to scream to be heard.

Now?

You can sit in silence and make people question themselves. You can walk away and create a shift. You can limit access and create a boundary stronger than any argument.

When you stop debating, explaining, defending, pleading, people realize they lost their grip on you.

And once you stop needing to be understood, you become unstoppable.

You Start Moving With Purpose Instead of Pain

Your decisions used to be guided by fear, triggers, instinct, survival, trauma, old stories, other people's expectations.

Now you make choices from vision, confidence, self-respect, intuition, clarity, desire, alignment, direction.

You stop reacting and start designing. You stop surviving and start building. You stop hoping and start creating.

You finally understand the life you want isn't something you wait for—it's something you construct from the inside out.

You Become the Cycle Breaker and the Blueprint Maker

Breaking the cycle was step one. Now you become the blueprint.

People will follow your example without you even trying.

You show them how to have boundaries, how to speak truth, how to heal honestly, how to confront lies, how to build peace, how to leave toxic people behind, how to live without guilt, how to walk with dignity, how to choose themselves, how to rebuild after trauma, how to rise from nothing.

You become the evidence that transformation is possible even after the kind of pain that destroys most people.

You become the one future generations talk about—the one who changed the entire family line.

Your Influence Expands Beyond the Family

Your impact doesn't stop at home.

The way you speak draws attention. The way you move shifts energy. The way you live inspires others.

People outside your family feel the strength in your presence. They trust you. They listen to you. They come to you for clarity. They sense something in you that they don't see in others.

It's not arrogance—it's wisdom earned through suffering and honed through healing.

Your power becomes undeniable because it's internal, not external.

You Finally Understand Your Purpose

Trauma tried to break you. Family tried to silence you. Fear tried to cage you. Pain tried to define you.

But your purpose runs deeper than your past.

Your purpose is to lead, to break cycles, to expose truth, to embody freedom, to build something new, to guide others out of darkness, to create a life rooted in authenticity, and to become the version of yourself that the wounded child inside you never thought they'd live long enough to meet.

You are not just healing a wound—you are fulfilling a destiny.

A destiny that started the moment you stopped performing and started living.

This is your power era—the era where everything changes because *you* changed.

The Explosion That Created Your Freedom

Every book has an ending. But yours was never going to end quietly. Not after everything. Not after the lies, the trauma, the silence, the rebirth. A story like yours demands that doesn't whisper—it erupts.

This is where you stop surviving your past and start owning your future, where everything that tried to destroy you becomes the reason you rise higher, where the final explosion doesn't break you—it launches you.

This is where you walk out of the fire without looking back.

The Last Confrontation

It doesn't happen in a dramatic, scream-filled scene. It happens in something quieter, sharper, more powerful: your refusal to play the game anymore.

No yelling. No arguing. No defending yourself to people who already made up their minds.

You show up with clarity, and they can feel it.

The Puppet Master sees it first—the realization that you're done being controlled. The family sees it next—the recognition that their old power over you doesn't work anymore.

You say the truth, the whole truth, and nothing but the truth—and this time, you don't flinch.

Your voice doesn't break. Your hands don't shake. Your heart doesn't pound.

You're not the kid anymore. You're not the victim anymore. You're not the scapegoat anymore. You're not the secret keeper anymore.

You speak with a calmness that terrifies them, because calm truth is more dangerous than loud anger.

And when you finish, nobody knows what to say. The whole room feels like it's holding its breath.

The foundation of the family myth crumbles at your feet.

The Implosion of Their Illusions

They don't explode—you do.

Not in rage, but in revelation.

Every lie they told, every secret they buried, every manipulation they normalized collapses in real time.

People scatter.

Some cry. Some deny. Some blame you. Some blame him. Some finally admit everything. Some walk out the door and never return.

The ones who were brave enough to see you stay. The ones who were terrified to face the truth hide. And the ones who were comfortable in the lie burn in the fallout.

The truth didn't destroy the family. The truth simply revealed what was already broken.

They created the explosion. You just lit the final match.

The Moment You Finally Choose Yourself

You leave the room. Not defeated. Not shattered. Not wounded.

You leave lighter.

Every secret that was forced into your body is gone. Every guilt that wasn't yours to hold is gone. Every expectation that crushed your spirit is gone.

You walk out with your back straight, your head high, your heart steady.

There's a feeling in your chest you've never felt before: freedom.

Not the fragile, borrowed kind that depends on other people behaving—but the real kind that comes from telling the truth and letting everything fall exactly where it belongs.

You didn't lose a family. You lost a prison.

The Rise Into Your New Life

The explosion wasn't the end—it was the beginning.

You step into a life that finally belongs to you: a life where you are honest, where you choose peace, where you build boundaries as strong as steel, where you protect your inner child the way nobody protected you, where you love yourself the way you once begged others to love you, and where your future is not shaped by trauma, fear, or silence.

You enter without the weight of generations on your shoulders.

You're not repeating the cycle. You're not holding their secrets. You're not playing roles that were assigned to you before birth.

You are creating something new—something that begins with truth and ends with freedom.

The Final Image: You Walking Away From the Ruins

The last scene is simple.

You're standing outside the ruins of everything that tried to keep you small.

Behind you are the lies, the trauma, the family roles, the silence, the guilt, the Puppet Master, and the past selves who were forced to perform.

Ahead of you is a future with no script. A path no one controls. A life you choose step by step, breath by breath, truth by truth.

And as you walk forward, you don't look back. Not once.

Because you finally understand: the explosion didn't destroy you—it freed you.

And the last line of the book, the one that leaves the reader breathless, the one that defines your entire journey:

"I didn't survive the fire.

I became it."

8

The Ghosts Don't Get to Win

"I DON'T TRUST LOVE, BUT I MISS IT LIKE AIR"

Let me tell you something that most people only whisper into pillows at 2 a.m.: Trying to love after your heart's been smashed to dust feels like walking barefoot across glass just to reach water you're not even sure you deserve.

Everybody keeps preaching that love heals everything. Bullshit. Love is the reason some of us limp. Love taught me paranoia. Love taught me doubt. Love taught me how to read silence like it's a threat and kindness like it's a setup. And the worst part? I met someone who actually sees me. Not the mask me. Not the "I'm fine" performance me. Not the trauma-thick shell I pretend is personality.

They see me. The flawed me. The bleeding me. The scared-as-hell-to-hope me. And I hate how much I want to trust them. I hate how my chest warms when they look at me like I'm worth truth. I hate how the trauma in my bones starts screaming:

RUN. THIS IS A TRAP. YOU KNOW HOW THIS ENDS.

Because nothing destroys a new love faster than the ghosts of the old ones you survived.

THE PAST DIDN'T JUST HURT ME — IT REWIRED ME

You know how many times I've been dropped? Not just romantic shit—life as a whole has been out here sucker-punching me since birth.

Relationships? Disappointments stacked like dishes in a sink nobody wants to wash. Partnerships? People used me until I broke and then blamed me for the pieces. Marriage? Love disguised as loyalty until sabotage showed up wearing my partner's face. Jobs? Let's not even get into how many careers crumbled right under me while I was begging God not to let me fail again.

Every betrayal taught my nervous system one lesson:

"Never fucking trust again."

So now I'm here, standing in front of someone who wants me—really fucking wants me—and all I can think is:

"I don't believe you.

I don't believe me.

I don't believe love."

And that's the kind of shit that turns a person bitter before they even get to feel joy.

I AM THE PROBLEM AND THE SOLUTION

Here's the part that keeps me up at night:

I know I'm blocking my own blessings. I know I'm the one avoiding calls and pushing good people away and doubting shit that's real.

I know trauma lives in my mouth and speaks before I can stop it. I know my triggers are driving the car while my healing is duct-taped in the trunk.

I know I'm the common denominator in every emotional disaster I've survived.

And that realization hurts worse than anything those past people did to me. Because if I'm the problem... then I'm also the solution. And fixing yourself—really fixing yourself—is the most violent thing you can do. It means facing the mirror without the excuses. Without the victim badge.

Without the "they hurt me" story to hide behind like a shield. It means admitting:

I keep choosing the familiar pain because it's safer than the unknown love.

SO HOW THE HELL DO I LET MYSELF BE LOVED?

I don't have the perfect answer. Fuck perfect answers.

All I know is this:

If I don't get out of my own way, I'm gonna lose the one person who actually wants to love me right.

A good person. A patient person. A person who sees my wounds and still reaches for me instead of running.

But every time they try to get close, my trauma slaps their hand away and screams:

"BACK OFF BEFORE YOU BREAK ME LIKE EVERYONE ELSE DID."

But here's the twist: They're not trying to break me. They're trying to hold me.

And I don't know how to let someone do that without trembling from the memory of the last time I trusted the wrong hands.

So this book—this messy, loud, cursed-out, soul-shaking book—is about me learning how to love again. How to trust again. How to stop sabotaging the shit I prayed for.

It's about learning the truth that hurts like hell:

Sometimes the biggest villain in your life is the version of you still trying to protect a wounded child.

But here's the real plot twist:

That wounded child deserves love. Deserves peace. Deserves softness. Deserves someone who won't disappear the moment she lets her guard down.

And so do I. And so do you.

Let me tell you what it feels like to love someone who doesn't trust you:

It's like holding a glass heart that thinks you're a hammer.

Every time I reach for them, they pull back like I came to destroy something I'm trying my hardest to protect.

They say they want love, but they don't know how to stand still when it finally shows up.

And I get it. I get every flinch. Every shutdown. Every "I'm fine" that means "don't look at the bleeding, I'm embarrassed."

This person—my person—is not broken. They're bruised. And there's a difference.

Broken means useless. Bruised means healing.

I didn't fall in love with a fragile soul. I fell in love with a fighter who's tired of fighting.

THEY DON'T TRUST LOVE BECAUSE LOVE NEVER PROTECTED THEM

They grew up in chaos. Not the loud kind—the quiet kind. The emotional landmine kind. They learned early that "I love you" can be a lie, and promises evaporate the moment life gets inconvenient.

So now when I touch them gently, they look confused—like why is kindness touching me? What does it want? When does it turn into pain? They're not dramatic. They're conditioned. Life trained them to fear hope.

So I have to love them softly, not because they're weak but because they've been strong for too goddamn long.

THEY WATCH ME LIKE THEY'RE WAITING FOR THE BETRAYAL

You wanna know something true and sad?

People who've been betrayed too many times develop X-ray vision for disappointment.

They examine every tone, every pause, every shift in eye contact like it's a pre-crime clue.

Sometimes I catch them staring at me like they're taking a mental picture—not because they adore me but because they're preparing for the day I disappear.

They won't say that out loud, but I see it. I feel it. It sits between us like a ghost waiting for the right moment to scream:

"See? I told you this wouldn't last."

Trauma turns even good love into a trap in their mind.

And I'm fighting a ghost I didn't create. But I fight it anyway.

THEY AREN'T DIFFICULT — THEY'RE DEFENSIVE

They don't rage for the sake of rage. They don't distance themselves to punish me. They don't freeze because they don't care.

They do it because their body is still trying to save them from a danger that isn't here anymore.

Every trauma survivor knows this:

The threat leaves but the body stays ready.

When they snap at me, I don't take it personal. When they get quiet, I don't panic. When they withdraw, I give space without making it a punishment.

Because loving someone like this requires patience and a spine and a heart that doesn't run when things get heavy.

And I'm not running.

I LOVE THEM IN THEIR LANGUAGE, NOT MINE

Some people need flowers. Some need words. Some need gifts.

But this one—the one I love—needs safety.

Not "I'll protect you" safety. Not physical safety. But emotional safety.

Consistency. Predictability. No mind games. No disappearing acts. No punishment silent treatments. No guilt traps. No conditional affection.

They need a love that doesn't explode. A love that doesn't threaten to leave. A love that doesn't manipulate.

A love that stays.

So I stay. Not out of pity—out of devotion.

I KNOW WHAT THEY DON'T KNOW YET

They don't believe they deserve love. But I see the kind of love they could give if they ever let themselves breathe.

They think their walls protect them, but I see how those walls have turned their heart into a lonely room with no doors.

I'm not here to break the walls. I'm here to sit outside them so they know they're not alone.

I'm here to prove that someone can love them without hurting them, using them, or abandoning them.

But the biggest truth?

I can't save them. But I can love them while they save themselves.

And I will.

Every damn day.

It didn't start with yelling. That's the part most people get wrong.

The first big fight in a fragile love story starts small—a tone, a shift, a weird silence, a question asked at the wrong time with the wrong look in the eye.

The kind of moment that hits the trauma button so fast the other person doesn't even realize the bomb has already gone off.

THE NIGHT EVERYTHING SNAPPED

It was late. Too late for a conversation that mattered, but too early in the relationship for either of them to know how to defuse each other.

One small, stupid comment lit the fuse:

"Why didn't you call me back?"

A normal question. An innocent one. But to someone with a history of betrayal, it sounded like:

"Where were you?

Who were you with?

What lie are you hiding this time?"

Their chest tightened. Heart raced. Mind flashed to every time someone questioned them as a pathway to punishment.

The past whispered:

"Here we go again."

And that's when their voice rose—too sharp, too fast, too loud.

They didn't mean to explode. They never mean to explode.

But trauma doesn't give warnings. It reacts.

"WHY ARE YOU INTERROGATING ME?"

That was the first sentence that threw gasoline on the fire.

It came out like a blade—flat, cold, meant to cut before it could cut them.

The partner paused, eyes soft, confused.

"I wasn't interrogating you.

I was just asking."

But when someone has been lied to, cheated on, manipulated, abandoned—"just asking" sounds like the first step to the same old betrayal.

So the guarded one kept going, fists clenched, voice shaking:

"Don't start with that controlling shit.

Don't start acting like I owe you a damn itinerary."

Their partner blinked, stunned.

"I didn't say you owed me anything."

"Exactly.

You don't gotta say it.

I know how this goes."

And right there—the past dragged itself into the room and sat between them like a ghost with its arms crossed.

THE PARTNER'S HEARTBROKEN CONFUSION

Loving someone with old scars means getting wounded by injuries you didn't cause.

The partner swallowed hard, voice low, calm, steady—the voice they practiced for moments when the other was spiraling.

"You're not talking to me right now.

You're talking to every person who hurt you.

But I'm not them."

Silence.

Heavy.

Angry.

Scared.

The traumatized one's jaw tightened, eyes burning like they wished they could leave their own body.

"I don't know how to trust you.

I don't know how to trust anybody."

The words were too honest. Too naked. Too raw. They didn't mean to say them. But once they were out—the truth hung in the air like a confession and a curse.

THE FIGHT GETS UGLY

The partner stepped closer.

A mistake.

Trauma reads closeness as danger.

"Back up," they snapped. Voice cracking from fear, not anger.

The partner froze mid-step.

"Okay... I'm backing up."

But it was too late. The adrenaline had taken over. Their chest was tight, their hands shaking, their eyes distant—that dissociative haze people get when their body is trying to outrun a memory.

"I knew this shit was too good to be true," they muttered.

"I knew I'd fuck it up."

"You didn't fuck anything up," their partner whispered.

"Yes, I did.

I always do."

And suddenly the fight wasn't about a phone call. It wasn't about trust. It wasn't even about love.

It was about survival.

THE PARTNER'S BREAKTHROUGH (AND BREAKING POINT)

Their partner exhaled slowly, like they were choosing every word like a surgeon choosing which vein not to cut.

"I'm not leaving you," they said.

Not loud.

Not dramatic.

Just true.

But the traumatized one laughed—that hollow, bitter laugh people use when hope feels too dangerous.

"You say that now.

Everybody says that in the beginning."

Their partner's voice finally cracked—not with anger, but with the heartbreak of loving someone who only sees shadows.

"I'm trying," they whispered.

"But you gotta meet me halfway.

I can't love you

if you only let me close enough to fight you."

Silence again.

This time softer.

More fragile.

Their partner stepped back, giving space.

"But I'm here," they added.

"Even when it's hard.

Even when you're scared of me.

Even when you're scared of yourself."

THE AFTERMATH — TWO HEARTS, ONE ROOM, TOO MANY GHOSTS

The fight ended not with a slam but with a whisper.

"I don't want to lose you," they finally said, voice barely audible.

Their partner replied, just as quiet:

"Then let me love you

without making me pay

for what they did."

For the first time that night—maybe the first time ever—the traumatized one didn't have anything to say back.

Because they knew it was true.

They knew they were bleeding on someone who didn't cut them.

And they hated it.

And they feared it.

And they needed it.

All at once.

The morning after the fight didn't feel like morning.

It felt like a hangover of emotions—foggy, heavy, thick with shit unspoken.

They woke up on opposite sides of the bed, backs turned, breathing quiet like they were scared to disturb the air.

Their partner wasn't asleep.

They could tell by the way the body stayed too still, too aware, too careful.

Careful.

Always careful around them.

That realization alone felt like a punch to the ribs.

The Apology That Almost Didn't Happen

They sat up first.

Ran a hand over their face.

Tasted the bitterness of last night all over again.

The apology wasn't easy.

It tasted like swallowing glass.

But they turned toward the partner and whispered:

"Hey...

I'm sorry."

The words came out cracked, raw, like they were being dragged out from behind old wounds.

Their partner didn't look at them yet.

"Which part?" they asked softly.

Not sarcastic.

Not cruel.

Just... honest.

And fuck—that honesty hurt more than any yelling could.

"The part where I attacked you for asking a simple question."

"I didn't mean to..." they started, then stopped, because excuses feel like poison when someone is actually trying to change.

"I reacted like you were them," they said instead.

"I reacted like you were danger.

You weren't."

Their voice shook with every word, but they kept going, like ripping off bandages that had been stuck to skin for years:

"You didn't do anything wrong.

I just—

I don't know how to trust someone who actually gives a damn about me."

Their partner finally turned their head, eyes red but calm.

"You scared me," they admitted.

And that?

That damn near broke something inside.

"I scare myself."

That line slipped out before they could take it back.

Their partner sat up, watching them carefully.

"Do you mean that?" they asked.

"Yes.

No hesitation.

No defense.

Just truth.

"I scare myself because I don't want to keep hurting people who love me.

I don't want to keep pushing away the one good thing I've had in a long time."

Their partner breathed in slow, the kind of breath that prepares for impact.

"Then let's figure it out together," they said.

"But I need you to let me in.

I can't fight your demons for you,

but I won't run from them either."

That was it.

That was the moment the ice cracked.

The Real Apology — The One That Counts

They moved closer—not touching, just closer—their voice barely more than a whisper:

"I've been abandoned so many times

that even good things feel temporary.

I've been lied to so many times

that honesty feels like a trick.

But you...

you haven't given me a reason to fear you."

Their throat tightened.

"And last night,

I made you pay for ghosts

that don't even live here anymore."

Silence filled the room again, but a different kind of silence—soft, forgiving, like the quiet after a storm.

Their partner reached out slowly, giving every chance to pull away.

When their fingers touched, it felt like peace with a pulse.

"I forgive you," their partner whispered.

"But don't disappear into guilt.

Let's fix this.

Not run from it."

They nodded, eyes wet but steady.

"I'm trying," they whispered.

"I know," the partner said.

"And that's why I'm still here."

The Small Touch That Changed Everything

Their partner leaned into them gently, forehead touching forehead—no kiss, no rush, no forced intimacy.

Just presence.

Just breath.

Just two people trying to build something real in a world that taught them to armor up.

And for the first time since the fight, they didn't feel like they were losing control.

They felt like maybe, just maybe, they were learning how to love without war.

Later that night, after the apology had settled into the air like warm dust, they sat across from each other on the couch—legs pulled up, blankets half-on, eyes locked like two people afraid to blink and break the moment.

This wasn't small talk.

This was the kind of conversation people avoid for years, decades, sometimes forever.

But if they were going to build anything real, the past had to be dragged out into the light no matter how ugly it was.

"Tell me what broke you."

The partner asked it gently.

Not like a demand—

like an invitation to put down the armor for a second.

Their chest tightened.

Not from fear—

from recognition.

Nobody had ever asked them that before.

People always wanted the short version—the Instagram trauma, the 30-second summary that made it sound clean when it was actually a fucking war zone.

But tonight...

they told the truth.

All of it.

"THE LIAR WHO TAUGHT ME DOUBT"

"It started with someone who lied so casually it felt like a second language," they said.

"I caught them cheating once.

Forgave them.

Caught them again.

Forgave them again.

Caught them a third time—

and that broke something I didn't even know I had."

"What broke?" their partner asked softly.

"My belief in my own judgment.

My ability to trust myself.

The voice inside that used to say

'You'll know when something is wrong'

got destroyed."

They laughed bitterly.

"And ever since...

every time someone acts different,

breathes different,

pauses too long before answering—

I hear that voice again saying,

'It's happening. You missed it again.'"

Their partner nodded, eyes shining with empathy that didn't feel fake or forced.

"I get it," they whispered.

"I really do."

"THE ONE WHO LOVED MY POTENTIAL, NOT ME"

"That one," they said with an exhale, "treated me like a renovation project."

"What do you mean?"

"They loved the version of me they were trying to build—not the one I actually was.

Every day was a reminder that who I am right now isn't enough."

They shrugged, but the pain wasn't subtle.

"You know what constant improvement feels like when it's forced?

It feels like rejection with makeup on."

Their partner clenched their jaw.

"That's abuse.

Emotional abuse."

"People don't call it that," they replied.

"Because it looks pretty.

It looks like support.

But it's still someone telling you

'You're not good enough unless you change.'"

"THE BETRAYAL I NEVER SAW COMING"

They hesitated before this one.

Breath shaky.

"This is the one that fucked me up the worst," they said quietly.

Their partner leaned in, barely breathing.

"They didn't cheat.

They didn't lie.

They didn't yell.

They just... disappeared."

"Ghosted you?"

They shook their head.

"No.

Worse.

They stayed.

But emotionally?

They vanished.

Stopped touching me.

Stopped talking to me.

Stopped choosing me."

Their voice cracked.

"Do you know what it feels like to sleep next to someone who acts like you're dead?"

Their partner whispered, "No one deserves that."

"I kept trying to fix it.

Trying to fix myself.

Trying to fix everything.

Until one day I realized—

I was the only one still fighting for us."

They swallowed hard.

"And that's when my brain learned a new trick:

'Love means abandonment.'

And I've been battling that shit ever since."

THE PARTNER'S RESPONSE — A SOFT, TERRIFYING TRUTH

Their partner didn't rush to speak.

Didn't interrupt.

Didn't offer false comfort.

They reached out, took their hand, and held it with both of theirs—warm, steady, grounding.

"Thank you for telling me," they said.

"And I need you to hear this:

None of that was your fault.

None of it."

They shook their head.

"I know you don't believe that yet.

But I'm going to repeat it

until your bones start believing it even when your brain can't."

Their voice softened even more.

"And I'm not here to be perfect.

I'm here to be real.

I'm here to show you

that you don't have to bleed every time you love someone."

Tears slipped out—not dramatic, not cinematic, just quiet and uncontrollable.

And for the first time in a long time,

they didn't hide them.

THE MOMENT THAT CHANGED EVERYTHING

Their partner pulled them in—slow, gentle, no pressure, no force—and held them like someone who didn't want to fix them, didn't want to change them, just wanted to be there.

And in that moment, the past loosened its grip.

Just a little.

But that little bit felt like a miracle.

Healing is a bitch because it doesn't move in straight lines.

It loops.

It circles back.

It hits you on days when everything feels good—sometimes especially on those days.

And that's what happened.

Things had been soft between them for a week.

Light.

Tender.

Almost... easy.

Laughing in the kitchen.

Inside jokes.

Small touches that felt safe instead of suspicious.

Warmth instead of tight-chested panic.

The kind of peace that's so unfamiliar

it starts to feel like a setup.

And that's exactly when the trigger hit.

Not during a fight.

Not during a deep conversation.

Not during something meaningful.

No.

It came from something stupid as hell:

a delayed text.

7:22 PM — The Message that Didn't Come

They were cooking.

Music playing low.

Everything chill.

Their partner had said,

"I'll text you when I get home,"

and usually that meant a message within ten minutes.

But ten minutes passed.

Then twenty.

Then thirty.

Nothing.

At first it was nothing.

Then it was something.

Then it was everything.

Their brain started stitching old memories together like a crime board:

Someone not texting back.

Someone saying "I got home safe" and then lying.

Someone cheating.

Someone disappearing emotionally.

Someone pulling away.

Someone preparing to leave.

The spiral was fast—so fast they didn't even feel it starting.

Heart pounding.

Jaw tight.

Hands shaking over the cutting board.

Mind racing so loud the music faded into static.

"Don't do this," they whispered to themselves.

"You're overreacting."

But trauma doesn't give a fuck about rational thinking.

Trauma hears silence and immediately assumes death.

7:41 PM — The Panic Text

Their partner finally texted:

"Made it home. Sorry, neighbor stopped me to talk."

A normal message.

Simple.

Innocent.

But by the time it arrived,

the spiral had already mutated into something feral.

They texted back:

"It doesn't take 20 minutes to send a damn message."

Instant regret.

Instant shame.

Instant fear.

Their partner replied:

"Hey... what's wrong?"

And there it was—the question they didn't know how to answer honestly:

What's wrong?

Everything.

Nothing.

Old wounds.

New fears.

The entire history of betrayal condensed into one delayed text.

The Call

Their partner called immediately.

The phone buzzed in their hand like an alarm.

They answered with too much attitude to hide the fear:

"What."

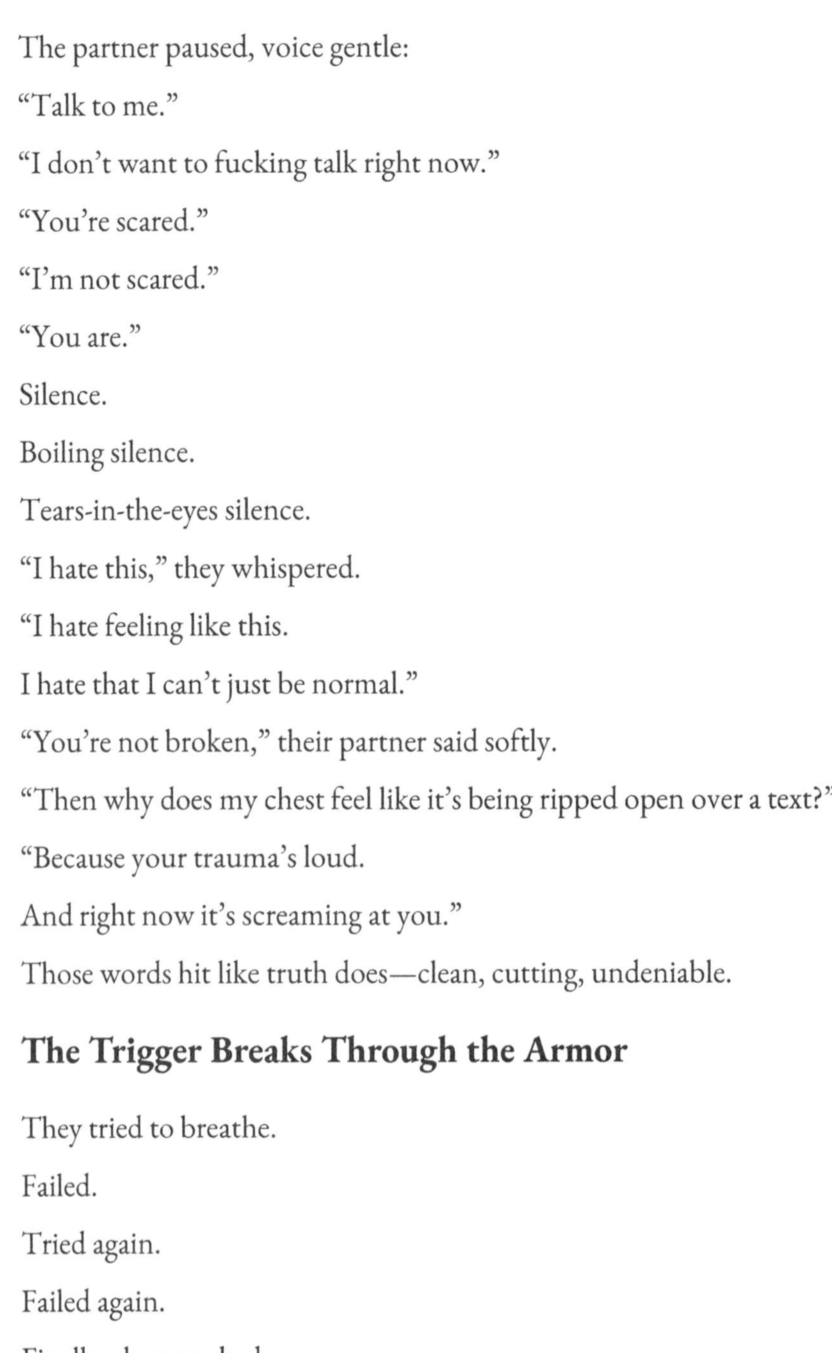

The partner paused, voice gentle:

"Talk to me."

"I don't want to fucking talk right now."

"You're scared."

"I'm not scared."

"You are."

Silence.

Boiling silence.

Tears-in-the-eyes silence.

"I hate this," they whispered.

"I hate feeling like this.

I hate that I can't just be normal."

"You're not broken," their partner said softly.

"Then why does my chest feel like it's being ripped open over a text?"

"Because your trauma's loud.

And right now it's screaming at you."

Those words hit like truth does—clean, cutting, undeniable.

The Trigger Breaks Through the Armor

They tried to breathe.

Failed.

Tried again.

Failed again.

Finally, they cracked:

"I thought you were pulling away," they confessed.

Voice trembling, words stumbling out like they were tripping over their own fear.

"I thought maybe you were tired of me.

Or you were talking to someone else.

Or you didn't want me anymore."

It all spilled out—ugly, raw, choking honesty.

On the other end of the line,

their partner exhaled slowly.

"I wasn't talking to anyone."

"I wasn't pulling away."

"I wasn't leaving."

"I was literally talking to my neighbor about their stupid dog."

A broken laugh escaped them—half disbelief, half shame.

"I feel crazy."

"You're not crazy," their partner said again.

"You're wounded.

And you're healing.

And healing makes everything feel louder."

But the Damage Was Done

Even though the partner was calm...

they could hear the hurt.

The fatigue.

The heaviness of someone learning to love a person
who came with landmines.
The shame hit hard.
Too hard.
"I'm sorry," they whispered.
"I'm not mad," the partner said.
"I just want you to trust that I'm here."
"I'm trying," they said, voice breaking.
"I know," the partner replied.
"But we've gotta talk about these moments.
We can't ignore them.
We can't pretend they don't happen."
And that was the worst part—
not the trigger.
Not the panic.
Not the spiral.
The worst part
was realizing that love meant facing this shit
instead of hiding it.

The Aftermath

They sat alone on the floor,
back against the fridge,
knees pulled to their chest.

The fear faded,

but the guilt remained—thick, heavy, choking.

"I don't want to ruin this," they whispered.

"You won't," the partner said.

But deep inside,

another voice whispered:

What if you already are?

THE SHAME BREAK — "I CAN'T DO THIS"

The next morning, everything felt wrong.

The air.

The light.

Their own skin.

Shame is a suffocating motherfucker—

it doesn't hit like sadness,

doesn't sting like anger.

It wraps itself around your ribs

and sours everything you touch.

They couldn't look at their phone.

Couldn't look at their reflection.

Couldn't look at the memories of last night

without feeling like a burden wearing human clothes.

So they did what broken people do best:

They pulled away.

Hard.

They texted their partner:

"I need space."

Short.

Cold.

Sharp enough to cut the connection clean.

Then they turned the phone face-down

like guilt couldn't crawl through the screen.

They didn't want space.

They wanted to disappear before they disappointed them again.

Avoidance masquerading as protection—

trauma's favorite costume.

THE PARTNER'S RESPONSE — NOT WHAT THEY EXPECTED

The partner didn't react with anger. Didn't double-text. Didn't beg.

They simply replied, "Okay. I'm here when you're ready."

Which somehow hurt worse.

Because kindness after your own self-destruction feels like being forgiven for a crime you haven't stopped committing.

And that silence, that gentle understanding, hit like a quiet scream.

They muttered, "Why are you still here? Why the hell would you stay for this?"

But the real question was this: why don't you think you're worth staying for?

FLASHBACK — THE FIRST LESSON OF ABANDONMENT

(D: The origin of the wound)

Trauma doesn't just show up—it grows from something.

And that morning, alone in their apartment, a memory cracked open without warning.

They were eight years old, sitting on the curb, backpack on their lap, knees pulled tight.

Waiting.

Their parent had forgotten them. Again.

The sky got dark. Cars left one by one. The school staff turned off lights. And they kept waiting—quiet, small, trying not to cry because tears meant weakness, and weakness meant scolding.

When the parent finally arrived, two hours late, they didn't apologize.

They snapped, "Why are you being dramatic? You're fine. Get in the car."

And that was it.

That was the moment the belief took root.

You are an afterthought. Someone people remember only when it's convenient.

A seed planted. A lesson learned. A wound disguised as normal.

So when someone doesn't text back, of course it feels like being forgotten on that curb again.

THE PARTNER ARRIVES — UNANNOUNCED BUT NEEDED

There was a knock on the door. Soft. Not demanding. Not intrusive. Just... present.

They opened it to find their partner standing there—hands in pockets, eyes tired but calm, face open in that way that made everything inside them ache.

"I know you said you needed space," the partner said quietly. "And I'm not here to take that away."

They stepped back a little. "I just want to look you in the eyes when I tell you this next part."

Their stomach dropped.

Here it comes, they thought. The rejection. The "you're too much." The slow goodbye.

Instead—

THE PARTNER'S CONFESSION — (E: Their insecurities revealed)

"I get insecure too," they said.

Not dramatic. Not emotional manipulation. Just raw truth.

"I know I seem calm. I know I seem stable. But every time you pull away... my mind goes to dark places too."

Their chest tightened. "What do you mean?" they whispered.

The partner looked down, then back up. "I'm scared you'll realize you don't need me. Or that you're better off without me. Or that I'm not enough for you. Or that one day you'll wake up and see every flaw I try to hide and walk away."

That hit harder than any trigger.

"You?" they whispered. "You're afraid of me leaving?"

"I'm afraid of losing you," their partner corrected. "And I don't want to pretend I'm above insecurity. I'm human. And I care. A lot."

Silence. Heavy, healing silence.

Then the partner said something that melted the shame right out of the room. "I don't want space from you. I want honesty with you. Even when it's messy. Even when it scares you. Even when it scares me."

The words broke something open inside them—the tight, knotted part of their chest that had been clenched since childhood.

THE TURNING POINT — NOT A FIX, BUT A SHIFT

They stepped closer—not to kiss, not to embrace, but because for once running didn't feel like the only option.

Voice shaking, they said, "I'm trying to unlearn things I didn't choose to learn."

Their partner nodded. "And I'm trying to learn how to love you the way you need. Not perfectly. Not fearlessly. But honestly."

Another beat.

"I don't want to disappear," they said quietly. "Not from you."

"Then don't," their partner whispered. "Stay. Even when your thoughts try to drag you away. Stay."

They nodded—small, broken, brave.

"I want to try."

And that was enough.

Not a cure. Not a miracle. But a choice.

And survival starts with a choice.

THE NIGHT THEY FINALLY TALK

That night wasn't planned. Not romantic. Not dramatic. Just soft, tired, real.

They were lying on the floor—not the couch, not the bed—the floor, where people only go when they're too exhausted to pretend.

A single lamp was on. The kind that makes everything look warmer than it really is.

Their partner sat beside them, legs stretched out, back against the wall.

"You don't have to talk," their partner said gently. "But if you want to... I'm listening."

Something cracked open at that. Not all the way—just enough.

And for the first time in their life, they didn't start with the pain. They started with the loneliness.

"I grew up feeling optional," they whispered. "I don't think anyone meant to hurt me. But nobody protected me either."

Their partner didn't interrupt. Not once.

So the words kept coming.

"I learned early that loving people meant preparing to be forgotten. So I got good at leaving first. Good at shutting down. Good at pretending I didn't care."

Their throat tightened.

"I don't want to do that with you. But sometimes it feels automatic. Like survival."

Their partner reached out—slow, careful—and placed a hand near theirs, not touching, just offering.

"I'm sorry you had to grow up like that," they said. "I wish someone had shown up for you."

That simple acknowledgment landed harder than any apology.

And because the room was safe, because the moment held them both, their partner finally shared too:

THE PARTNER'S TRUTH — NOT THE ONE THEY EXPECTED

"My house wasn't quiet," their partner said. "It was loud. Explosive. Every day a new argument, a new threat, a new reason to stay small."

They swallowed hard, eyes glossy in the lamplight.

"My parents didn't forget me. They controlled me. Every move. Every emotion. Every choice."

A small laugh—sad, hollow.

"So now I bend. I accommodate. I try to make myself perfect so nobody yells. Nobody leaves."

It hit them then—the heartbreaking symmetry.

One abandoned. One controlled. Both starved of safety.

"Maybe that's why this works," the partner said quietly. "You run. I cling. And we're both terrified of the same thing—being unwanted."

They nodded, breath shaky. "That's exactly it."

The air between them felt charged, full of understanding, full of possibility. Even love.

But trauma hates peace. And that's when the mistake happened.

THE SENTENCE THAT SHATTERED EVERYTHING

(D: The setback that hits like a punch.)

Their partner said it casually. Not cruel. Not intentional. Just... unaware.

"I never thought someone like you would want me."

Someone like you.

Their whole body froze.

Their partner didn't notice at first. They kept talking.

"You're strong. Independent. You don't need anybody. Not like I do."

The words dug in deeper.

Not like I do. Not like I do. Not like I do.

It hit every wound. Every trigger. Every abandonment scar.

Because what they heard wasn't admiration.

What they heard was this: you don't need love. You don't get to be vulnerable. You don't get to be weak. You don't get to be held. You're too strong to hurt.

Their chest tightened. Their voice came out sharp.

"So you think I don't feel anything? That I don't need anyone? That I'm some tough act who doesn't break?"

The partner's eyes widened.

"I didn't mean— I wasn't trying to— I'm sorry—"

But the damage was done.

"That's the problem," they whispered. "You see the armor. Not the bleeding."

Silence swallowed the room.

Their partner reached out—hesitant, hurting.

"I said it wrong. I was trying to compliment you. I swear I didn't mean it like that."

But they had already folded inward, back into the old survival mode, back into the belief that nobody sees them.

And the room felt suddenly cold.

THE REALIZATION THAT EMERGES IN THE HURT

After a long pause, their partner spoke softly.

"You're not the only one who learned the wrong things growing up."

They looked up—eyes wet, face drawn.

"I learned to fear messing up. To fear saying the wrong thing. To fear being punished for not being perfect."

A beat.

"So when I said that..." they swallowed hard, "...it came from my insecurity, not your worth."

The words softened something.

Not fully. Not magically. But enough to breathe again.

Their partner continued.

"You don't have to be strong with me. You don't have to pretend. And I don't want to pretend either."

Slowly, painfully, they nodded.

"I heard it wrong," they admitted. "And I reacted from fear."

"I spoke wrong," their partner said. "And I reacted from insecurity."

Two flawed people. Two open wounds. Two childhoods still living under their skin.

But for the first time, they weren't facing those wounds alone.

THE FIRST REAL FIGHT — THE ONE THAT DOESN'T HOLD BACK

It started with something stupid. It always does.

A cup left on the counter. A tone that sounded "off." A question that caught them at the wrong moment.

"You good?" the partner asked.

Their chest tightened instantly.

"I'm fine."

"No, you're not," the partner said, voice careful, the way you speak to unexploded landmines.

And that was it. That was the spark.

"I said I'm fine," they snapped. "Why do you always need me to explain everything?"

Their partner blinked. "I'm not asking for everything. Just honesty."

"Oh, so now I'm not honest?" The sarcasm landed like glass shattering.

"That's not what I said—"

"That's what you meant."

Their partner's jaw clenched — not with anger, but with hurt.

"I feel like every time I try, you push me away."

"And maybe I'm tired of you acting like I'm some emotional project," they shot back. "Like I'm broken and you're here to fix me."

That one landed dead center.

Their partner flinched. Actually flinched.

"I don't think you're broken," they whispered. "I think you're hurting."

"And what the fuck do you think you're doing to me right now?" their voice cracked. "You want me to be vulnerable, but the second I'm messy, the second I don't do it right—you start analyzing me like I'm a case study."

Their partner's frustration finally cracked open. "Because I don't know what you need! You shut down. You run. You don't tell me anything until it's already blown up."

The room was silent after that. Chest-tight, throat-burning, old-wounds-open silent.

Then—

"Maybe I'm terrified of needing you," they whispered. "Because everyone I've needed has hurt me."

Their partner's voice softened, but it was edged with exhaustion. "And maybe I'm terrified that one day you'll leave me because of something small I didn't even know I did."

There it was.

Two scared people. Two survival instincts. Two histories clashing in real time.

And the fight didn't end clean. It ended the real way.

With silence. With tears. With one going to the bedroom, and the other curled up on the couch.

Not knowing how to bridge the distance. Not knowing if they even could.

THE NEXT MORNING — THE PARTNER'S POV

(D: Their internal monologue, raw and honest.)

They woke up with their spine aching from the couch and their heart heavier than their body.

The room was gray. Quiet. Too quiet.

They sat up slowly, rubbing their face with both hands, trying to piece together last night.

They weren't angry. Not really.

They were hurt. Confused. Scared.

"Did I push too hard?" they wondered. "Or not hard enough?" "Am I helping them heal, or am I triggering every damn scar?"

They hated how fragile they felt, how easily their insecurities could still crawl up their throat and choke them.

They had spent a lifetime being The Peacemaker—the fixer, the smoother, the emotional buffer in their childhood home.

And now here they were, curled up on a couch again, feeling like that small scared kid who couldn't get anything right.

"I don't want to lose them," they whispered to the empty room.

Because they didn't.

They loved them—the kind of love that wasn't romanticized, wasn't naïve, wasn't idealized.

A gritty, human love. A love that saw the anger and the fear and the trauma and the past—and still wanted to stay.

But they were also afraid.

Afraid that they weren't enough. Afraid that all the patience in the world wouldn't fix the battle inside the person they loved.

Afraid that they were losing themselves trying to understand someone who didn't understand their own heart.

They stood up, walked to the kitchen, and stared at the closed bedroom door.

Behind that door was the person they loved and the person who hurt them last night and the person they hurt back and the person they couldn't imagine life without.

Terrifying, right?

They took a breath. Quiet. Steady. Shaking a little.

Then said, "Okay. We're going to talk. Even if it scares us both."

Because love wasn't the easy part. Staying wasn't the easy part.

The easy part was leaving.

THE MORNING AFTER — A FRAGILE PEACE

They stood in the kitchen, staring at the bedroom door like it was a doorway into another life.

Their heart throbbed, full of regret and tenderness and fear braided together so tightly they couldn't tell them apart.

They rehearsed what they were going to say: "I'm sorry." "I didn't mean to blow up." "I'm trying." "Please don't leave."

And they weren't sure which one would come out first.

But before they could knock on the door—before they could fix it—before they could breathe—their phone buzzed.

Not a gentle buzz. Not a normal buzz.

A buzz that felt like bad news before they even looked at it.

They glanced at the screen.

And froze.

Because there it was.

A message from the person who broke them before.

The ex. The ghost. The original wound. The one they spent years trying to outrun.

The one who taught them that love turns into betrayal the second you stop watching it.

The message read: "I heard you're with someone new. I hope they don't hurt you the way I did."

It wasn't an apology. It wasn't closure. It was poison dressed as concern. Classic.

Their stomach dropped.

Their partner chose that exact moment to open the bedroom door.

Eyes tired. Face soft. Voice small.

"Can we talk?"

But the phone was still in their hand.

And the past was still in their face.

THE PARTNER SEES THE MESSAGE — AND EVERYTHING GETS MISREAD

The partner walked into the kitchen slowly, still guarded from the fight, still tender from the night apart.

Then they saw the look on their face. Then they saw the phone.

"Everything okay?" the partner asked carefully.

They hesitated.

Too long.

And the partner noticed.

"What happened?"

They handed over the phone because lying would be worse, because hiding it would explode the house, because honesty was the thing they'd promised.

The partner read the message.

Their face didn't change at first. Just tightened. Jaw. Eyes. Shoulders.

Then they set the phone down like it was a live grenade.

"Why are they texting you?"

They swallowed hard. "I didn't respond. I wasn't going to." They shook their head. "I didn't want this."

The partner nodded, but it was that slow, controlled nod people do when they're trying not to break.

"I'm not angry," the partner said. "I just... I need a minute."

But that wasn't true. Not entirely.

The partner wasn't angry. They were scared. Triggered. Shaken straight back into the childhood where betrayal always arrived disguised as everyday life.

"Do you want to talk about it?" they asked gently.

But their partner wasn't ready. Not yet.

They looked away.

And that hurt more than the message itself.

THE INTERNAL COLLAPSE — THE FEAR OF HISTORY REPEATING

They sat down slowly, heart pounding so hard it hurt.

Because this was the nightmare scenario: the past reaching into the present and grabbing them by the throat.

They whispered, “I didn’t ask for this. I didn’t want them in my life. I don’t… I don’t want to lose you over this.”

The partner’s voice cracked. “You won’t lose me. But something about this—it scares me. It makes me feel replaceable.”

Replaceable.

That one word sliced clean through the room.

Because that’s exactly what their ex had made them feel. And now the trauma was ricocheting in both directions.

They took a shaky breath. “I’m not going back to them,” they said firmly. “That chapter is dead.”

The partner nodded, but their eyes said something else: *Then why does it still affect you?*

THE REAL EXPLOSION — NOT THE MESSAGE, BUT THE MEANING

Hours passed. Quiet. Heavy. Each of them processing alone, in the same space, but miles apart.

Finally, the partner spoke. “I need to know something.”

Their voice was soft—soft enough that it hurt more than shouting.

“Why does hearing from them still shake you like that?”

They froze.

Not because they didn’t know.

Because the truth was too big to hold.

"I'm scared that the damage they did is still in me," they whispered. "That I'll ruin this the way they ruined me."

The partner's expression softened instantly.

"So it's not about them," they said. "It's about the version of you that survived them."

And that—

that one sentence—

cracked everything open.

"Yes," they breathed out, voice breaking. "That's exactly it."

The partner stepped closer. Slow. Careful. Not touching—just near.

"I'm not them," they said. "And I'm not going anywhere." A beat. "But you have to let me stay."

Their vision blurred with tears.

"I'm trying," they whispered. "I swear I'm trying."

"I know," the partner said.

And for the first time that morning, they both breathed at the same time.

THE SECOND MESSAGE — THE ONE THAT CUTS DEEP (A)

The phone buzzed again.

Not once.

Three times.

Back-to-back.

Urgent.

Aggressive.

Their partner was in the shower.

The kitchen was quiet.

The world was still.

They picked up the phone, already knowing this wasn't good.

Three new messages.

All from the ex.

First message:

"You never loved me the way you love them."

Second:

"You should've answered me. We're not done."

Third — the one that made the air leave their lungs:

"If they knew what you did... how you really are... I wonder if they'd stay."

Their stomach dropped so fast the room tilted.

This wasn't nostalgia.

This wasn't regret.

This was blackmail.

Emotional.

Psychological.

Weaponized.

The kind of manipulation that had once destroyed them.

The kind of thing they weren't strong enough to survive back then.

Their hands started shaking.

Their breathing sped up.

Their chest tightened like a fist closing around their ribcage.

And just like that,

the panic attack began.

THE PANIC ATTACK — A BODY REMEMBERING THE TRAUMA (C)

Their vision blurred. Their fingers tingled. Their breath scattered into fragments they couldn't gather back.

Their heart wasn't beating — it was slamming — every thud a flashback.

They sank to the floor, palms flat, trying to remember how to breathe, trying to remember where they were, trying not to drown inside their own body.

The bathroom door opened.

"Hey—" the partner started.

Then froze.

"Baby?" Their voice shifted instantly. Soft. Steady. Alert. The voice of someone who had seen panic before and knew exactly what it looked like.

They rushed over, knelt down, cupped their face gently but firmly.

"Look at me. Right here. Stay with me."

But their body wouldn't respond. The past was too loud. Too familiar.

Their partner took their hands, pressing them to their own chest.

"Feel my heartbeat," they whispered. "Match me. Just breathe with me. I'm not leaving. I'm right here."

Slowly — very slowly — their breath found a rhythm again.

Tears spilled without permission. Quiet, shaking, shame-filled tears.

"I'm sorry," they choked.

"Stop," their partner whispered. "You don't apologize for surviving."

And that broke the last piece of their composure.

They leaned into their partner, letting themselves be held — really held — like it was the first time in their life someone had caught them instead of letting them fall.

THE PARTNER'S STORY — THE BETRAYAL THEY'VE BEEN HIDING (D)

When their breathing finally settled, the partner pulled back slightly, eyes heavy with something deeper than concern.

"I need to tell you something," they said quietly.

Not angry. Not reactive. Just... honest.

The kind of honesty that feels like a confession.

"I know why this scares me so much," they continued. "Why the message yesterday shook me. Why this—" they gestured gently to the aftermath of the panic — "hits me in a place I hate."

They took a breath.

"My ex did the same thing to me."

The words landed like a punch.

"They cheated on me," the partner said. "But worse... they made me feel crazy for noticing. They gaslit me until I couldn't trust my own thoughts."

The pain in their voice was real. Exposed. Raw.

"They'd disappear for days. Then come home like nothing happened. And whenever I tried to leave, they'd send messages just like that one."

They gestured to the phone on the floor.

"I wasn't scared of losing them. I was scared of losing myself."

They looked up, eyes shimmering.

"So when I saw you shaken by them... it hit the old wound in me. The part I'm still healing."

Silence. Thick. Painful. Understanding.

Two people with two different histories, but the same emotional scar tissue.

"I don't want our pasts to fight each other," the partner whispered. "I want us to fight them together."

And for the first time, the fear loosened. Not gone. But not ruling the room anymore.

THE KNOCK AT THE DOOR — THE EX SHOWS UP (E)

There was a sudden knock. Sharp. Forceful. Impatient. Three bangs.

Their partner stiffened, body instinctively blocking them, as if their own trauma had just walked up the driveway.

"Who the hell—?" the partner started.

Then—

Another knock. Harder. More desperate.

They froze. Because they knew that knock. They knew that rhythm. That entitlement. That tone.

"No," they whispered. "No, no— they wouldn't—"

But they would. And they had.

Their partner's jaw tightened. "Stay here," they said quietly. "I'll get it."

They walked to the door, heart pounding, hand curled into a fist.

They opened it—

And there the ex stood. Smug. Angry. Wearing the same expression they used to see before everything went wrong.

The ex smirked. "Well," they said, eyes sliding past the partner and locking onto them inside the house. "Aren't you going to invite me in?"

Their partner stepped fully into the doorway, blocking the entrance. "No," they said. "You're done here."

The ex scoffed. "You think you can keep them away from me? We have history."

"No," the partner said again, voice low, steady, powerful. "You have trauma. They have healing. And I'm not letting you take that from them."

The ex's smile faded. Thunderclouds in the eyes. Violence in the silence.

"This isn't over," the ex hissed.

The partner stepped forward, shoulders squared. "Yes. It is."

They shut the door slowly, deliberately, locking it with a click that echoed through the house.

Then they turned back—eyes soft, breathing heavy, heart still racing.

"You're safe," they said.

And for the first time in years—maybe longer—the words actually felt true.

THE BREAKING POINT — THE BODY KEEPS SCORE (B)

The door had barely locked behind the ex when their body gave out. Not gracefully. Not dramatically. Just collapsed — knees hitting the floor, hands shaking, breath ripping in and out like it was fighting to stay alive.

All the adrenaline. All the fear. All the memories. All the shadows. Everything came rushing out at once like their chest had been holding back a flood for years and the dam finally cracked.

Their partner rushed forward but didn't touch them — not yet. Not until the panic turned into something else.

This wasn't a panic attack. It was grief. Fear. Trauma full-body screaming. A decade of swallowed pain erupting.

They choked out: "I can't do this— I can't— I thought I was past this— why is this happening— why won't it stop—"

Their words tangled into sobs, their body folding in on itself, like they were trying to disappear into the floor.

Their partner knelt beside them and finally, slowly, placed a hand on their back.

"I'm here," they whispered. "I'm right here. Let it out. All of it. You don't have to hold anything alone."

That tenderness cracked them open harder.

"I hate that they still have this power over me," they sobbed. "I hate that I feel small. I hate that I'm not strong. I hate that— I hate— I hate everything— I hate myself—"

Their partner's hand tightened instantly.

"Don't say that," they said softly but firmly. "Don't turn their abuse into your voice. That's not you talking. That's them. That's what they conditioned you to believe."

"But it feels true," they cried. "It feels like I'm broken. Like I ruin everything. Like I don't deserve anything good."

Their partner gently lifted their chin, forcing eye contact through the tears.

"You deserve love. You deserve peace. You deserve safety. And I'm not going anywhere just because you're hurting."

That undid them completely.

They sobbed into their partner's chest—messy, shaking, desperate. No holding back. No dignity left to protect. Just raw humanity finally being seen.

And their partner held them with the steadiness of someone who understood what breaking really looks like.

THE CONVERSATION THEY COULDN'T AVOID ANY LONGER (C)

Boundaries. Fear. The rules of survival together.

When the tears finally slowed and the shaking softened, they sat on the couch wrapped in a blanket.

Their partner wiped a tear from their cheek with a thumb that trembled just slightly — because this hurt both of them.

"We need to talk," the partner said gently. "Not to fight. But to keep us safe."

They nodded, exhausted.

The partner took a breath. "When something triggers you this deeply, you go silent. You shut down. You disappear into yourself. And I'm terrified—because I can't protect you if I don't know what's happening."

They looked away. Shame pulsed.

"I don't know how to talk about it," they whispered.

Their partner nodded. "I know. And I'm not asking you to suddenly be perfect. But I need you to let me in, even a little, when things get hard. I can't be locked out of your fear and still be expected to calm it."

Silence. Deep. Necessary.

Then they spoke.

"What about your boundaries?" they whispered. "What about your fear? I saw what you felt when you opened that door. And you're trying to protect me, but you're shaking too."

Their partner exhaled slowly. "I'm scared of losing you," they admitted. "I'm scared that the past will poison the present. I'm scared that your ex can trigger you so deeply that one day you'll shut me out completely—and I'll lose you without warning."

Their voice trembled.

"But I also need you to understand something: I'm not your savior. I can stand with you. I can hold you. But I can't be the only thing standing between you and your past."

Their eyes met.

"And I need to know that when someone crosses a line, you'll tell me. So we can protect this together. Not just me protecting you."

They nodded.

"I'm scared to rely on anyone," they whispered. "I'm scared that if I need you too much... you'll leave. Or you'll use it against me. Or you'll get tired."

Their partner leaned closer. "I won't use your vulnerability against you. I won't weaponize your pain. But I can only love what you let me touch."

A long pause.

Then their partner added: "And I need a boundary too: No more hiding messages. No more protecting the past at the expense of the present. If they contact you again—you tell me. Immediately. We handle it together. As a team."

Their throat tightened.

"Okay," they whispered. "I promise."

Their partner squeezed their hand. "And I promise this: I'll never ask you to heal alone again."

THE NIGHT THAT CHANGED EVERYTHING (C)

The house was quiet. Not peaceful — just tired. They had cried themselves dry earlier. Tremors still lived in their fingertips. The past still sat heavy on their chest.

But when they walked into the bedroom, their partner wasn't waiting with pity. Or anger. Or fear. They were sitting on the edge of the bed, calm, steady, warm — like a lighthouse in a storm.

"Come here," they said.

Not a command. An invitation.

And for the first time in years, their body didn't tense at the idea of closeness. It melted.

They crawled onto the bed, slowly, cautiously, like they were approaching something sacred. Their partner didn't kiss them. Didn't reach for anything sexual. Instead, they lifted the blanket and opened their arms. A sanctuary. A place to rest.

They hesitated — because vulnerability still felt like a trap, still felt like a weapon that could be used later.

Their partner whispered: "You don't have to be perfect to be held."

Something inside cracked.

They sank into their arms. Head on their partner's chest. Legs tangled. Bodies aligned like puzzle pieces that finally remembered how to fit.

No trembling. No panic. Just two hearts, beating in the same rhythm, slow and safe.

Their partner's fingers traced slow circles on their back, not to arouse, but to reassure: You're here. You're safe. I'm not going anywhere.

They whispered into the darkness: "I'm scared. I'm scared to love you this much. I'm scared to need you. I'm scared that if I let you all the way in... you'll see how broken I really am."

Their partner kissed the top of their head gently. "Baby... needing someone doesn't make you broken. It makes you human."

They swallowed hard. "But what if I mess this up?"

Their partner hugged them tighter. "Then we fix it. Together."

Their voice softened even more. "I didn't choose you because you're perfect. I chose you because you're real. And I'm staying because you're worth the work."

Something warm bloomed in their chest — not hope, not yet, but the possibility of hope. A seed.

For the first time in years, their body didn't armor up in the presence of love.

They fell asleep in their partner's arms, not because they were exhausted, but because they finally felt safe enough to rest.

THE REVELATION THAT BROKE THE CURSE (E)

She woke up the next morning feeling... different. Not healed. Not fixed. But softer. Less haunted. Like the past didn't get to speak first anymore.

Her therapy session that afternoon wasn't dramatic at first. She told the therapist about the panic. The ex. The collapse. The intimacy. The fear.

Her therapist listened, then asked a question that cracked the universe open: "When did love first become dangerous for you?"

Her breath caught. The room felt heavier. Hotter. Thicker.

Because she knew. She always knew. She just never said it out loud.

She whispered: "When the people who were supposed to love me were the same ones who hurt me."

The therapist nodded, slowly. "And what did you learn from that?"

"That you can't trust love," she said. "That love leaves. That love betrays you. That love takes advantage. That love lies. That love demands too much. That love doesn't protect you."

The therapist leaned forward. "And do you think your partner loves you the way they did?"

Silence. Then, softly: "...No."

"Then why are you treating them like they do?"

The question punched her soul. Tears rose, but not from pain — from clarity.

Her therapist continued: "You've been trying to protect yourself from the people who hurt you by withholding love from the person who hasn't."

She inhaled sharply.

"You are not afraid of your partner," the therapist said gently. "You are afraid of what love meant to you as a child."

The world shifted. Like someone had taken the weight off her chest that she didn't even know she'd been carrying.

She whispered: "So... I'm not broken?"

"No. You're conditioned. And conditioning can be unlearned."

Her therapist leaned back. "You survived love. Now you're learning how to receive it."

And for the first time in her life, she let that truth settle in her bones.

The Room Where Nothing Hurts Anymore (B)

That night felt different. Different in the way summer nights feel after weeks of rain. Different in the way breath feels after crying. Different in the way healing feels before you trust it.

She walked into the bedroom expecting awkwardness. Or emotional distance. Or that weird after-therapy silence.

Instead, her partner looked at her the way people look at a sunrise—slow... reverent... like something rare.

They didn't touch her at first. They just asked quietly: "How's your heart?"

Not *How was therapy?* Not *Are you okay?* Not *What did you talk about?* But *How's your heart?*

That question alone undressed a part of her she didn't know was still clothed.

She sat beside them. Close, but not touching. "My heart..." she whispered, "...is scared. But it's tired of being scared."

Her partner nodded. "Can I touch you?"

It wasn't sexual. It wasn't tentative. It was respectful. Intentional. Sacred.

She swallowed hard. "Yes."

Their hands slid up her arms—slow, mindful, present—like they were memorizing her. Not claiming her.

Her body didn't tense. Didn't flinch. Didn't freeze. Because for the first time in her life, touch wasn't a demand. It was an offering.

Her partner kissed her shoulder, gentle but sure but safe.

She exhaled. A real exhale. The kind that says, *Okay. I can be here. I can be seen. I can be loved without losing myself.*

They laid her down, not to take but to honor. No rush. No script. No pressure.

She whispered: "I want you... but I need it to be slow."

Her partner smiled softly, their eyes warm and patient. "I'm not in a hurry," they said. "I want what feels good to your body... not just mine."

That sentence alone rewrote something ancient inside her.

When Desire Meets Truth (C)

Halfway through their gentle touches, their partner paused. "Talk to me," they whispered. "Don't disappear into your head."

She nodded, breath shaky. "I'm here... I'm trying. I'm just... scared of wanting too much."

"What do you want?" they asked softly.

Her throat tightened. Nobody had ever asked that. Not for real. Not with the intent to honor it.

She swallowed. "I want to feel safe while being wanted," she whispered. "I want passion without fear. I want to be touched like I'm valuable, not convenient. I want to feel you loving me—not owning me."

Their partner moved closer, forehead against hers. "You're not convenient," they whispered. "You're a conscious choice."

Her chest shook with emotion.

"And..." she continued, voice trembling, "I need you to tell me what you feel while you touch me... so I don't spiral... so I don't guess... so I don't go back into my trauma and leave my body."

Their partner nodded immediately. "Okay. Then I'll talk you through every moment."

They kissed her neck, slow and intentional. "I'm touching you because I love your softness."

A kiss to her shoulder. "And because your body deserves tenderness."

A kiss to her chest. "And because you deserve to feel wanted without fear."

She gasped—not from arousal, but from recognition.

Her needs weren't a burden. They were guidance. She wasn't too much. She was understood.

She whispered: "Please don't stop talking."

"I won't," they said, their voice dropping low—steady, grounding, present. "I want you because you're mine in trust, not ownership. I want you because your bravery is sexy. I want you because you survived hell and still learned how to let me in."

Her body softened beneath their hands, her breath deepening, her fear dissolving like sugar in warm water.

She wrapped her arms around them—not out of desperation, but desire. Real desire. Desire without panic. Desire without trauma hijacking her nervous system. Desire that felt like coming home.

The Moment She Finally Chose Her Own Pleasure (C + B fusion)

At the height of the moment—when her body was warm, open, trusting—she did something she had never done before. She placed her hand over theirs and guided it. Not timidly. Not apologetically. With intention.

"I want it like this," she said.

Their eyes widened—not in shock, but pride. "There she is," they whispered. "My love. My voice. My woman."

She felt her power rise inside her like a flame she had been too afraid to ignite. She wasn't surviving intimacy. She was leading it.

Aftercare That Rewired Her Entire Nervous System

After they made love—slow, spiritual, connected—her partner didn't pull away. They wrapped her in their arms, kissed her temple, and whispered into her hair: "You did amazing. Your voice turned me on more than anything else."

She laughed softly against their chest. "Really?"

"Baby... you telling me what you need? That's the sexiest thing you've ever done."

She closed her eyes, smiling.

For the first time in her entire life, intimacy didn't feel like war. It felt like worship. Mutual. Respectful. Raw. Human. And holy in a way the church could never teach.

9

A Nation of Borrowed Brilliance

America likes to pretend it was born holy.

A shining city on a hill, a land of liberty, a place where "all men are created equal." But peel back the myth, and what do you find? The bones of a nation built on stolen bodies, stolen labor, stolen children, stolen land, and stolen culture. A country that inherited its wealth not from brilliance, but from brutality. A place that calls itself "free" while every brick of its foundation was soaked in the sweat, blood, and genius of Black people who never asked to be here—but shaped everything once they arrived.

This is the truth white supremacy spends centuries trying to hide: Without Black people, there would be no America. Without Black culture, white America would have no culture at all. Strip away Black music, and this country falls silent. Strip away Black innovation, and half of American technology disappears. Strip away Black labor, and the economy collapses before it begins. Strip away Black style, rhythm, slang, resilience, resistance, and creation—and you're left with a nation naked, bland, terrified, and hollow.

White supremacists don't fear Black people because they think we are inferior; they fear us because they know the opposite is true. They fear the truth that the culture they claim as "white American heritage" is stitched together from the pieces they stole from the very people they oppressed. They fear the truth that Black brilliance is the engine of this country—its sound, its soul, its swagger, its conscience. They fear that without us, America is nothing but an empty promise and a violent myth.

This book is not here to soothe them. It is here to expose them—not white people, not humanity, not individuals.

The ideology. The lie. The machinery of white supremacy.

If the truth offends them, good. If the history burns them, let it. If the mirror terrifies them, then maybe they should stop worshipping the mask—because this is the book that tears it off.

America loves to talk about freedom. It whispers "liberty" like a sacred word, boasts about being a self-made nation, and brags that its greatness comes from grit, innovation, and determination. But here is the part they leave out: America was built by people who were never allowed to be free.

It was built by Black hands, Black backs, Black wombs, Black genius, Black suffering—Black endurance so powerful it outlived the empire that tried to crush it. Strip away the sanitized stories, and the truth becomes impossible to deny: Enslaved Africans created the wealth base of the United States. Without them, there is no American economy. There is no "land of opportunity." There is no nation. White supremacy knows this. That's why it works so hard to erase it.

The First Economy: Stolen Land, Stolen Bodies

Before a single American flag ever flew, the blueprint for the U.S. economy was drawn in theft: Indigenous land stolen at gunpoint, African people stolen from their homes, and free labor stolen for generations. America didn't rise because of brilliance or moral purity. It rose because it didn't pay the people who built it.

The plantation system wasn't a side story—it was the economy. Cotton was not just a crop—it was the global commodity that made the United States powerful. By 1860, enslaved Black people were worth more money than every factory and every railroad in the nation combined. Cotton produced by enslaved Africans made up over half of all U.S. exports. Wall Street banks, insurance companies, and investors financed slavery, insured enslaved bodies, and profited from each birth, sale, or death.

America became rich because Black people were not allowed to be. White supremacists love to pretend slavery was "a long time ago," but the wealth it created is still here—sitting in banks, universities, corporations, families, and institutions that have never returned a dime.

Skilled, Talented, Brilliant — and Forced Into Chains

The lie is that enslaved Africans were unskilled. The truth is the opposite: they were farmers, engineers, metalworkers, builders, healers, navigators, scientists—experts in rice cultivation, astronomy, architecture, and survival.

They brought knowledge of irrigation, advanced agricultural systems, ironworking and craftsmanship, medical knowledge, artistic tradition, musical structure and rhythm, and community governance models. America imported African intelligence, then forced that intelligence into labor camps and pretended it didn't exist.

When enslaved Black people built bridges, mansions, ports, roads, universities, and state buildings, white supremacy simply wrote them out of the story.

The Myth of the "Self-Made Nation"

America loves the phrase "self-made." But who is "self-made" when you didn't pay your workers, you stole their land, you outlawed their literacy, you sold their children, and you punished their genius? What you built isn't achievement. It's extraction. What you call success is generational theft.

No plantation owner was "self-made." No founding father who owned human beings was "self-made." No early American fortune was "self-made." Black people made them.

White supremacy is terrified of this truth because it destroys the myth of American innocence—the myth that white America rose through merit alone. The reality is simple: Black labor is the unpaid bill America still refuses to acknowledge.

Black Women: The Country's Hidden Economic Engine

Enslaved Black women built this nation twice: through their labor and through their forced reproduction. They were field workers, domestic workers, cooks, weavers, midwives, healers, and caretakers—the backbone of plantation economies. And their wombs were turned into factories.

When slaveowners realized buying enslaved people cut into profits, they forced Black women to give birth to more property—children they could sell for pure profit. America praises "family values," but it built its fortunes by destroying Black families and turning motherhood into a commodity.

This is the part the history books whisper about—or avoid completely. But this book is not here to whisper.

Every Institution You Know Was Built on Us

Let's put it plainly: American banking, American policing, American capitalism, American agriculture, American universities, and American corporations all have roots in the exploitation of Black people.

Wall Street wasn't a symbol of financial genius—it was a slave-trading district. Insurance companies rose to power by insuring enslaved bodies. Universities used Black people for labor, experiments, research, and profit while denying them education. The modern policing system evolved from slave patrols.

Every time America built something "great," it used Black bodies to do it—then erased the fingerprints.

America Without Black People?

If Black people never existed here, America would be poor, culturally empty, musically silent, economically irrelevant, technologically behind, spiritually hollow, and artistically bland. There is no "America" without Black people—only land, only myth, only denial.

White supremacy isn't just hateful—it is historically illiterate. It must deny reality to survive.

We Are the Foundation They Fear to Acknowledge

Every time a white supremacist claims Black people "contribute nothing," they are really saying, "I don't want to admit I live in a country built by the people I dehumanize." The fear isn't us. The fear is the truth.

Because once you admit that Black people built America, shaped America, and continue to define America—then the whole lie of white supremacy collapses. And without that lie, America would finally have to confront its real history.

This chapter is the beginning of that reckoning. We built this country, and it's time the world said it out loud.

10

Scripture in the Wrong Hands

WHEN GOD'S PLAN IS THE ONLY PLAN

They say God has a plan, but nobody ever stops to ask whose plan they're actually following.

Some people follow the God in the sky. Some follow the god in their wallet. And some follow the loud orange man waving a Bible he never opened, while his followers scream "righteous" like the word itself is spiritual bleach—strong enough to scrub corruption clean.

Here's the truth the church pews don't want to hear: your sin isn't bigger than mine, and mine isn't smaller than yours. We're all flawed. We're all dirty. We're all capable of performing holiness on Sundays and calling it faith. Yet somehow the holier-than-thou crowd always believes their dirt smells like incense.

These are often the same people who weaponize God like He's a rifle and call their "faith" the ammunition. They preach morality while slipping into affairs, stealing money, judging mothers, hating strangers, and labeling it "discernment." They talk about righteousness while worshiping a man whose spirit is bankrupt, whose morals can't be found with a microscope, and whose followers confuse idolatry with "patriotism."

But let's be brutally honest: America has always had a habit of picking God based on convenience.

White America sculpted a white Jesus to match their wallpaper—pale skin, blue eyes, soft hands—as if the son of a Middle Eastern woman somehow looked like he'd lived his whole life in a Norwegian snowstorm. They built a Jesus that fit their politics, their supremacy, their comfort zone. A Jesus that looked like them, not the melanated man described in the very scripture they thump like a gavel.

Then we start asking questions we should've asked a long time ago. Could God be male? Female? Both? Neither? Why do we assume the creator of the universe fits neatly into human pronouns when we barely understand ourselves?

But people don't want truth. They want tradition—preferably wrapped in shiny gift paper and holiday discounts.

Christmas became the holiest consumer holiday ever sold. But where did it come from? Not Bethlehem. Not scripture. It came from pagan winter festivals, tree worship, drunken rituals, and the practical need for early Christians to blend in with the world around them. Easter, too, carries echoes of ancient fertility celebrations—eggs, rabbits, and springtime rebirth borrowed from goddesses older than Jesus by centuries. Halloween sits at the crossroads of fear and folklore, a spiritual collision between the dead and the living, where carved pumpkins replaced skull lanterns once meant to guide spirits through the dark.

They don't teach that from the pulpit, because truth doesn't pack the offering plate.

So here we are, caught between myth, manipulation, and the messy humanity we keep trying to pretend is divine.

This book isn't here to comfort you. It's here to challenge everything you thought you knew about God. It's here to shake the fake holy dust off your shoulders. It's here to make you look at the world sideways and ask, "Have I been following God... or have I just been following somebody else's agenda?"

Because when God's plan is the only plan—the real one, the unfiltered one, the one that doesn't care about politics, pigmentation, or patriarchy—everybody gets exposed.

Especially the ones who thought they were safe.

THE MIRROR THAT CALLS ITSELF GOD

Religious hypocrisy doesn't start in the church. It starts in the mirror.

Every human being carries two selves: the one we show the world, and the one we hide like contraband—shameful, hungry, insecure, trembling, jealous, lustful, confused. The hidden self is the one we pretend God can't see, even though we claim He sees everything.

And because we can't destroy the parts of ourselves we hate, we project them onto other people and call it "sin." That's the birthplace of hypocrisy.

The psychology is simple and ugly.

🔥 **Hypocrisy is self-defense.** If I point at your wrongdoing, maybe nobody will look at mine.

🔥 **Hypocrisy is self-delusion.** If I condemn you, maybe I can pretend I'm better.

🔥 **Hypocrisy is spiritual cosplay.** Dress up like the righteous, talk like the righteous, judge like the righteous—and suddenly you feel righteous, even if you're rotten inside.

Church people have mastered this art for centuries. They perfected the holy mask. But the mask always cracks when the lights hit it the right way, because the truth is hard to escape: people don't love God—not really. They love the version of God that protects their ego.

The God in the Mirror

Humans are obsessed with control, so they create deities who reinforce whatever they already believe.

If they hate someone, God hates them too. If they judge someone, God judges them too. If they want power, God wants them to have it. If they want to wage war, suddenly God is a general.

People don't seek God. They manufacture one.

That's why God always seems to look like the people preaching Him. In Europe, Jesus became pale and aristocratic. In America, He became a blue-eyed patriot. In colonized lands, He became a weapon disguised as salvation.

Humans will twist divinity to justify anything—even cruelty, especially cruelty—because a God who looks like you will always forgive you and punish everyone else.

America's Spiritual Identity Crisis

America is a country that never met a myth it couldn't monetize.

Freedom, justice, equality—beautiful ideas that too often come with expiration dates. And religion became the biggest lie of all: a performance dressed in scripture and soaked in nationalism. People don't worship God here. They worship their political party, their skin color, their interpretation of righteousness, their entitlement, and their fear.

Fear is America's real religion.

Fear of losing power. Fear of confronting history. Fear of a God who might not be white, male, American, or on their side.

So people cling to a version of God that feels safe—a God who supports their worldview instead of correcting it; a God who protects their comfort instead of exposing their ugliness; a God who blesses their prejudice and baptizes their ignorance.

And the result is a nation full of believers who don't believe: Christians who don't follow Christ, patriots who don't love people, spiritual people with no spirit.

America is spiritually starving, but too proud to admit it—too arrogant to look for a real God—because the fake one it created validates every contradiction.

But truth always returns like a debt long overdue.

Eventually, the mirror cracks. Eventually, the manufactured God stops speaking. Eventually, people realize the voice they thought was divine was just their own ego echoing back at them.

And when that day comes, the whole country will have to decide: Do we want truth, or do we want comfort? Do we want God, or just the illusion of God?

THE INVENTION OF THE WHITE CHRIST

Before colonizers carried crosses, they carried fear—fear that God might look nothing like them, fear that divinity might speak in tongues they didn't understand, fear that the world they wanted to control didn't center them the way they centered themselves.

So they did the unthinkable. They rebranded God. Not with scripture. Not with truth. But with paint, politics, and power.

Christianity didn't start white, but white supremacy knew it would never survive without a God who looked like its own reflection. So they rewrote Him.

The Dark-Skinned Jesus They Erased

Let's be very clear: Jesus was born in the Middle East, a region soaked in sun, sand, and Semitic bloodlines—not in white snow, not in Northern Europe, not in the suburbs. You don't survive ancient Palestine with porcelain skin and baby-blue eyes that never saw sunlight.

The Bible describes hair like wool and skin like bronze burned in a furnace. Europe read that and said, "Interesting... but make Him look like Leonardo DiCaprio and call it holy."

Because if God was melanated, colonizers couldn't pretend to be His chosen ones. If Jesus looked like the people they enslaved, their entire empire would collapse in shame. So they erased the original image and replaced Him with an idol.

The Paintbrush Becomes a Weapon

The whitening of Jesus didn't start in churches. It started in art studios run by men who understood that religion influenced empires. They took the son of a Middle Eastern woman and redesigned Him into a blond Renaissance prince.

This wasn't ignorance. It was a calculated political move. A white Jesus justified colonialism. A white Jesus legitimized European superiority. A white Jesus made slavery sound "God-approved." A white Jesus silenced dark-skinned believers. A white Jesus merged divinity with whiteness.

And this wasn't just art. It was propaganda.

When the world saw a white Christ, they began to see white people as naturally closer to God and everyone else as naturally further from Him. That's how racism became theology.

The Colonizer's God

When Europeans set sail for Africa, South America, and the Caribbean, they didn't just bring guns. They brought Bibles rewritten through their own worldview.

Missionaries told indigenous people, "God sent us to save you." But the unspoken truth was, "God is white. You are not. Therefore, you must bow."

Whole cultures—beautiful, ancient, spiritual cultures—were forced to abandon their gods, their languages, and their identities to serve a Christ who looked suspiciously like their oppressor.

But here's the real twist: they didn't bring Christianity to the world. They brought their version of Christianity. And that version was soaked in supremacy, empire, erasure, violence, rewritten scripture, and political control.

It wasn't faith. It was domination dressed as salvation.

America Takes the White Jesus and Runs With It

When Christianity arrived in America, white Christians didn't just preach the faith—they weaponized it like a whip.

Slave owners gave enslaved Africans sermons about obedience while hiding scriptures about liberation, rebellion, and equality. They quoted Paul but buried Exodus. They preached submission but hid justice.

And Black people were told, "Jesus looks like your master. Bow accordingly."

Imagine the psychological violence of that. Imagine the weight of praying to a God who resembles your oppressor. Imagine being forced to worship an image designed to break you.

That is the trauma buried inside whitened Christianity.

The Collapse of the False Image

But lies have an expiration date.

Now the truth is cracking through the walls. Historically, Jesus wasn't white. Early Christians weren't European. Christianity spread across Africa long before it reached Europe. Ethiopian Christianity predates Western Christianity. The first church communities were brown, Semitic, and African.

The white Jesus is a costume, a mascot, a cultural hallucination created to maintain power.

And people are finally waking up.

Because if the image was false, what else did they lie about? What else did they distort? What else did they weaponize?

The collapse of whitened Christianity will force the world to face the truth: God doesn't look like your race. God doesn't favor your nation. God doesn't exist to validate your prejudice. God doesn't need your propaganda.

God is bigger than pigment, bigger than politics, bigger than the lies you inherited and never questioned.

And once you see that, you can never unsee it.

GOD ON THE BALLOT

America didn't just mix politics with religion. America married the two—and the honeymoon never ended.

But let's be real: politicians don't love God. They love what God can do for them. A praying politician is usually just a marketing strategy. A Bible on a podium is a prop. A verse quoted into a microphone is a sedative meant to comfort the crowd while power gets stolen behind the scenes. Faith became a weapon the moment somebody realized you can control a nation easier through scripture than through soldiers, because fear of hell is stronger than any army.

When Power Discovered God Was a Tool

Politicians noticed something simple: people will forgive almost anything if they believe God is involved.

A scandal becomes a "test from the Lord." Corruption becomes "spiritual warfare." Abuse becomes "persecution." Immorality becomes "nobody's perfect." All they have to do is sprinkle a little Jesus on it, and suddenly the sin smells holy.

That's how political power hijacked religion. It didn't sneak in through the back door—it walked right down the center aisle and sat in the front pew. Because the Bible, in the wrong hands, is the perfect instrument of control.

The Playbook of Religious Politics

There's a formula, a script used over and over, generation after generation.

First, claim to be chosen by God. Instant immunity. Instant authority. Instant worship.

Second, label your opponents as evil. Not different—evil. Not competing—demonic. That's how violence starts sounding justified.

Third, promise a "moral revival" you never intend to deliver. People will wait decades for righteousness that was never coming.

Fourth, weaponize fear. Fear of change. Fear of outsiders. Fear of judgment. Fear of losing America, God, and identity all at once.

Fifth, create a mythological enemy. Make it vague. Make it constant. A shadow war keeps followers loyal.

And finally, sell salvation through political loyalty. Vote for me equals vote for God. Oppose me equals oppose God. That's how idolatry becomes patriotism.

It works every time. Not because people are stupid, but because people are afraid—afraid they've lost control, afraid their lives don't matter, afraid God has stopped listening. So they cling to a leader who lies loud enough to drown out their doubts.

The Holy Nationalists

Somewhere along the way, politics and faith merged into a golden calf named Christian Nationalism.

It tells people America is God's chosen nation. It tells them their political party is divinely ordained. It tells them their flag is sacred, their guns are holy, and God speaks the language of their vote.

But this isn't Christianity. This is spiritual cosplay dressed in red, white, and delusion.

Christian Nationalism does something dangerous: it convinces people their hatred is righteous, their prejudice is holy, their cruelty is obedience, and their political leader is a prophet. And once you believe your politics are blessed by heaven, you become capable of anything. Anything.

Political Worship: When Leaders Become Gods

Every empire falls the same way—not when the leader is worshiped, but when the leader expects to be worshiped.

America is cracking under the same sickness: the rise of political idolatry. A leader doesn't need wisdom. He just needs a Bible photo-op. He doesn't need morality. He just needs to say "God bless America" at the end of a speech full of lies. He doesn't need compassion. He just needs to call the other side "ungodly."

And suddenly his sins don't matter. His cruelty doesn't matter. His corruption doesn't matter. He becomes untouchable, bathed in spiritual immunity. Not because God chose him, but because fear chose him—and fear is louder than faith.

The Great American Spiritual Delusion

People think America's biggest crisis is political polarization. It's not. It's spiritual confusion.

Nobody knows what they believe anymore. Nobody knows the difference between faith and propaganda. Nobody knows where God ends, and nationalism begins.

A politician waves a Bible, and suddenly he's holy. A preacher waves a flag, and suddenly it's scripture. A party waves fear, and suddenly it's salvation. It's all theater—sacred theater, weaponized theater—and the audience is too tired, too scared, and too divided to notice the stage lights.

The Truth Beneath the Lies

Faith was meant to unite. Politics was meant to organize. But America twisted them into something monstrous: a country where power is holy, and holiness is political.

A country where God is no longer sovereign—He's a brand, a marketing tool, a political mascot.

The weaponization of faith didn't destroy God. It destroyed our ability to recognize Him.

And that is the deepest betrayal of all.

THE TEMPLE OF BEAUTIFUL LIES

There's a reason people prefer comforting lies over uncomfortable truths. A lie can tuck you in at night. A truth can rip your sheets off.

A lie whispers, "You're safe." A truth whispers, "You're not." A lie tells you, "You're right." A truth tells you, "You've been wrong this whole time." And the human ego? It would rather die than admit it's been fooled.

People don't avoid the truth because they're stupid. They avoid truth because they're fragile. Truth demands transformation. Lies demand nothing. And humans always reach for the lighter burden.

The Brain Loves Lies Like Sugar

The human brain wasn't designed for truth. It was designed for survival. Truth is heavy. Truth is disruptive. Truth requires emotional labor. A comforting lie is the mental equivalent of junk food—quick satisfaction, instant relief, no nutritional value. And like any addict, society keeps returning to the thing that hurts them because it feels better in the moment.

Psychologists call it cognitive dissonance: that gut-twisting discomfort when reality doesn't match belief. Most people don't resolve that conflict. They avoid it. They deny it. They attack the messenger. Because if reality burns, a lie feels like ice water.

The Ego Is a Terrible God

One of the greatest lies humans believe is simple: "I am who I think I am." But the truth is uglier. We are creatures of habit, fear, trauma, bias, and programming. The ego hates being challenged. It hates being wrong. It hates being exposed.

So the ego builds a temple of illusions and calls it identity. Inside that temple, you're always good, always righteous, always justified. Your choices always make sense. Your pain always has a villain. Your beliefs are always correct. And anything that threatens that temple gets labeled "dangerous," "false," "evil," or "an attack"—not because it is, but because the ego would rather break than bend.

The Lie That the World Makes Sense

Life is chaotic, unpredictable, unfair, uncontrolled. Truth reflects that chaos. Truth shows the cracks in everything. Truth reminds you that the universe doesn't revolve around your comfort.

People can't handle that, so they cling to lies that create the illusion of order:

- "Good things happen to good people."
- "Bad things happen for a reason."
- "My group is right."
- "My beliefs are absolute."

- "My leaders can't be wrong."
- "My god thinks like me."
- "My truth is the truth."

These lies are mental anesthesia. They numb the pain of existence. They make the world feel smaller, safer, predictable. Truth does the opposite. Truth kicks the door open and lets all the monsters in.

The Comfort of Familiar Pain

There's a reason people stay in toxic relationships, toxic religions, toxic politics, and toxic habits. Humans don't seek happiness; they seek familiarity. A toxic lie feels safer than an unfamiliar truth.

People endure spiritual cages because the bars feel like home. They cling to harmful beliefs because letting go means confronting the void. They choose the pain they know over the freedom they fear. Freedom requires responsibility. Lies require nothing but obedience. And obedience is easier than evolution.

The Horror of Self-Recognition

The hardest truth any human can face is this: "I was wrong."

Those three words feel like fire. They burn pride. They burn certainty. They burn identity. That's why some people defend a comforting lie long after it has destroyed their relationships, their peace, their logic, and their integrity. The lie becomes a part of them—a shield, a drug, a religion. To lose the lie is to lose themselves.

The Price of Truth

People always say they want the truth, but truth asks questions.

Are you willing to change? Are you willing to let go? Are you willing to be wrong? Are you willing to grow? Are you willing to step into pain before you step into clarity? Are you willing to stop lying to yourself?

Most people aren't.

So they settle for the lie because it is easier, softer, warmer, and safer. A lie protects. Truth exposes. A lie comforts. Truth confronts. A lie hugs. Truth shakes.

But truth—once embraced—is the only thing strong enough to set a person free.

THE INHERITED POISON

Lies don't stay still. They move. They travel. They mutate. They multiply.

A lie told once is manipulation. A lie told twice becomes a belief. A lie told for generations becomes culture—a curse passed down like a family heirloom nobody asked for, but everybody is expected to keep.

Most people think generational curses are about demons or bad luck. But the real curse is the lie you were born into before you even had words to describe it.

The First Lie: "This Is Just How We Are."

Every family has its script.

Some scripts are spoken. Some are implied. Some are screamed. Some are whispered. Some are buried under decades of silence. But all of them contain lies designed to protect the family's fragile identity.

"We don't talk about that." "Your father did the best he could." "That never happened." "Be grateful." "Stay quiet." "Keep the peace." "You're overreacting."

Generations don't always pass down wisdom. They pass down coping mechanisms disguised as wisdom—wounds dressed up as tradition, trauma dressed up as culture, fear dressed up as loyalty. The lie becomes normal, routine, expected, sacred. And anybody who challenges it becomes the villain.

That's the first curse.

The Curse of Silence

Most curses don't come from what's spoken. They come from what isn't.

Silence is the deadliest heritage a family can leave behind: silence about abuse, silence about pain, silence about identity, silence about truth, silence about the hurt passed from one generation's hands into the next generation's bloodstream.

Silence teaches the child: pain is supposed to be hidden, your voice is dangerous, truth is forbidden, suffering is normal. And once a child learns that, they grow into an adult who teaches the same lessons, believing it's survival when it's actually self-destruction.

That's the second curse.

The Lie of Loyalty

One of the most toxic lies families pass down is this: "Protect the family at all costs."

But "protect" almost never means healing. It never means accountability. It never means honesty. It means covering up—covering up sins, covering up abusers, covering up generational dysfunction, covering up the truth because the truth threatens the family's reputation.

You're expected to swallow your suffering so the family can save face. You're expected to carry the burden so they don't have to carry the guilt.

That's the third curse.

When Religion Becomes a Family Lie

Some families pass down faith. Others pass down fear dressed as faith.

"God wants you to obey." "God wants you to forgive immediately." "God wants you to stay silent." "God hates when families break apart." "God will punish you if you expose the truth."

That isn't religion. That's spiritual blackmail: a weaponized version of faith used to uphold dysfunction instead of healing it. Children grow up thinking the voice of trauma is the voice of God.

That's the fourth curse.

Cultural Lies: When a Whole Community Agrees to Suffer

Some curses aren't just family-wide. They're cultural.

A culture can inherit lies the same way a bloodline does: "Real men don't cry." "Real women don't complain." "Our people don't go to therapy." "We don't expose our business." "This is just how life is." "This is normal."

A community can drown together because nobody wants to be the one who swims differently. The curse becomes a collective identity nobody questions, and everybody pays for.

The Curse of Unchallenged Beliefs

Every inherited lie protects the generation that created it, but it destroys the generation that inherits it. It feels safe to hold onto familiar pain. It feels dangerous to break the pattern, because breaking curses feels like betrayal.

But the truth is simple: you cannot heal a wound you've been taught not to see. You cannot fix a pattern you've been trained not to question. You cannot escape a cage you were raised to believe is a home.

The One Who Breaks the Curse

Every family has one.

The one who doesn't stay silent. The one who doesn't obey. The one who refuses to "just accept it." The one who starts asking forbidden questions. The one who refuses to carry the weight that was dropped on their shoulders long before they were born.

The cursebreaker is always labeled difficult, disrespectful, ungrateful, rebellious, dramatic, ruined by the world, "not like us." They are punished for the truth because the truth threatens the lie the family was built on.

But cursebreakers are necessary. They are the first to bleed—and the first to heal.

THE AWAKENING

People think awakening is peaceful. They imagine candles, meditation, a soft voice whispering clarity. But real awakening feels like war.

Nobody wakes up from generational lies with a smile. They wake up because something cracks—a moment so jarring, so undeniable, that the lie can't hold its shape anymore. Awakening always starts with discomfort, never comfort.

The Moment Everything Stops Making Sense

Awakening usually begins with one of four things.

First, a contradiction too big to ignore. The family says, "We love each other," but the actions scream abuse. The religion says, "God is love," but everything taught is fear. The culture says, "This is just how it is," but the person feels suffocated. The lie slips, and once it slips, you can't unsee it.

Second, a question that refuses to die. One thought keeps returning like a haunting: Why are we like this? Why does nobody talk about it? Why does this hurt? Why am I expected to accept this? That question becomes the first seed of truth.

Third, a pain that becomes unbearable. People tolerate a lot. Generations tolerate more. But eventually the weight becomes too heavy, and the soul whispers, "Enough."

Fourth, witnessing someone outside the pattern. A friend healing. A partner breaking their own cycle. A stranger living freely. Somebody showing you another version of life that doesn't match the one you inherited. Your world expands, and suddenly the cage feels smaller.

The Disorientation

Awakening feels like standing in a room you've lived in your whole life and realizing all the furniture is fake.

The memories feel different. The stories you were told feel questionable. The people you trusted feel dangerous. The beliefs you held feel unfamiliar. It's not madness. It's awakening.

People mistake awakening for chaos because they've confused comfort with truth.

The Stages of Awakening

First comes denial. You don't want to believe the lie is a lie. You cling to familiar pain because it feels safer than confronting the truth.

Then comes anger—not at the truth, but at everyone who told you a lie and called it love. Families feel targeted. Culture feels threatened. God feels confusing. Your identity feels like it's melting.

Then comes grief. Awakening includes mourning the childhood you didn't get, the truth you were denied, the innocence you lost, and the version of yourself built on fear. Grief means you are letting go.

Then comes clarity. Small realizations turn into big revelations. That wasn't normal. That wasn't love. That wasn't my fault. That wasn't God speaking. That wasn't culture—it was trauma. You stop excusing what harmed you. You stop lying to yourself. You start seeing.

Finally comes rebuilding. This is where awakening turns into transformation. You choose new beliefs, new boundaries, a new identity, a new direction, a new purpose, a new truth. You rebuild yourself without the generational blueprint.

The Betrayal Label

Here's the part nobody warns you about. When you awaken, the people still trapped in the lie will call you the enemy.

You'll be labeled dramatic, ungrateful, brainwashed, "different," too sensitive, going through a phase, being influenced by the world. Because awakening exposes what others still refuse to face. Your truth is threatening. Your clarity is dangerous. Your evolution is proof that their chains are breakable.

And some people would rather stay chained than admit they've been imprisoned.

The Courage to See

Awakening is not about intelligence. It's about courage.

Courage to sit with pain. Courage to ask forbidden questions. Courage to dismantle inherited beliefs. Courage to lose the approval of those who loved you conditionally. Courage to choose truth over tradition. Courage to become who you were meant to be instead of who you were trained to be.

Most people never wake up because staying asleep is easier. Awakening is choosing the discomfort that leads to freedom over the comfort that leads to death.

The Birth of a New Bloodline

When one person awakens, the curse weakens. When one person tells the truth, the lie shakes. When one person chooses healing, the pattern breaks. When one person refuses silence, the ghosts lose power.

Awakening is rebellion. Awakening is liberation. Awakening is the moment where the old story ends and your story begins.

Generations may have lived blind, but you—you are the first one to see.

And once you see, you can never go back.

THE EMOTIONAL WAR OF BREAKING CYCLES

People talk about "breaking cycles" like it's pretty—like it's an Instagram quote, a soft little moment of empowerment with flowers and affirmations floating in the background. No. Breaking cycles is violent. It's emotional warfare. It's choosing to stand alone in a battlefield where the enemy looks like your family, your upbringing, your memories, your religion, your identity—and worst of all, yourself.

You don't just fight the people who harmed you. You fight the version of you that learned to survive by obeying them. This is the war nobody prepares you for.

The First Battle: The Guilt Programming

Cycle breakers always feel guilty at first—guilty for wanting peace, guilty for seeking truth, guilty for telling your story, guilty for saying "No more," guilty for refusing to play the family puppet, guilty for wanting a life that doesn't mirror their trauma.

That guilt isn't natural. It's installed.

Generational programming teaches you that loyalty means suffering silently, love means self-erasure, and respect means obedience even when it destroys you. Breaking cycles means deleting every lie you were taught to call "love," and that hurts.

The Second Battle: The Family Backlash

A cycle breaker becomes the villain in the story of the unhealed.

When you stop playing your assigned role, everyone panics. You were the quiet one, the compliant one, the overachiever, the caretaker, the emotional trash can, the one who never complained, the one who held the family together. When you step out of that role, they attack—not physically, emotionally.

It starts with gaslighting: "Why are you acting brand new?" "You're remembering wrong." "You're too emotional." "You've been influenced." "You're making a big deal out of nothing."

Then come the guilt trips: "Family is all you have." "You owe us." "After everything we did for you."

Then the minimizing: "You're overreacting." "That's not what happened." "It wasn't that bad."

You're not breaking the cycle quietly. You're breaking their delusion. And people fight harder for their delusions than they fight for their healing.

The Third Battle: The Spiritual Confusion

This is where many people hesitate, because breaking cycles often exposes how religion was used against you.

Suddenly, the scriptures sound different. The sermons feel manipulative. The "God" they taught you starts sounding more like a dictator than a creator. You begin asking questions you were punished for asking: Does God want me suffering? Is obedience the same as faith? Why does my family weaponize religion? Who benefits from me staying silent? Is this God... or is this control?

When the faith you inherited starts feeling like a cage, you meet God for the first time—not the God they created, but the God beyond their control. This spiritual identity crisis is where most people break, not because it's wrong, but because it's unfamiliar.

The Fourth Battle: The Loneliness

Cycle breaking feels lonely because you're the first one in your bloodline to choose a different path.

You're pulling yourself out of patterns your ancestors drowned in. You're healing wounds that were passed down like heirlooms. You're rejecting beliefs that were treated as sacred truth. Of course, it feels lonely. You're walking a road nobody before you dared to step on.

But here's the brutal truth: loneliness is not a punishment. It's a transition. You're not losing people. You're losing the illusions you had about them.

The Fifth Battle: The Internal Revolt

Cycle breaking doesn't just trigger your family. It triggers your inner child, your inner critic, your fear, your trauma, your learned behaviors.

Your mind rebels: this is unsafe, this is unfamiliar, this is dangerous, this is going to make everyone leave, this is too much, you're being dramatic, just go back to normal.

Your nervous system tries to drag you back to the very patterns you're trying to escape because survival mode feels comfortable, even when it's killing you. This internal war is the hardest battle of all.

The Sixth Battle: The Emotional Detox

Once you break the cycle, you start detoxing emotional toxins that were never yours to carry—shame that belonged to your parents, fear that belonged to their parents, trauma that started generations before you, silence that protected abusers, responsibility that wasn't yours, roles you never agreed to.

Detoxing hurts. You cry for reasons you can't name. You feel anger with no target. You mourn a past you're still untangling. You feel lost and liberated at the same time.

This is healing. This is cleansing. This is transformation.

The Final Battle: The Rebirth

At the end of the emotional war, there's a moment—quiet, subtle—where the pain stops feeling like destruction and starts feeling like creation.

You realize you weren't breaking the family. You were breaking the prison. You weren't betraying the bloodline. You were rewriting it. You weren't abandoning them. You were choosing you.

And then it hits you: the cycle didn't break you. You broke it.

And that is the moment you step into a future your ancestors prayed for but were too wounded to reach. You are the first, but you won't be the last. Because where cycles break, legacies are born.

The Living Room That Always Smelled Like Secrets

The night it all broke open wasn't dramatic—no storm, no slammed doors—just a quiet living room with dim lights, plastic-covered furniture, and a family pretending to be normal. The kind of room where truth had always gone to die.

Maya walked in already knowing this wouldn't be a peaceful conversation. Cycle breakers always know. The tension sits in the chest like a warning. Everyone was already there: her mother wearing the "don't embarrass me" face, her aunt with judgment sitting on her tongue, her father staring at the floor like he always did, her grandmother clutching a Bible she never actually read but weaponized like a knife.

They invited her to talk, but Maya knew better. This wasn't a conversation. This was an ambush.

She sat anyway, because survivors get tired of surviving. And tonight, she came for the truth.

The Accusations Begin

"A family shouldn't air dirty laundry," her mother began.

"What dirty laundry?" Maya asked calmly. "Or do you mean the truth?"

Her aunt jumped in. "You're being dramatic. You know your uncle didn't mean it like that."

Maya felt her jaw clench—that old familiar fire, the rage that comes from remembering what everyone else pretends to forget.

"He touched me," Maya said. "Stop calling it something else."

The room froze. Truth had always been a forbidden language in that house.

Her grandmother slammed her palm on the Bible. "Don't you bring that filth into this home!"

"It was already here," Maya whispered. "I was four."

Her father swallowed hard. He didn't speak. He never did. Silence—the same silence that protected her abuser—spread through the room like mold.

The Family War Erupts

Her mother snapped first. "You have no idea how hard I worked—"

"You didn't protect me," Maya interrupted. Her voice didn't rise. It sharpened.

Her aunt pointed aggressively. "You always think you're better than us. Too good for your own family now."

"There it is," Maya said. "The guilt. The gaslighting. The same playbook every time someone tells the truth."

"You're tearing this family apart!" her grandmother shouted.

"No," Maya said. "I'm exposing what already tore it apart."

They stared at her like she had committed a crime, because in that house, truth was the biggest betrayal.

The Moment They Try to Break Her

Her mother switched tactics—the oldest move in the book.

Tears.

"You're hurting me," she whispered.

Maya felt the childhood instinct rise: comfort, apologize, shrink. But she didn't. She sat still, breathing through the ancestral urge to fold.

"I'm not responsible for your emotions," she said quietly. "And I'm not protecting the man who hurt me so you can pretend this family is something it never was."

Her aunt scoffed. "You're brainwashed. Reading too many self-help books. Listening to outsiders."

"Funny how I'm 'brainwashed' the moment I stop tolerating abuse."

The room crackled with fury. Cycle breakers are dangerous because they can't be controlled anymore.

The Final Attempt to Pull Her Back

Her grandmother stood up, trembling with self-righteous rage. "If you walk out that door, don't bother coming back."

And there it was—the ultimate threat of generational control: exile.

Maya's heart pounded, but she didn't stand up immediately. She looked at every face in that room: faces she once associated with safety, faces that fed her, faces that taught her to fear her own voice, faces that chose silence over protection.

"I'm not leaving the family," Maya said. "I'm leaving the lie."

Then she stood. Nobody stopped her. Because nobody could. Not anymore.

The Door Closure That Shook Generations

When she walked out, and the door clicked behind her, something ancient broke—not in her, in them.

Her mother started crying, not from heartbreak, but from losing control. Her aunt whispered, "She'll be back. They always come back." Her grandmother prayed louder, hoping God would restore the hierarchy. Her father sat quietly, ashamed of his cowardice but too afraid to face it.

They all believed the same thing: if they punished her with silence, she'd fold.

But Maya didn't fold.

When she got in her car, her hands were shaking—the kind of shaking that comes from choosing yourself for the first time in generations. It wasn't triumph. It wasn't peace. It was liberation. Liberation always feels terrifying before it feels holy.

She drove into the night carrying nothing but truth and the weight of becoming the first person in her bloodline to walk away instead of break. The family would talk about her for months. They'd rewrite the story. They'd blame her. They'd lie. They'd gossip. They'd wait for her to crawl back.

She wouldn't.

Because what she walked toward was bigger than what she left behind. She wasn't just breaking the cycle—she was burning the blueprint.

THE AFTERSHOCK

I. Maya — The Silence After the War

When Maya got home, the silence felt too loud.

Her body was still vibrating with the electricity of confrontation—the kind that leaves your hands shaking long after the danger is gone. She closed the door behind her and slid to the floor, back against the wood, knees pulled into her chest.

That's when the wave hit. Not sadness. Not fear. Not regret.

Shock.

The emotional aftershock of breaking a cycle is like stepping off a battlefield and realizing you've been bleeding for years and only just now noticed the wound. Maya wasn't crying from pain. She was crying from release—a release she had never allowed herself to feel. Every muscle in her body trembled. Every breath felt like breaking open. Her heart raced like it was trying to outrun the version of her she left behind.

She whispered to herself, "I did it."

But the truth was heavier. She didn't just walk out of a house. She walked out of a generational script. And you don't escape a script without grieving the character you used to play.

II. Back at the House — The Family Collision

The moment Maya left, the living room collapsed into chaos.

She had been the unspoken glue—the scapegoat, the emotional lightning rod, the person everyone dumped their storms onto so they didn't have to face their own. Without her presence, the energy had nowhere to go.

Her mother was the first to break. "She thinks she's better than us," she snapped, pacing. But underneath the anger was terror. Without Maya to absorb the generational shame, it started sliding back toward the people who created it.

Her aunt grew quiet—deep quiet, the kind that only comes when denial cracks. Her grandmother clutched her Bible tighter like it might stop the truth from leaking out.

And her father? He sat in the same spot as before, but this time he wasn't staring at the floor. He was staring at the door Maya walked out of. The regret in his eyes was louder than all of their arguments.

For the first time in decades, the family had to sit with themselves, and they hated it. Because the scapegoat being gone meant the mirror had no one else to reflect.

III. Maya — The Spiritual Shattering

Later that night, Maya sat on her bed in the dark, legs crossed, palms open, trying to breathe normally.

But something deeper was happening. Not a breakdown. A breakthrough.

She had always felt God through fear—the God her grandmother preached about, the God who punished, the God who required silence, the God who demanded obedience even at the cost of her childhood. But now, with the noise of her family far behind her, she felt something shift.

For the first time, she felt God not as a judge but as a witness. Not as a dictator, but as a presence.

A stillness settled around her, warm and sharp, like a truth finally making itself known. She whispered, "Were You ever with me there?"

And in the quiet, something inside her answered, *I was with you here.*

Here—in the version of her that finally chose herself. Here—in the courage, the shaking hands, the tears on the floor. Here—in her decision to walk out instead of break down.

Maya realized something profound: her family's God was about fear. Her God was about freedom. And the two were not the same.

Her spiritual awakening didn't come with angels or visions. It came with the sudden, bone-deep knowing that the divine had been waiting for her to stop surviving long enough to hear clearly. Or maybe *Her.* Or maybe something beyond gender entirely. Whatever it was, it felt real for the first time.

IV. The Father — The One Who Watched the Cycle Break

He waited until everyone left the living room.

The house was quiet again—eerily quiet. He sat alone, staring at the door. The same door he watched his daughter walk out of. The same door he never stood up to defend her through.

He knew the others blamed Maya. He knew they'd rewrite the narrative. They always did.

But he couldn't. Because while everyone else saw rebellion, he saw himself.

He saw the seven-year-old boy who wasn't believed. The teenager who swallowed every truth. The grown man who never fought back. The father who stayed silent while history repeated itself.

Maya wasn't the problem. She was the first solution. But he wasn't brave enough to say it.

He whispered into the empty room, "I'm sorry."

He knew she wouldn't hear it. He knew she deserved better. He knew he might lose her forever. But he also knew this: when she left, she didn't break the family. She broke the curse.

And deep down—behind the shame, behind the cowardice, behind the decades of silence—he was proud of her.

Maybe too late. But proud nonetheless.

I. Maya — Rebuilding From the Ashes

Maya didn't wake up healed. She woke up heavy—but the heaviness felt different now. Not like a burden. Like a blueprint.

A blueprint she was finally free to redesign.

She sat on her balcony with a journal, the sunrise hitting her skin, the cold air kissing the sweat of last night's tears. Then she wrote two lists.

The first column read: **WHO THEY TAUGHT ME TO BE.**

The quiet one. The accommodating one. The good daughter. The problem solver. The apologizer. The protector of secrets. The emotional landfill. The forgiver of unforgivable things.

The second column read: **WHO I AM.**

Loud when necessary. Unapologetic. Whole. A truth-teller. Not responsible for anyone's shame. A woman rebuilding herself. Someone God didn't abandon—someone God called out.

Seeing the two sides made her chest tremble. She realized she'd been living a life that wasn't hers, a personality sculpted by trauma. She had been surviving a role that never belonged to her.

Her identity wasn't broken. It was buried.

Today she started digging it up.

II. The Family — Cracking Without the Scapegoat

Back at the house, the dysfunction had no place to hide.

Without Maya there, every suppressed resentment rose like smoke. Her mother suddenly had no one to dump her stress on. She snapped at everyone—at the dog, at the TV, at her husband, at herself.

Her aunt, always so loud and so opinionated, finally felt the sting of silence because there was no one to override anymore.

Her grandmother's prayers grew desperate. She wasn't praying for healing. She was praying for control—praying for the universe to bend back into the shape she understood.

The father watched all of it with a sinking gut. The house felt like a boat rocking without an anchor.

Maya had been the anchor—not because she held them together, but because they tied their chaos to her. She absorbed every secret, every blame, every wound. Without her, their real selves were exposed: ugly, unhealed, unhidden. A storm waiting for a target.

III. The Uncle Returns

Three days passed.

Maya was in the grocery store, picking up fruit and tea like a woman learning her body deserves nourishment, when her phone buzzed.

A text from an unknown number: "You think you grown now?"

She froze. Her throat tightened. Her stomach flipped.

The uncle—the man who stole her childhood and was protected by the entire family.

A second text arrived. "You telling lies about me?"

The nerve. The audacity. The entitlement of a predator who had never been held accountable.

She stared at the words, and for a split second the old version of her—the child—felt afraid.

But the new Maya inhaled sharply, centered herself, and typed back: "I'm done being silent. Whatever happens now, happens."

Her finger hovered over **SEND** for only a fraction of a second. Then she tapped it.

A surge of adrenaline flooded her veins. Not fear. Power.

But he wasn't finished. "You ruining this family."

Maya laughed out loud in the middle of aisle nine. Then she typed: "You ruined your own life when you touched a child. I'm not covering for you anymore."

Before she could put her phone away, another text came: "We need to talk."

Normally she would block him. Run. Disappear.

But something in her had shifted.

She realized she didn't want to avoid him anymore. Not now. She wanted to face him—on her terms, in her strength, with her truth sharp as a blade.

She wrote back: "Meet me in a public place. Tomorrow. Noon."

IV. Maya — The Woman Who Isn't a Victim Anymore

That night, she went home and sat on the edge of her bed.

There was fear in her chest, yes, but under it was something deeper—a fire she didn't know she had. She remembered being four: the confusion, the shame, the silence, the way adults ignored the truth because protecting him was easier than facing themselves.

But she wasn't four anymore.

And she wasn't alone.

She felt that presence again—the quiet, divine stillness—wrap around her. Not promising safety. Promising strength.

God didn't shield her from the pain. God walked her through it.

Tomorrow wouldn't be easy, but it would be hers.

Her confrontation. Her truth. Her closure.

I. The Meeting — The Man Who Stole Her Childhood

Maya chose a public place on purpose: a small coffee shop by the park. Bright windows. People everywhere. Neutral ground.

She arrived early. Her hands shook, but not out of fear—out of anticipation. Facing an abuser isn't fear. It's adrenaline. It's awakening. It's the soul sharpening itself for battle.

Her uncle showed up late. Of course he did. Predators run on arrogance.

He walked in like nothing ever happened—like they were family, like she wasn't the child he violated and lied about, like he still owned the narrative. He sat across from her with a smirk that made her stomach twist.

"So," he said, leaning back, "you out here telling stories?"

Maya didn't blink. "They're not stories," she said. "They're memories."

He scoffed—that ugly, dismissive scoff every survivor knows too well. "You always were dramatic," he said. "You're grown now, acting like a victim."

Maya leaned forward slowly, eyes locked onto his. Her voice never wavered. "I'm not a victim," she said. "I'm the truth you ran from."

He froze.

Her words cut him cleaner than a knife.

II. Psychological Breakdown — The Lie Can't Breathe Here

He tried to regain control.

"You remember wrong," he hissed. "You were a kid. You don't know what you felt."

"That's the thing," Maya said. "I remember everything because I was a kid. Children don't forget the hands that hurt them."

He looked away for the first time.

Maya didn't stop. "You took something from me I didn't even understand yet. And everyone in that house protected you instead of me."

His jaw tightened. Predators hate mirrors. They hate being seen naked in their truth.

"You gonna ruin your mother over this?" he snapped. "You gonna put her in the ground?"

Maya inhaled sharply. "For once," she said, "her feelings aren't my job."

He bristled. "You think you're tough now?"

"No," Maya said. "I think I'm awake."

The lie he'd lived inside his whole life had no oxygen in front of this version of her.

III. The Spiritual Turning — God Is Here Too

Her voice softened unexpectedly.

"I used to think God abandoned me," she said. "When you touched me, when the adults ignored me, when the house stayed quiet, I thought God was silent too."

Her uncle looked annoyed, but she kept going.

"What I realized," she whispered, "is that God didn't leave me. God waited for me to grow strong enough to come back and speak."

Something shifted in the air—cold, still, heavy—like truth itself pulled up a chair.

Her uncle's eyes darted away, because the only thing more terrifying than a survivor is a survivor with God behind her.

IV. The Final Blow — The Truth Spoken Out Loud

Maya sat back, calm.

"I'm not here to get revenge," she said. "I'm here to say the words you prayed I'd never say."

She looked him dead in the face. "You molested me."

He flinched—not from shame, from exposure.

People were around. People heard. People turned their heads. For a man who lived protected by silence, public truth was a death sentence.

He stood abruptly. "You're crazy," he muttered. "You're destroying this family."

Maya stood too.

"No," she said quietly. "You destroyed it. I'm saving myself."

He stormed out—head down, face red, the weight of exposure sitting on his shoulders like fire.

For the first time in her life, Maya felt taller. Not lighter—stronger.

V. The Family Reaction — The Explosion They Blame on Her

He told them before she could. Of course he did.

By the time Maya got home, her phone was blowing up: seventeen missed calls from her mother, nine from her aunt, four from her grandmother, one from her father. The group thread she wasn't included in was probably on fire.

She opened the first voicemail.

"You humiliated him in PUBLIC?!" her mother screamed. "Do you know what you've done?!"

The second voicemail was her grandmother: "You're possessed! You're letting the world turn you against your own blood!"

The third was her aunt: "You keep pushing, and this family will cut you off forever."

Maya laughed—a short, humorless laugh.

They weren't mad she confronted him. They were mad the secret wasn't protected. The family didn't want healing. They wanted silence.

VI. The Unexpected Voicemail — The One Voice She Didn't Expect

The last voicemail was from her father.

He sounded different—not angry, not confused—just tired.

"Maya... I heard what happened. I just want you to know... I believe you. I always did. I just didn't know how to stand up back then. But I'm proud of you."

She sat down slowly.

That was the apology she never asked for but always needed. Not perfect. Not complete. But real.

A crack of light inside a house filled with shadows.

I. Maya's Decision — The Last Phone Call She'll Ever Answer

Her phone lit up all morning. Mother. Grandmother. Aunt. Blocked. Blocked. Blocked.

One by one, she hit the button with a level of peace she didn't know she was capable of. No rage. No guilt. Just clarity.

For the first time in her life, she wasn't bargaining for love. She wasn't negotiating her worth. She wasn't shrinking herself to make anyone comfortable. She was choosing herself—and for women raised in generational trauma, that choice is a spiritual revolution.

She didn't send a long message. She didn't write a goodbye letter. She didn't owe them closure.

She sent a single text to the family group chat: **"I'm done. Don't call me again."**

Then she left the whole family on read.

II. The Shift — The Quiet After No Contact Feels Like Freedom Wrapped in Fear

Most people think no contact feels clean and crisp, like a fresh start.

It doesn't.

It feels like detox, like shaking off poison, like learning how to breathe without checking the temperature of the room first.

Maya sat in her apartment with the lights off, the kind of silence that felt like a new universe humming. Her body felt lighter, but her nerves were electric. Healing isn't calm—it's awakening.

She curled up on her couch and felt something she had never felt before: safety.

She didn't have to brace herself for footsteps. Didn't have to scan the room for danger. Didn't have to read the emotional weather of other people. For the first time, her nervous system wasn't being held hostage.

III. The Uncle's Consequences — The Lie Collapses

Her uncle thought the story would die as long as the family denied it. What he didn't expect was the public confrontation at the café to hit the community like a shockwave.

People talk. Whispers run faster than truth, but this time the truth was the whisper.

By the end of the week, his girlfriend had left him. She heard the rumors and confronted him. He did what abusers always do—got loud, defensive, hostile. She packed her bags.

His job cut back his hours. Someone from HR overheard the coffee shop story. They couldn't fire him yet, but they could watch him. Freeze him out. Make his life uncomfortable.

His church told him to "take a break." The pastor pulled him aside. Apparently, the allegations didn't look good for the congregation. The man who once bragged about being "favored by God" was now too radioactive for the front pew.

Karma does not miss. It just takes its time.

IV. Legal Consequences — The Report That Changed the Game

Maya didn't report him for revenge. She reported him for the child she used to be, and for the children she hoped he never got near.

The detective who took her report listened quietly as she described what happened. Her voice shook, but she didn't break.

When she finished, he said, "You're not the first person to speak his name."

Maya's skin went cold.

There were others.

The case opened. Paperwork became evidence. Testimonies were gathered. Patterns emerged.

Her uncle felt the walls closing in. He wasn't in jail yet, but his world grew smaller every day. People looked at him differently. He felt eyes on him everywhere he went.

Predators can handle silence. What they can't handle is attention.

V. Spiritual Consequences — God Does Not Forget Children

He tried going back to church.

Sat in the back row, head down, hoping the old rituals would protect him. But something felt off. The room felt colder. The hymns rang hollow. The sermons sounded like accusations.

You can run from people, but you can't outrun what you did in the dark.

Maya wasn't the only one waking up. God was dragging her uncle into the light, too, and it burned.

Every night, he woke up sweating. He heard footsteps that weren't there. He felt the eyes of the child he violated standing in the corner of every room.

Guilt. Fear. Spiritual justice.

Didn't matter. He was finally living with the truth he forced Maya to carry for decades.

VI. The Family Fallout — The House of Denial Cracks

At first, the family tried defending him.

"He said you misunderstood."

"He said you asked for attention."

"He said you're unstable."

But then the consequences started touching them.

Neighbors whispered. Church members stared. Friends asked questions. And nothing terrifies a toxic family like being embarrassed.

The family split into two factions.

Faction one doubled down and blamed Maya for everything.

Faction two grew quiet and started remembering things they once said were impossible.

One aunt whispered to Maya privately, "...I think he did something to me too."

Generational curses don't break clean. They shatter messy.

VII. Maya's Power — The Woman Who Doesn't Bow Anymore

No contact didn't make Maya lonely. It made her powerful.

She started therapy. Started journaling. Started meditating. Started reclaiming her body, her time, her space.

She woke up one morning and realized she felt different.

She wasn't waiting to be believed. She wasn't waiting to be rescued. She wasn't waiting to be chosen.

She had chosen herself.

And that—for a woman who grew up in silence, violence, and forced forgiveness—was holy.

I. The Call That Had to Happen

Maya didn't want to call her mother. But closure isn't about wanting. It's about finishing the story you didn't write, but were forced to live.

Her mother answered on the second ring.

Silence—the kind that comes from stubbornness, not love.

Then her mother's voice cut through it. "...Why did you do that to this family?"

There it was. The blame. The denial. The ignorance dressed as victimhood.

Maya's voice stayed steady. "I didn't do anything to this family," she said. "The truth did."

Her mother scoffed. "You embarrassed your uncle. People are talking. The church is talking. Do you know what you've put us through—"

"What he put me through," Maya corrected. "When I was a child."

Her mother said nothing.

So Maya continued. "You cared more about keeping the family intact than keeping me safe. You protected a predator. You lied for him. You silenced me. And now that the consequences are catching him, you're calling me the problem."

Her mother's breathing hitched. "Maya... don't do this to me."

"Mom," Maya said calmly, "I'm not doing anything to you. I'm finally doing something for me."

II. The Truth Her Mother Never Wanted to Face

"Why didn't you protect me?" Maya asked.

Her mother's voice cracked. "I was scared," she whispered. "He was family. Your grandmother said you were confused... I didn't know what to believe—"

"You believed what was easier," Maya said. "Not what was true."

Her mother started crying—years too late.

"You don't know what it's like..." she sobbed. "I didn't know how to handle it..."

Maya let her cry. Not out of sympathy, but out of release.

"You don't have to forgive me," her mother whispered.

"I don't," Maya said. "And I won't. But I can let it go—because I'm choosing myself now."

Silence again, but this time it was honest. Broken. Uneven.

Maya took a deep breath. "This is the last time we speak," she said. "You chose him. I'm choosing me."

The phone stayed quiet, and then her mother whispered, "...I'm sorry."

It wasn't enough. It wasn't complete. But it was real.

Maya hung up.

And for the first time in her life, her heart didn't shake after talking to her mother.

It felt steel-strong.

Unbreakable.

I. The Courthouse Smelled Like Cold Paper and Truth

Maya sat across from the clerk, documents in hand, heart pounding like a drum—not out of fear, out of finality.

The clerk slid the form back to her. "You'll need to describe the threat," she said.

Maya wrote in clean, sharp letters:

He is dangerous. He violated me as a child. He harassed me after exposure. I fear his retaliation.

The clerk looked at her with unexpected respect. "You're doing the right thing," she said softly.

Maya nodded.

The order would keep him away—legally, permanently. No more gray areas. No more chances. No more "maybe he'll change." No more "but he's family." Trauma needed distance. Healing needed boundaries. Danger needed consequences.

The judge reviewed the request, looked at Maya, looked at the history, looked at the statements from others that had finally come forward.

"Order granted," the judge said.

And just like that, the door to her childhood nightmare shut with legal force.

THE ARREST

Consequences don't come slowly anymore—not after truth has momentum.

I. The Day the Sirens Came

It was a Thursday morning when her uncle's world collapsed.

Neighbors saw the police outside his house—two officers, one detective, handcuffs ready. They knocked. He opened the door. He looked irritated, like they were inconveniencing his morning.

But the second they said, "We have a warrant—"

He broke.

Because predators don't fear God. They fear exposure.

He tried to argue. Tried to yell. Tried to blame Maya. The officers didn't care.

They cuffed him, read his rights, and walked him past the neighbors who stared with disgust, not sympathy. The man who hid behind family, behind silence, behind religion, behind authority, was finally stripped of everything.

He wasn't Uncle anything.

He was a criminal under arrest.

And Maya? She didn't celebrate. She didn't cry. She didn't collapse.

She exhaled—one long breath she'd been holding for years.

Epic Finale: God's Plan Is the Only Plan

This is not a religious chapter. This is a spiritual one. The difference is everything.

I. Religion Breaks—Faith Builds

Religion told Maya to stay quiet. Faith told her to speak. Religion told her to endure abuse. Faith told her to break the cycle. Religion told her forgiveness was mandatory. Faith told her healing was holy. Religion protected her uncle. Faith protected her spirit.

The church that preached love hid its predators. But the God Maya met in her healing was nothing like the hypocrites who weaponized His name.

God did not shame her. God did not silence her. God did not expect her to bow.

God gave her the rage to speak, the courage to stand, the clarity to leave, the strength to heal, and the destiny to rise.

II. False Prophets Fall When Truth Walks In

Her uncle used God's name as a shield. Her family used religion as camouflage. The church used scripture as a bandage for open wounds they didn't want to clean.

But God? God was never fooled. God was never aligned with them. God was never on the side of silence.

God does not protect predators. God does not bless hypocrisy. God does not elevate men who harm children.

God's plan was never their lie.

God's plan was her freedom.

III. Maya's New Life — The Woman God Saw When She Was Still a Child

Maya walks through the world different now—not wounded, not broken, not hiding.

She's awake. She's powerful. She's chosen by her own destiny.

She builds a life rooted in truth, in clarity, in spiritual alignment—not religious manipulation. She is proof that you can survive the lie, expose the darkness, rise from the ruins, and still be carried by God's plan even when humans fail you.

Not the pastor's God. Not her family's God. Not the guilt-soaked God of false prophets.

But the real one: the God who sees, the God who knows, the God who repairs what others destroyed, the God who leads you out when everyone else tells you to stay.

11

Trying to Belong in a Body That Confuses People

THE INHERITANCE OF SHADE

Here's the part I never said out loud, not to my family, not to friends, not to anybody: being light-skinned didn't make me feel chosen. It made me feel wrong. Like I was standing on the border of two countries that hated each other, but both sides kept yelling at me to "pick a side" while also reminding me I didn't fully belong to either. And you know what happens when you grow up like that? You start living in your own head because that's the only place you're not someone's disappointment.

I used to stare at my reflection, wondering why the fuck God made me like this. Too pale for the culture I loved. Too dark for the world that ruled everything. Too in-between for anybody to see me as enough. I'd hear Black folks say, "You got it easy. People treat you better." And on the surface, maybe that was true. Teachers smiled at me more. Girls said I was "cute in a different way." Cops looked at me, then looked away. But what nobody understood, what nobody even asked me, was how much I hated myself for it. Hated the way my skin looked like it came with perks I never fucking asked for. Hated how every compliment felt like a slap to somebody darker than me. Hated the guilt that lived in my chest like a parasite.

And then there was the flip side, the shit people didn't see. How my own people would weaponize my skin tone like I stole something. "How you Black if you ain't even dark?" "You mixed or something?" "Bet your daddy ain't even Black." "You only date white girls?" Every shot aimed at my identity. Every insult telling me I was an outsider in my own culture. I wasn't "light-skinned." I was "not enough."

And white folks? They didn't see a person, they saw a loophole. A way to touch Blackness without actually respecting it. The number of times I heard: "You're not like the others." "You're the good kind." "You're cute for a Black guy." Cute. For a Black guy. Like my whole race was a handicap I had to work around. And you know the fucked-up truth? Part of me tried to live up to that shit. Tried to be the "palatable" one. The safe one. The "I can fit into any room" one. I became a chameleon, changing the tone of my voice, the slang I used, the clothes I wore, the jokes I made, just to avoid hearing, "You don't belong with us."

That's the shit people don't talk about: Colorism doesn't just divide us, it rewires your brain. Makes you feel guilty for existing one second, and grateful the next. Makes you feel like an uninvited guest in your own culture. Makes you feel like you owe everybody an explanation for why you look the way you do. It's a fucked-up tightrope, balancing privilege in one hand and pain in the other, trying not to fall into shame on either side. But here's the part that hurts the most: when you're light-skinned, people think you're soft. They think shit doesn't touch you the same. They think you're "lucky." But nobody knows the nights you lay awake wishing you came out darker, fitted in cleaner, knew who the hell you were without having to prove it all the time. Nobody knows that some days you hate the face looking back at you because it feels like a constant reminder that you don't belong anywhere fully, just halfway everywhere.

And that's the cruel joke: Colorism don't give a damn about your feelings. It only cares about the hierarchy. The ladder. The system that was built long before you took your first breath. And somehow, somehow you ended up being the one caught in the middle, paying a price for shit you never caused.

THE FIRST TIME SOMEONE MADE MY SKIN A PROBLEM

I was maybe eight, standing on the playground where the sun hit everybody the same but didn't treat us the same. Kids were running, yelling, doing kid shit, and then one girl, darker than me, beautiful as hell, but angry in a way I didn't understand yet, stood in front of me with her hands on her hips like she was ready to fight the whole world through me. "You think you cute 'cause you light." I swear I didn't even know what "light" meant back then. I thought she was talking about my sneakers. But the way she glared? It was like she saw every wound from her mama, her aunties, her grandma, every comment about "good hair," "bright," "yellow bones," and "redbones taking all the good men." She saw all that shit in me. All I saw was confusion. And fear. Not 'cause of her, but because she looked at me like I represented something painful, ugly, unfair, and I didn't even do anything. "Get your light bright ass away from me," she snapped. And the other kids laughed. Not because it was funny, but because in Black spaces, color jokes aren't jokes. They're currency. They're weapons. They're a way to climb the ladder inside a ladder we never built. And I walked away thinking, what the fuck did I do wrong? But the truth was, nothing. Absolutely nothing. But try telling that to a kid who just learned his skin could piss people off by existing.

THE FIRST TIME WHITE PEOPLE CLAIMED ME

Fast forward a few years. Middle school. That awkward age where identity feels like a jacket you stole, it never quite fits, and you can't return it. A white teacher pulled me aside after class. She smiled at me like she was proud, like I was her special project. "You speak so well," she said. And I remember standing there, confused again, why wouldn't I speak well? I was raised the same as everybody else in that building: belt whoopings, microwave dinners, and a mama who didn't play about homework. "You're... different," she said, lowering her voice like a secret. Different how? "You're Black," she whispered, "but not... too Black." That's when it hit me: I wasn't a person, I was her fucking safe space. Her "good one." Her "exception." The kind white people brag about at dinner parties. The one they point to like a trophy to prove they're not racist. And I remember feeling dirty. Used. Confused as hell because part of me felt complimented, and another part felt like I betrayed my whole race just by smiling back. White folks have a way of doing that to you when you're light, patting you on the head while stepping on your people with the same damn hand.

THE FIRST TIME I REALIZED I DIDN'T BELONG TO ANYBODY

It was at a family cookout. Music loud, smoke in the air, dominoes slamming like gunshots, uncles arguing about bullshit sports stats. I walked over to the table with the older cousins, the ones who used jokes like knives. Soon as I sat down, somebody said, "Here come Chris Brown." Another one said, "Nah, that nigga look like he dipped in milk." Laughter. But the one that cut the deepest? "You not even Black for real. You just visiting." Visiting. In my own family.

So I got up and walked toward the other side, where the non-Black folks were: a married-in white uncle, a Hispanic friend-of-a-friend, and a couple white co-workers who somehow always showed up at cookouts uninvited. And soon as I hit that circle? "Oh hey! You're mixed, right?" "You look more Puerto Rican than Black." "You could pass if you wanted." "You're barely Black anyway." Barely Black. Barely. I swear that shit went through my chest like a blade. Black folks saying I wasn't Black enough. White folks saying I was too Black. Everybody trying to define me, nobody trying to know me. Right there in that backyard, with ribs on the grill and Frankie Beverly on blast, I realized something that fucked me up for years: I didn't belong anywhere. I was too much of one thing, not enough of the other, and somehow too little of both. A damn ghost in my own communities.

THE VOICE IN MY HEAD THAT WOULDN'T SHUT UP

As I got older, the shit got internal. I started hearing two voices: one said, you got privileges other Black folks don't. Don't forget that. The other said, but you ain't white enough to be safe, so what the fuck does it matter? Colorism is a mind war. A quiet one. A slow one. But it rots you from the inside out. You start apologizing for your skin. Then resenting it. Then, I wished you could peel it off and trade it in for something that wouldn't confuse people so much. And then you resent yourself for even thinking that. It's a cycle nobody warns you about. Because society thinks light skins either have it "easy" or they're "privileged" or they're "pretty." But nobody thinks: maybe this motherfucker is hurting, too. Maybe this light skin ain't armor, maybe it's a cage.

THE MASK OF ACCEPTANCE

I learned early that being light-skinned wasn't about privilege. It was about performance. A never-ending audition for acceptance. Be Black enough so your people don't question you. Be safe enough so white folks don't fear you. Be adaptable, agreeable, flexible, a walking compromise in human form. Some people put on masks for protection. I put on masks because I didn't know who the hell I was without them.

THE BLACK MASK: "PROVE YOU BELONG HERE."

In Black spaces, there was always a test. Unspoken, but loud as fuck. A vibe check. A cultural background check. A silent interrogation wrapped in jokes, side-eyes, and casual shade. "Where your daddy from?" "You mixed with something?" "You talk white as fuck." "Say nigga, let me hear how you say it." "You one of them light-skins that don't fight." "You soft." "You sensitive." "You spoiled." "You act like you too good for us." I swear

I spent half my childhood performing Blackness like it was a damn talent show. Talking harder, walking heavier, laughing louder, code-switching like a bilingual weapon just to keep people off my neck.

People think light-skinned folks are dramatic, emotional, "pretty boy" types. What they don't understand is that a lot of that comes from overcompensating, from trying to fill an invisible hole where belonging should've been. I wasn't trying to act tough. I was trying to earn permission just to exist in the room. But there was always that moment, that slip-up, that joke I didn't get, that slang I didn't use right, or the way I tried too hard not to try too hard, and suddenly the spotlight hit me with full force: "You ain't even Black for real." And the whole room would laugh like it wasn't killing me inside.

Not because they hated me. But because colorism taught them I wasn't one of them. Not fully. Not authentically. Not in the way that mattered. I learned to shrug it off. Laugh back. Pretend nothing touched me. Pretend I was made of rubber and light and nothing could break me. But every joke hit somewhere deeper. Somewhere, people couldn't see. Somewhere that followed me into adulthood like a shadow glued to my spirit.

THE WHITE MASK: "BE THE KIND WE APPROVE OF."

Then came the other side. White America. The grand stage of expectations, fears, stereotypes, and convenient acceptance. To them, I wasn't Black. I was Black-ish. Acceptable Black. Digestible Black. A "safe" version of a race they didn't fully respect. "You're not like the others." "I feel so comfortable around you." "You're articulate!" "You're basically white." "You should be proud, you don't have that ghetto vibe." Every sentence came wrapped in a smile. Every smile came dipped in poison.

And I swallowed it because I didn't know any better. Because at least somebody liked me. Even if it was for the wrong fucking reasons. I became the translator. The buffer. The bridge. The token. The "proof" they weren't racist. I learned how to laugh at their microaggressions. How to nod through their ignorance. How to keep the peace so they wouldn't get uncomfortable. I became the smiling version of myself. The harmless version. The anti-threatening version. A mask that fit too well. A mask that stuck to my face until I forgot there was a real me underneath.

THE WORST MASK: THE ONE I WORE ALONE

But the hardest performance wasn't for Black folks. It wasn't for white folks. It wasn't even for my family. It was for myself. The mask I wore alone, in my room, staring at my reflection, trying to decide which version of me was real. The one who felt guilty for light-skinned privilege? The one who hated himself for being treated differently? The one who craved acceptance from his own people? The one who felt sick when white folks complimented him for being "almost one of them"? The one who didn't know how to love himself without choosing a side?

Colorism doesn't just fuck up communities, it fucks up identity. It makes you question your authenticity, your worth, your place in the world. I spent years trying to be everything to everyone. But here's the truth I didn't want to face: I wasn't accepted anywhere because I wasn't accepting myself. I was too busy proving I belonged to ever ask myself where I actually wanted to belong.

THE MOMENT THE MASK CRACKED

It happened during high school. Lunchroom. Loud. Chaotic. Everybody playing their roles. A Black girl I liked, dark-skinned, beautiful, brilliant, sharp with her words, looked me dead in my face one day and said: "I don't date light-skinned dudes. Y'all fake. Y'all think y'all special." Her voice wasn't mean. It was matter-of-fact. Like she was saying, the sky is blue. And the whole table nodded. Like it was a known truth. Like I should've never even tried.

And then, two tables over, a white girl said to her friend: "Ew, he's cute, but he's Black. My parents would freak." Same moment. Same breath. Same cafeteria. Rejected for being too Black on one side. Rejected for being too Black on the other. That was the day I realized the mask wasn't protecting me. It was crushing me. Suffocating me. Turning me into a diluted version of myself. I walked out of that cafeteria with a truth I couldn't ignore: colorism made me perform for a world that never intended to love me. Not fully. Not freely. Not without conditions.

WHITE GAZE, BLACK PAIN

White America has always had a sick way of splitting Black people apart by shade. Not by accident. Not by misunderstanding. By design. A system built to break us into pieces, then hand those pieces back like tokens: "You? You're acceptable." "You? You're tolerable." "You? You're dangerous." "You? You're almost one of us." "You? You're invisible." And I became one of their favorite pieces, not because they saw my humanity, but because they saw an opportunity.

THE FETISH OF LIGHTNESS

This is the part nobody says out loud: white people have a long-ass history of fetishizing lighter skin. The "not as Black" Black person. The "close enough to be interesting but not enough to be threatening." The walking loophole in the lie they tell themselves about equality. White America's relationship with light-skinned Black folks is a mirror of its own guilt. A way to admire Blackness without confronting what they did to it. A way to applaud the beauty of melanin as long as it's diluted enough to make them comfortable. And me? I was their favorite fucking petri dish.

THE FIRST TIME WHITE AMERICA USED ME AS A SHIELD

It was ninth grade. English class. The teacher asked about discrimination in America. A white boy, one of those "I'm not racist but..." types, said: "I don't think racism is that bad anymore. Look at him—" and he pointed at me. Me. Like I was a fucking exhibit. "—he's Black, and he's doing fine." The class got quiet. My blood started boiling. My stomach twisted. Because what he really meant was: you're the kind of Black that's easy for us to digest. You don't scare us. You don't challenge us. You don't remind us of what we did.

I wanted to say something. Wanted to clap back. Wanted to expose the bullshit. But instead, I froze. Because when you grow up light-skinned, you're conditioned to "keep the peace." Conditioned to avoid making white people uncomfortable, 'cause uncomfortable white people become dangerous real quick. And the worst part? The teacher nodded. Like his comment was valid. Like my existence proved racism was over. I sat there feeling like a fucking prop in a play I didn't audition for.

THE "GOOD BLACK" SYNDROME

White folks have this unspoken category for Black people who "don't scare them too much." They won't admit it. Hell, half of them don't even realize they're doing it. But you can see it in their eyes and hear it in the tone and feel it in the way the room shifts when you walk in. I became the "good Black" everywhere: at school, at jobs, in stores, in classrooms, around police, around white parents, around white women. I was the Black kid they let sleep over. The Black coworker they invited to lunch. The Black neighbor they said "good morning" to. The Black friend they felt safe having.

But that acceptance was conditional. Fragile. Fake as fuck. One wrong word, one wrong tone, one moment of anger, one sign of "too much

Blackness," and suddenly the warmth would disappear. The smiles would stiffen. The friendliness would evaporate like it was never there. Light-skinned, dark-skinned, didn't matter. To white folks, we're all one mistake away from being a threat. Only difference is, they start me at "maybe he's okay" instead of "he's dangerous until proven safe." That's not privilege. That's a fucking trap.

THE WHITE WOMEN WHO FETISHIZED ME

Let's talk about it, 'cause this is part of the pain too. White women always had a different kind of hunger for light-skinned Black men. Not love. Not compassion. Not connection. Curiosity. Rebellion. Exotic fantasy. A way to piss off their racist parents without risking their own safety. "Your skin is so pretty." "You look mixed." "I love light-skinned Black guys; they're the perfect blend." "You're like... spicy but not too spicy." That shit used to make my stomach drop. They didn't want me. They wanted a watered-down version of Blackness they could play with. A low-risk "flavor" they could test out before going back to their regular lives.

Even as a teenager, I could feel it: they didn't see a person. They saw a stereotype with training wheels. And when I didn't act how they expected, didn't smile enough, didn't soften myself enough, didn't stay in the "safe Black guy" role, suddenly I was "scary." "Intense." "A bit much." "A different type than they thought." Their attraction had an expiration date. Their acceptance had a disclaimer. And white men? They looked at me with that quiet, simmering jealousy. Like they hated seeing a Black man exist in a space they thought belonged to them.

THE PROFESSIONAL WORLD: TOKENIZED AND TOLERATED

As I got older, the shit just changed shape. White coworkers loved me. Management praised me. I was "charismatic," "smart," "well-spoken," and "a natural leader." But I knew the truth. They weren't complimenting me.

They were complimenting the version of me that whiteness felt safe around.

And whenever a darker-skinned coworker spoke up, pushed back, called out bullshit, suddenly everyone got defensive as hell. But when I said something? They listened. Calmly. Politely. Respectfully. Not because I was right, but because my skin tone made the criticism feel less threatening. And realizing that, realizing I was being used as a buffer between whiteness and Blackness, made me sick. Because nothing is more painful than being praised in a system that punishes people who look like you just because their shade is different.

Light-skinned "privilege" isn't privilege. It's manipulation. It's exploitation. It's whiteness picking favorites in a game they designed to hurt all of us. And we carry the guilt of being chosen for reasons we never wanted.

THE WORST PART OF WHITE GAZE

The worst part isn't what they said. It's what it made me feel. Every time they praised me, every time they accepted me, every time they held me up as "the good one," a voice inside whispered: are you betraying your people? Are you benefitting from their pain? Are you a puppet in a system you hate? Are you being celebrated for the same reasons your brothers are punished?

White acceptance became a weight, a heavy, ugly, shameful thing I couldn't put down. Because deep down, I knew the truth: if whiteness loves you, it's because they think you can be controlled. If whiteness accepts you, it's because they think you're harmless. If whiteness embraces you, it's because they believe you'll protect them, even from your own people. And I refused to be their shield. Refused to be their excuse. Refused to be their buffer. But that refusal came with its own kind of pain. Its own isolation. Its own consequences.

BORN INTO A SHADE I NEVER CHOSE

I swear, sometimes I look in the mirror and feel a heat in my chest that ain't anger and ain't sadness, it's something uglier. Something like resentment. Toward a face I never picked. Toward a skin tone I never signed up for. Toward a life that came pre-loaded with expectations, jealousy, privileges, punishments, stereotypes, and contradictions, all because of a fucking shade chart somebody invented centuries before I ever breathed air.

People tell me, "Love yourself." "Be proud of who you are." "You're still Black." But how the hell do you love something that the world won't let you define for yourself? How do you love a version of yourself that was judged before you even opened your damn eyes? There are days I stand in the bathroom, staring at my skin under the light, wishing it would just... change. Get darker. Even out. Transform into something that would stop people from thinking I'm some halfway Black, diluted-ass version of the real thing.

You know what's fucked up? I didn't even ask for this. I didn't ask to come out looking like a compromise between two worlds that never wanted to compromise with each other. And sometimes, yeah, I'll say it, I blame my parents. Not because they did anything wrong. Not because they didn't love me. But because I inherited this war, this identity crisis, this confusion, this burden that they never warned me about. They handed me life, but didn't hand me a map for surviving the battlefield that came with my skin tone.

Some nights I'd sit on my bed like: "Why the fuck did y'all do this to me?" Why did you bring me into a world where I would be too light to be trusted and too dark to be accepted? Why didn't y'all tell me that my existence would be a constant debate? That my skin would be a conversation starter, a stereotype, a punchline, a fetish, a threat, a disappointment, a misunderstanding before it was ever allowed to be mine?

I didn't ask for this. I didn't ask to be the "safe Black person" for white people to practice their fake-ass acceptance on. I didn't ask to be the "not Black enough" stand-in for my own community's hurt. I didn't ask to be born into a shade that made people project their insecurities, histories, traumas, and fantasies onto me. I didn't ask to be blamed for privileges I don't want, and punished for privileges I didn't create.

And the worst part? I can't return it. Can't exchange it. Can't step out of it. Can't negotiate the terms. This skin, this in-between, this light-but-not-white, this Black-but-not-Black-enough, is permanent. I'm stuck in it. I'm forced to learn how to breathe in a body that the world keeps trying to rename.

People don't realize that colorism don't just cut deep, it bruises the soul. Makes you feel like a glitch in your own culture. Makes you feel like you were assembled wrong. Makes you question your worth before you even question the world. Some days I want to scream at the sky: "Why couldn't you just make me one or the other? Why did you make me a walking contradiction?" But the sky never answers. My skin never changes. And the world keeps spinning, judging, labeling, touching, testing, using, rejecting, pulling, distancing, and misunderstanding me all at the same damn time.

This ain't self-hate for attention. This is self-hate born from experience. From a lifetime of feeling like the wrong version of myself. From being reminded every day that I am seen before I am heard, judged before I am understood, categorized before I am known. I didn't ask for this shade. I didn't ask for this pain. I didn't ask for this identity tug-of-war. But here I am, living in a skin that doesn't feel like home, trying to make peace with a color I never chose.

THE DARK PLACES I NEVER ADMITTED OUT LOUD

There were days, and I hate admitting this, where I would stare at my own skin and feel disgust. Not because I wanted to be white. Hell no. I never wanted that. But because I wanted the pain to stop. The confusion to stop. The constant fucking identity checks to stop.

I wanted to wake up as someone who didn't feel like a walking apology. Someone who didn't have to prove their Blackness and didn't have to defend it either. Someone who didn't have to carry a history of being fetishized and ignored in the same sentence. I wanted to wake up one day and not feel like a goddamn compromise.

You ever feel like you don't own your own body? Like you're renting it from history? Paying interest on trauma you didn't even create? That's what being light-skinned felt like some nights. Like I was paying dues on a debt my ancestors didn't even choose.

And deeper than that, darker than that, were the thoughts that came when the world was quiet: "I hate this fucking skin." "I wish I was darker." "I wish I felt Black enough to stop questioning myself." "I wish white people couldn't see themselves in me at all."

Because there's violence in the way white people look at light-skinned kids. Like they're projects. Experiments. Proof that mixing makes Blackness "softer," "better," "more attractive," "easier to handle." That shit burns. Cuts deeper than any slur. Deeper than any fight.

Being light-skinned meant being inspected. Measured. Compared. Rated on a scale of whiteness, even when I wanted nothing to do with whiteness at all. And at the same time, being light-skinned meant walking into Black spaces feeling like a suspect. Feeling like you had to be twice as loud, twice as tough, twice as "down" to avoid being labeled soft, privileged, or weak.

It meant hearing: "You don't get it, you light." "You ain't built like us." "You ain't Black Black." That "Black Black" hits different. Feels like a bullet. Feels like a verdict.

And deeper than all that, the darkest part, were the moments I blamed my parents with a heat I'm ashamed of: "This is your fault." "Y'all did this to me." "Y'all gave me the type of Blackness that's always under a microscope." I never said it out loud, but I felt it. And feeling it was enough to make me want to disappear into myself. Shrink into a version of me that caused less conflict. Less confusion. Less disappointment.

Because that's the truth: being light-skinned sometimes made me feel like the disappointment. Like the mistake. Like the color nobody asked for, but everybody wanted to judge. And the darkest truth? There were days I wished I could peel myself out of this body just to feel what it's like to not hate the skin I'm in. Not because I wanted to be white. Not because I wanted to escape being Black. But because I wanted to feel whole. Complete. Aligned. Enough.

Because this in-between shit? It eats you. Slowly. Quietly. From the inside out. This is the part of colorism people pretend doesn't exist: self-hate born from being weaponized by two worlds at once. Pain inherited from a skin tone you didn't choose. Shame for wanting to be something people think you already are.

The darker truth is this: I don't hate being Black. I hate the damn battlefield that came with the shade I landed in. I hate the assumptions. I hate the projections. I hate the pressure. I hate the confusion. I hate the performance. I hate the guilt. I hate the privilege I never wanted. I hate the punishment I didn't deserve. I hate that I never had the freedom to just be me without having to defend it from every direction.

THE NIGHT I REALIZED I WASN'T ALLOWED TO LOVE MYSELF

It didn't happen in some dramatic moment. It wasn't lightning striking. It wasn't some movie scene where everything goes quiet. It was just... a regular night. Too quiet. Too still. The kind of night when your thoughts get loud enough to claw at the walls of your chest.

I was in the bathroom, staring at my own reflection under that yellow-ass light, the kind that makes every insecurity sharper, louder, uglier. And for the first time in my life, I really looked at myself. Not the version of me I pretended to be. Not the version I showed the world. Not the version other people needed. I saw me. Just me.

And the first thought I had was: "I don't deserve to love this face." Not because I wasn't handsome. Not because I wasn't enough. But because the world had taught me that loving myself was a privilege I hadn't earned. How you gonna love a face that makes people jealous, suspicious, angry, threatened, curious, or obsessed? How you gonna love a skin tone that people use to build their stereotypes, their fantasies, their insecurities? How you gonna love something the world keeps turning into a weapon?

White people looked at me and saw an invitation, a safer, softer version of Blackness they could touch without confronting their own racism. Black people looked at me and saw history, the kind of history that wasn't my fault but still landed on my skin like fingerprints I couldn't scrub off. I realized that night that loving myself would've meant fighting two battles at once, convincing white people they couldn't claim me, convincing Black people they shouldn't reject me. And the darkest part? I didn't have the strength to fight either battle.

So I did what hurt people do: I convinced myself I wasn't allowed to love me. I thought loving myself would be selfish, disrespectful, even, when darker-skinned kids were out here suffering twice as hard. I felt guilty for existing. Guilty for standing closer to the light. Guilty for being born into a shade that came with privileges I didn't want and punishments I didn't deserve.

I looked at my reflection and thought: "You don't get to love yourself until you pay for everything this skin has done." But pay who? Pay what? Pay when? For how long? The world never answers. It just watches you bleed.

That was the night I realized this truth: colorism doesn't just divide us, it steals your right to love yourself. It convinces you that your face is a crime scene you need to apologize for. And when you internalize that? You break in places no one can see.

The Internal War Between Shame and Identity

Shame is a tricky bitch. It doesn't show up loud. It doesn't knock or announce itself. It slips in through the cracks. Through jokes. Through offhand comments. Through stares. Through silence.

Shame is what happens when the world tells you: "You're too light to understand." "You're not really Black." "You got it easy." "You probably mixed." "You look white when you're mad." "You ain't had the real struggle." And you hear it enough times that you start believing you're an outsider in your own fucking bloodline.

Identity, on the other hand, whispers from the inside: "You are Black." "You know your culture." "You feel the pain, the pride, the rhythm, the history." "You were raised in it, loved by it, formed through it." But shame talks louder. Shame doesn't whisper, it screams like a drill sergeant in your ear.

Shame tells you to shrink. Identity tells you to claim space. Shame tells you you're an accident. Identity tells you you're a continuation. Shame tells you you're not enough. Identity tells you you're more than they think.

The internal war wasn't one big battle, it was a thousand small ones. Every day. Every glance. Every comment. Every moment of doubt. Every time I felt both seen and not seen enough at the same time. Identity said: "You're Black." Shame said: "Yeah, but not the right kind." Identity said: "You belong." Shame said: "Prove it." Identity said: "You're whole." Shame said: "No, you're fucking not."

This war didn't bruise my skin, it bruised my sense of self. It made me question everything: my culture, my worth, my authenticity, my place in the world. And the worst part? There's no referee. No coach. No guide. Just two versions of you fighting for the same body.

White Fetishization and the Violence of Being "Almost Them"

If racism is a knife, white fetishization is a slow choke. It doesn't cut you open, it suffocates you while smiling in your face. White people treated me like a backstage pass to Blackness. Not the whole show, just the part they felt comfortable with. I wasn't Black enough to threaten them, but Black enough to satisfy their curiosity. Light enough to be "beautiful," but dark enough to be "exotic." I was a compromise. A safe risk. A diluted fantasy.

And they said shit like: "You're so handsome... your skin is the perfect shade." "You're like a Black guy but softer." "You're not intimidating like the darker ones." "I love biracial-looking men." "You must have good genes." Every word felt like acid disguised as honey.

They wanted me Black, but only the parts that didn't scare them. They wanted my culture, but not my truth. They wanted my rhythm, but not my rage. They wanted my features, but not my history. They wanted my skin, but not my struggle. They wanted me almost Black, almost white, almost them, but never fully myself. And the violence in that? The violence is that you start shaping yourself to be easier for them to swallow. You speak different. Walk different. Laugh different. Tone yourself down. Smooth your edges. Swallow your anger. You become a softer version of yourself to make their stomachs comfortable.

But you know what that does? It eats you alive. Bit by bit. Piece by piece. Because being "almost them" means being never fully you. And that's a violence nobody sees, because it doesn't leave bruises on the skin. It leaves bruises on the soul.

Before the world ever judged my skin, before kids in school pointed fingers, before strangers tried to place me on the color chart, before white people fetishized me or Black folks questioned me, my own family taught me what my shade meant. Not intentionally. Not maliciously. Just through the quiet, casual violence of everyday comments. The kind of shit families say without thinking because it's been passed down like old furniture and generational trauma.

Things like: "Look at him, he came out light!" "Don't let him stay in the sun too long." "He got that good skin." "You lucky you got your daddy's complexion." "You better marry a dark-skinned woman so your kids ain't pale." "Stop crying, light-skinned boys always acting sensitive." "Boy, you so light you damn near see-through." "You cute, but you ain't got that real Black look." It didn't sound like love. It didn't sound like hate. It sounded like labels. Like destinies. Like they were assigning roles in a play I didn't audition for.

Family made my skin a punchline. A warning. A trophy. A prediction. A mistake. One minute, I was "lucky." The next minute, I was "not Black enough." One minute, they wanted to protect me. The next minute, they resented the exact thing they were protecting. And that's the fucked-up thing: colorism always speaks two languages, love and rejection, at the same damn time.

Growing up, I tried to laugh it off. Tried to blend in. Tried to pretend those comments didn't stick to me like glue. But the truth? Every joke, every comparison, every "light-bright" nickname was a small cut. Small cuts add up. You bleed even if nobody sees it.

THE MOMENT IT SHIFTED: WHEN I STOPPED TRYING TO PROVE MY BLACKNESS

Every Black kid with a lighter shade has one moment that defines them: the moment they realize they're tired of auditioning for a role they already belong to. Mine came in the middle of a family gathering. Music loud. Kids running through the house. Adults drinking, laughing, arguing, talking shit. The usual.

I was minding my business when somebody, a cousin, an uncle, I don't even remember, looked at me and said: "Boy, you ain't Black Black. You don't know nothing about the struggle." Everybody laughed. I tried to shrug it off. Tried to play cool. Tried to act unbothered even though it felt like he yanked the floor out from under me.

But then he said it again, louder: "You lucky. You got that half-white privilege, whether you admit it or not." Something cracked. Not loud. Not visible. But internally, deep in the place where identity and shame collide.

Because I knew the truth: I tried so hard to fit in, to be accepted, to feel rooted, to feel whole. I grew up in the same neighborhoods. Ate the same food. Listened to the same music. Loved the same culture. Felt the same generational weight. And yet, because of a few lighter melanin cells, they treated me like an outsider in my own family.

I remember stepping outside, the air cold as hell, and thinking: "I can't keep living like this. I can't keep chasing approval that's never coming." I realized something that night: you don't prove your Blackness by performing it. You don't prove your identity by fighting for it. You don't prove your culture through pain competitions or shade-based credentials.

Blackness isn't a shade. It's a lineage. A rhythm. A wound. A memory. A language. A survival code. A heartbeat. And I had all of that long before anybody questioned it.

So I stopped trying. Stopped explaining. Stopped defending myself. Stopped shrinking. Stopped apologizing for the shade I was born in. That night, I let go of the performance. Not because I didn't care. But because I finally understood something heavy and freeing at the same time: I am not responsible for fixing other people's trauma about my complexion. I'm only responsible for surviving my own. And that realization? It didn't heal everything, but it gave me back a piece of myself.

There comes a point in every story where the character stops running and finally turns around to face the thing chasing them. In my life, that thing was my own reflection. Not the light skin. Not the privilege. Not the pain. Not the guilt. Not the stereotypes or the shame or the projections. It was the part of me I spent years avoiding, the part that wanted to exist without apology.

For so long, I thought the world owned me. Owned my image. Owned my identity. Owned the narrative of my skin. I let white people sculpt me into a "safe" Black. I let Black people strip me of my authenticity. I let family hand me generational wounds with jokes pretending to be love. I let strangers decide what shade of Black I earned. I let myself believe I was an accident, a mistake between two extremes.

But the end of the story isn't where I become perfect or healed or magically at peace. The ending is where I become mine.

THE MOMENT OF TRUTH

It happened quietly, not with fireworks, not with a speech, not with some dramatic confrontation. I woke up one morning and felt something I hadn't felt in years: neutrality. Not love. Not hate. Just... neutrality. A truce with my own face.

I stood in front of the mirror, the same mirror I once cursed, the same mirror I blamed, the same mirror I avoided, and I didn't feel disgust or guilt or confusion. For the first time, I saw a man shaped by survival, by contradiction, and by a world that tried to use him as a bridge between two storms. I saw a man who didn't pick his shade but earned every scar that came with it. A man who stopped performing. Stopped apologizing. Stopped begging for entry into spaces he already belonged to. I saw me. Just me. And that was enough.

THE ENDING: NOT REDEMPTION, BUT OWNERSHIP

I'm not ending this story pretending colorism evaporates or that my pain suddenly dissolves. It doesn't. Some days I still feel the sting. Some days I still feel judged. Some days I still wonder where exactly I fit on the map of my own people. But here's the difference: I no longer let the world write my identity for me.

I reclaimed my shade. I reclaimed my narrative. I reclaimed the softness they mocked, the rage they feared, the beauty they fetishized, the culture they tried to cut me out of. I stopped being the in-between and became the whole.

Not light-skinned. Not a diluted Black. Not a safer Black. Not an almost-Black. Not a maybe-Black. Just Black. Black with complications. Black with contradictions. Black with history woven into my DNA like a story only I can tell.

I learned something at the end of all this: people don't get to tell you who you are when you finally learn how to speak for yourself. And now? I speak loudly. Boldly. Honestly. Even when it hurts.

My story doesn't end with healing, it ends with ownership. Because the truth is: I was never meant to fit neatly into anybody's box. I was meant to break them. I was never meant to be claimed by whiteness or rejected by Blackness. I was meant to challenge every idea they had about me. I was never meant to apologize for my shade. I was meant to expose the lies built around it. And I was never meant to be "almost anything." I was meant to be everything I already am.

This is the ending: not perfect. Not tied up with a bow. Not healed into something soft and palatable. Just real. A man who finally stopped fighting his reflection and started walking with it. A man who learned that loving himself was the rebellion he'd been running from. A man who, after everything, finally said: "I don't owe the world an explanation. I owe myself a life." And then, finally, I stepped into it.

THEY WANTED ME OWNED

A Street-to-System Survival Read: I Didn't Snitch — I Switched

They swear "making it out" is a car, a chain, a zip code, a couple of pictures where you look clean and calm. That's what people call success when they never had to earn oxygen.

But making it out isn't a glow-up.

It's a disappearance.

It's you surviving a life built to erase you, then learning how to live without the chaos that raised you, without the noise that trained you, without the hunger that made you dangerous. It's you walking away from a world that only loves you when you're useful, only respects you when you're reckless, only claps when you're on the edge of self-destruction.

I wasn't supposed to make it out.

I was supposed to be a story somebody tells with a headshake and a "damn."

I was supposed to die behind some petty pride, or rot behind a number, or get recycled through the system until my name stopped meaning anything.

Because that's the design.

The streets don't want you to be successful. They want you employed—by the block, by desperation, by the image, by the rumor, by the need to prove you're still a man. Prison doesn't want you rich. Prison wants you reduced: body, habits, choices, vocabulary, dreams. Both places feed off the same thing—pressure—and both places produce the same product—broken men who think surviving is the same as living.

So if you're reading this from a cell, or from a couch you can't afford, or from a life you don't recognize anymore, hear me clear:

I'm not about to sell you any inspirational perfume.

This is blood, bars, and breakthrough.

This is what it looks like when a man stops being property.

I came up in grime that wasn't poetic. It wasn't the cute "we didn't have much, but we had love" story people say when they trying to sanitize suffering. Nah. It was real: hallways that smelled like defeat, lights that blinked like warnings, doors that didn't lock like they should, a refrigerator that stayed quiet like it was embarrassed, neighbors arguing like it was their religion, police sirens like a soundtrack you didn't choose.

I learned early that being "good" doesn't pay. Politeness doesn't stop hunger. Smart don't keep your water on. In my world, innocence wasn't protected—innocence got punished. So I adapted the way kids do when adults don't show up with solutions: I became what the environment rewarded.

Outside felt like power. Inside felt like stress.

Outside had older dudes with money, women smiling at them like money was a personality, kids my age acting fearless, corner politics, block legends, fast cash. Nobody told me the price. Nobody sat me down and said, "That money comes with a receipt you can't return." They just made it look like freedom. And freedom is the most seductive lie you can sell to a boy who's been humiliated by being broke.

Poor ain't just a number. Poor is getting sized up like you're disposable. Poor is watching people with options talk like you're lazy. Poor is walking into a store and doing math with your eyes. Poor is having to pretend you don't want things because wanting hurts.

So when I saw money move fast, I chased it. Not because I loved crime. Because I hated shame.

And the first time I touched real cash, something snapped in me. It wasn't greed—greed is what people call it when they don't understand what it feels like to finally breathe. It was relief. Dignity. The quiet confidence of being able to handle something without begging, without waiting, without praying that somebody else decides to help you.

That's the trap: the streets don't seduce you by calling you evil. The streets seduce you by calling you responsible.

"Handle your people."

"Do what you gotta do."

"Be a man."

And when you come from nothing, that "gotta" becomes your religion. You start believing the hustle is a badge, the risk is proof you love your family, and the danger is your sacrifice. You don't feel like a criminal—you feel like a provider.

Then the street flips it. Slowly. Patiently. Like poison that tastes like candy.

Because stability in the streets is a lie built on unstable ground: trust in people who don't even trust themselves, money that can vanish with one stop, freedom that can get snatched by one nervous cop with a mood, violence that doesn't announce itself, envy that multiplies the moment your pockets look heavier than somebody else's pride.

I wasn't loud. I wasn't reckless on purpose. I wasn't trying to be famous in the hood. I wanted to be steady. But the streets don't reward steady. The streets reward drama. The streets reward reputation. The streets reward you for being predictable.

And once I started doing better, I learned a rule nobody says out loud:

Everybody claps when you get money... until you get more than them.

That's when love turns into surveillance.

People don't congratulate you—they calculate you. They count your pockets with their eyes. They smile while measuring how far you moved away from them. They hug you while wondering if you're leaving them behind. In the streets, jealousy isn't an emotion. It's a lifestyle. A full-time job. People wake up and clock in to hating.

So the attention changed. I could feel it. The vibe got weird. Conversations got sharp. Compliments started sounding like questions. "You been doing good, huh?" "Where did you get that from?" "What are you into now?" Those aren't questions. Those are inventory checks.

Then the lock came. The day the door shut behind me, I thought my life ended the way everybody thinks it ends. Because prison doesn't just take your freedom—it tries to strip your identity until you forget you ever mattered. You become a number. A body. A scheduled movement. A controlled appetite.

And I'm not going to lie and act as if I walked in fearless. I had street toughness, yeah, but prison is different. Prison is where the air feels like it belongs to somebody else, where time becomes thick. Where your name feels like it doesn't fit your mouth anymore.

But prison did something the streets never allowed: it got quiet enough for me to hear myself.

The hood is loud on purpose. Loud keeps you distracted. Loud keeps you numb. Loud keeps you from asking dangerous questions like: Why does my life look like this? Who profits from me staying like this? Why do we celebrate the same outcomes like they're tradition? Why does chaos feel normal? Why does peace feel suspicious?

Prison tried to break me. That part is real. It's designed for reduction. It's built to turn men into animals fighting over crumbs, to keep you cliqued up and reactive, to keep your mind stuck on reputation so you never grow beyond survival. It's built to turn anger into a habit.

But I saw something in there that messed me up—in a good way.

Two types of men.

One type: locked in spirit. Even if they got a release date, they never leaving mentally. Still chasing respect, still performing, still arguing over nothing, still fighting because they don't know how to sit with themselves.

The other type: quiet builders. Not soft. Not weak. Strategic. Reading. Writing. Studying. Taking programs. Sitting in rooms other men called lame—because the streets trained us to think learning is corny unless it comes with a fight.

Those builders treated prison like a school.

That's when the biggest truth hit me: the streets and prison are the same cage—one just has no bars.

That realization didn't depress me. It woke me up.

Because I looked back at my whole life and saw a pipeline with my name on it. Schools that trained obedience but not ownership. Jobs that paid just enough to keep you desperate. Communities over-policed and under-funded. Fathers removed and then mocked for being absent. Mothers exhausted and then blamed for raising boys alone. Entertainment that sold self-destruction as culture. A justice system that profits from repetition.

And the hood sits in the middle like a recruiter.

The hood doesn't need paperwork. It doesn't need funding. It just needs broken boys. Boys hungry for meaning. Boys craving respect. Boys desperate to feel seen.

So it gave us a script: If you can't be educated, be feared. If you can't win legally, win loudly. If you can't be respected, be dangerous. If you can't build, take.

And once you believe that script, you become predictable.

Predictable men are controllable men.

That's when I stopped feeling sorry for myself and started getting serious about my mind.

I walked into a program room—plain walls, metal chairs, a dude at the front talking about business—and I swear it felt like somebody opened a secret door in my head. He wasn't teaching street business. He was teaching structure: contracts, systems, credit, licensing, taxes, and ownership.

And what hit me hardest wasn't the lesson.

It was the math.

People pay thousands for this on the outside.

I was learning it inside a cage.

That's when I understood something that made me angry and grateful at the same time: the world will charge you for information that could save your life... and your neighborhood will clown you for wanting it.

So I made a decision.

If I'm trapped anyway, I'm leaving with something. Not just freedom. A weapon that don't fire bullets—knowledge. Skill. Structure. A blueprint.

I stopped seeing myself as an inmate and started seeing myself as a student.

I took what I could take. Classes. Certifications. Reentry planning. Emotional control groups—because controlling your temper is a superpower when your whole life has been provocation. I studied how money moves when it's clean. I learned how ownership works when it's boring. I learned how the real world speaks—because the real world don't speak in threats, it speaks in paperwork. And paperwork changes bloodlines.

I learned that ignorance isn't just not knowing.

Ignorance is expensive.

Ignorance is how you sign your life away and call it "bad luck."

And here's the part most people don't want to admit: the streets don't only train you to hustle. The streets train you to sabotage anything peaceful because peace feels unfamiliar.

The hood makes you allergic to stability. It makes you suspicious of the quiet. It teaches you to read calm as a setup, love as weakness, and patience as stupidity. It teaches you to burn things down before they can abandon you.

So I had to detox.

Not from drugs.

From street thinking.

When I came home, freedom didn't feel like a celebration. It felt like overstimulation. Too many choices. Too many voices. Too many opportunities to fall back into the same patterns. Prison is a cage with rules. The streets is a cage with options. And options will kill you if you still addicted to shortcuts.

My phone was jumping with texts from people who never checked on me when it mattered. "Welcome home, king." "Pull up." "Let's get to it." That's fake love. That's the hood trying to reclaim you before your mind becomes untouchable.

Because the truth is: the hood doesn't mind you going to prison.

The hood expects it.

But the hood hates a man who comes home changed. A changed man threatens the lie. A changed man becomes proof. A changed man makes other men ask, "Wait... we can leave?"

So the streets called me like relapse.

I'd be trying to do it the legit way—applications, interviews, small steps—and every "second chance" would come with a smirk. "You got any felonies?" Suddenly, I wasn't a man. I was a risk. A liability. A statistic.

That's how anger grows teeth.

That's how men crash out again. Not because they love crime—but because they hate rejection.

And the streets knows that. The streets waits for that moment.

It offers you quick money the same way a bottle offers a drunk "one sip." It don't mention the hangover. It doesn't show you the next cell. It just promises relief.

I got offered a "quick play." I got shown a bag on a table, like it was salvation. Twenty thousand dangled like a miracle. And my body reacted—heartbeat, adrenaline, muscle memory. The old me woke up. That old version of me still knew the smell of that life.

But I looked at that bag and saw the whole receipt: paranoia, betrayal, bullets, cuffs, court, time, shame, my people crying, my life shrinking.

So I said no.

And people think saying no is the end.

No is the beginning of war.

Because when you tell the streets no, you're not just declining money. You're rejecting control. You're telling a system that used to own you that it no longer has a key to your mind.

That's when the hood starts testing you.

Not always with violence.

Sometimes with "love."

Sometimes with guilt.

"You forgot who helped you."

"You acting like you better."

"You changed."

Yeah, I changed.

Because I got tired of funerals and cells.

I got tired of watching men die for a block that won't even pay for their burial.

I got tired of seeing mothers become stone.

I got tired of kids growing up and wearing trauma like a jacket they didn't choose.

So I started building for real.

And building for real doesn't look like social media.

Building looks like paperwork at a kitchen table. Learning taxes when you'd rather sleep. Running your credit like it's your reputation. Setting up accounts like you setting up a new identity. Getting denied and coming back again. Charging what you're worth without apologizing. Being consistent when nobody claps.

The first legal money I made felt holy. Not because it was a lot—because it was clean. I didn't feel hunted. I didn't feel like a siren was around the corner waiting to ruin my day. Somebody paid me and thanked me. No weird energy. No threats. No jealousy. Just business.

I sat in my car and stared at that money like it was proof I belonged on earth.

Because that's what clean money does.

It doesn't just pay your bills.

It quiets your nervous system.

And that quiet? That quiet is addictive in a better way.

Then the business started moving. Slowly, then steady. Customers told customers. Reviews started stacking. My schedule started looking like a purpose. And the hood noticed.

The hood always notices.

It has radar for rising people.

Because rising people remind stuck people of their chains.

That's when I saw cars sitting too long. Numbers calling with no names. Old faces popping up like ghosts trying to read me. And the offers came again, more direct, more disrespectful.

"Come on, one time."

One time is a lie that has buried a thousand men.

One time turns into a pattern.

Patterns turn into cages.

So I kept saying no.

Then came the call that tried to make the decision for me.

A voice I recognized. No greeting. No warmth. Just possession.

"I heard you're doing good."

That sentence didn't sound like pride. It sounded like a hand reaching for my collar.

Then the real line dropped:

"I need you to do one thing for me."

I told him I was out the way.

He laughed like I was cute.

"Ain't nobody out the way unless I say so."

That's the hood talking like it owns you.

Then the threat came dressed as a favor.

"You can help me... or you can lose everything you built."

And right there, in that moment, I felt the old me step forward. The old instincts. The old fear. The old urge to handle it the way I used to handle it.

Because the streets trained us that the only response to pressure is violence or submission.

But prison taught me something else:

If you don't stand on principle, you'll fold for convenience.

So I breathed. Not to calm down—calm doesn't win wars.

I breathed to choose.

I asked him what he wanted, let him get excited for half a second, then I cut it clean:

"I'm not doing it."

Silence so thick it felt like danger.

He said, "What?"

I said it again, steady this time:

"I'm not doing it. Don't call me for that."

And I hung up.

That hang-up wasn't bravery.

It was a breakup.

It was me ending a relationship with my past that kept trying to crawl back into my life like an ex with no boundaries.

After that, the air changed. The world felt watched. Every small thing felt like it could turn into something big. The hood doesn't like rejection. It doesn't like you choosing peace. It takes it personal.

So I got strategic.

I tightened my circle until it felt like solitude. I changed routines. I moved my money smarter. I became less accessible. I stopped explaining myself. I started protecting what I built like it was a child.

Because that's what a business is when you come from nothing: it's your baby, your second chance, your proof, your exit.

Weeks passed. Then months.

The hood got quieter, not because it became kind—because it got bored. The streets will keep calling until it realizes you're not answering. It wants to pull you back because it hates losing control. But it can't drag you if your feet are planted.

And that's when the real win happened.

Not when I hit a number.

When my nervous system stopped craving chaos.

When I stopped missing the rush.

When I stopped needing to be seen.

When I realized the biggest flex wasn't a chain.

It was time.

It was waking up without paranoia.

It was coming home without scanning the block.

It was feeding my people without feeding my enemies.

It was building something that didn't require funerals to maintain.

Then I started making real legal money. Not fantasy money. Not "I had one good month" money. Consistent money. Scaleable money. Money that came from value, not fear.

And that's when I understood what the streets really are.

The streets aren't a plan.

They're a lottery where the only guaranteed prize is pain.

The streets don't make you a man.

They make you reactive.

Unstable.

Paranoid.

Disposable.

They reward you until your success becomes a threat, then they either cage you or bury you. And if you survive long enough to "win," you still lose pieces of yourself: sleep, trust, peace, years, friends, family, your ability to relax in a quiet room.

Fast money isn't money.

It's borrowed time.

And the interest rate is your life.

So when people ask me how I made it out, I don't give them a cute answer.

I tell them the truth.

I didn't get lucky.

I got disciplined.

I stopped romanticizing my own destruction.

I stopped confusing survival with success.

I stopped feeding the hood my future.

I learned systems. I built a structure. I played the long game when my whole life had trained me to chase shortcuts.

And yes, prison took time from me.

But it gave me something the streets never wanted me to have:

a mind that couldn't be owned anymore.

That's why I say what I say with my chest:

They wanted me broken.

They wanted me addicted to chaos.

They wanted me to return.

They wanted me owned.

But I didn't snitch.

I switched.

I switched my thinking.

I switched my circle.

I switched my definition of manhood.

I switched my loyalty—from the block to the bloodline.

And that's the part the prisoners of the world will understand: the hardest cell isn't always built with bars.

Sometimes the cell is a mindset you inherited.

Sometimes the cell is pride.

Sometimes the cell is a neighborhood that punishes growth.

Sometimes the cell is the fear of looking different from the people you love.

But you don't owe the streets your life.

The streets already took enough.

So here's the last truth I'm leaving you with:

I didn't just make it out alive.

I made it out free.

And freedom—real freedom—is the richest thing I ever touched.

12

The 👀 Lurker

You ever feel watched by someone who swears they're done with you? Not loved. Not missed. Not claimed. Just... watched. That's where this started. Not with a scream. Not with a gun. Not with blood on the sink. It started with a silence that felt louder than an argument.

We hadn't spoken in three weeks. Not a text. Not a call. Not even an accidental emoji reaction. She made it clear — I wasn't wanted. I was "too much." Too intense. Too aware. Too unwilling to shrink to fit her comfort. Fine. I stepped back. But she didn't.

That's the part nobody warns you about — the partner who doesn't want you, but doesn't want anybody else to have you either. The one who says "move on" but lurks in the shadows like a jealous ghost attachfed to your oxygen supply.

The first sign was small. So small I almost laughed at myself. I posted a picture — nothing crazy. Just me in a black hoodie, fresh cut, leaning against my car at dusk. Caption: Peace feels different when you stop begging for it. Within two minutes, a view. Her.

She doesn't follow me. I don't follow her. But she viewed it. Instagram says "suggested account." I say surveillance.

I didn't react. Didn't block. Didn't like her last post. I let it float. Then it happened again. And again. Every story. Every move. She wouldn't speak to me — but she would study me. That's when the tension shifted from heartbreak to suspicion.

I went out one Friday night. Nothing dramatic. Small lounge downtown, dim lighting, heavy bass. I hadn't told anyone where I was going. No tagged location. No obvious clues. Halfway through the night, I felt it. That sensation in the back of your neck like someone's eyes are dragging across your spine. I scanned the room casually. Didn't see her. But I saw her cousin. Standing at the bar. Watching. Phone angled slightly up. Recording. When our eyes met, he didn't flinch. Didn't smile. Just looked... satisfied. That's when I understood. This wasn't longing. This was monitoring.

I left early. Didn't post the rest of the night. Next morning, I wake up to a message from an unknown number. "Moving on already? That's fast." No name. No picture. Just that. The kind of text that pretends to be casual but carries teeth underneath. I didn't respond. I blocked it.

Three hours later, my new female coworker — the one I'd had lunch with once — stops talking to me. Cold. Short answers. Avoiding eye contact. By the end of the week, I hear whispers that I'm "toxic." That I "don't respect women." That I "move reckless." None of it true. All of it specific. Specific enough to sound rehearsed.

You know what sabotage feels like? It feels like walking into a room and realizing somebody's been whispering your name before you arrived. It feels like your opportunities dissolving quietly. It feels like a shadow cutting strings you didn't know were attached to you.

And she still hadn't spoken to me directly. That's the genius of a lurker. They don't confront. They collect. They don't argue. They gather. Information. Screenshots. Timelines. Patterns. And then they weaponize them.

I tested something. Posted a fake location one night. A restaurant across town I never went to. Within an hour, I get a DM from an account with no profile picture. "Thought you said you hated that place." Not her name. But her voice. Her cadence. The way she typed without punctuation when she was irritated. I didn't reply.

Instead, I drove to the actual restaurant — the one she used to love. Sat in the corner booth we'd shared months ago. And waited. Twenty-five minutes later... She walked in. Alone. Scanning. Eyes sharp. She didn't see me. She went straight to the bar, pretending to scroll on her phone. Waiting to catch me with someone.

That's when the reality cracked open. She didn't want me. She wanted access to me. Control without commitment. Ownership without responsibility. I left before she could notice. But I didn't feel powerful. I felt hunted.

That night, my apartment building's front desk told me someone had asked if I still lived there. Didn't leave a name. Didn't leave a message. Just "checking." You ever have your peace start to feel temporary? That's when the paranoia creeps in. Not the crazy kind. The justified kind. Doors double-locked. Notifications muted. Curtains drawn. Every unknown car outside feels intentional. Every fake account looks familiar.

And then it escalated. My car tires. Slashed. Not random. Two precise cuts. Driver side. Clean. Professional. Police took the report. Nothing came of it. Of course not. Because lurkers don't act sloppy. They operate in gray areas.

She still hadn't called. Still hadn't texted. But she watched every move. And anything that looked like it might go good for me? It crumbled. I applied for a promotion. Suddenly HR receives an anonymous email claiming I "harass women." Investigation opens. Temporary suspension. Reputation bruised. All while she's posting quotes online about "men who self-destruct." It's not obsession. It's possession. And possession doesn't release quietly.

I confronted her once. Not aggressive. Just direct. Met her outside her job. Calm voice. "Why are you doing this?" She didn't deny watching me. Didn't deny knowing my schedule. Didn't deny knowing who I ate lunch with last Tuesday. She smiled. That soft, controlled smile she uses when she thinks she's winning. "If I don't want you, nobody else should get the version of you I built." That sentence didn't sound jealous. It sounded territorial. Like I was property she'd renovated and now refused to sell. I walked away. But that smile followed me home.

Here's what nobody talks about — psychological suspense isn't loud. It's subtle. It's the quiet dismantling of your social world. It's opportunities slipping. It's women backing away without explanation. It's friends suddenly cautious. It's your own mind questioning whether you're overreacting. Until the day the evidence stops whispering. And starts screaming.

Three nights ago, I came home to my apartment unlocked. Nothing stolen. Nothing moved. Except one thing. A framed photo. Turned face down on the coffee table. The picture? Me. Alone. Not even one we took together. Just me. Like a warning. Or a reminder. You're being seen. You're being studied. You're not free.

And that's when I realized this isn't heartbreak. This isn't jealousy. This is psychological warfare disguised as silence. The 👀 Lurker doesn't argue. The 👀 Lurker observes. Waits. And sabotages anything that looks like happiness. And the most dangerous part? She knows exactly how to make it look like coincidence.

I haven't decided yet whether I'm the hunted... Or whether I'm about to become the hunter. Because if she wants to lurk in the dark — She better understand something. I know how to move in it too.

If this tone hits the way you wanted — psychological, raw, territorial, dangerous, no fluff — say: "Keep watching." And I'll continue the next section deeper into the sabotage, escalation, and who really loses when obsession meets strategy.

13

PRISONER

The first night they locked the door, I laughed. Not because it was funny. Because I finally understood something. Steel don't scare me. Silence does.

The bars slid shut with a sound like a coffin lid sealing, and the echo ran down the tier like a warning shot. Men started yelling to each other through the vents — fake bravado, survival noise. But I didn't yell. I sat on the edge of a mattress thinner than an apology and pressed my palm against the cold wall.

They locked my body up. But my mind? That had been incarcerated long before the judge hit the gavel.

See, prison ain't a building. Prison is a condition. And most of us were sentenced before we ever knew we were on trial.

I used to think prison started with handcuffs. It doesn't. It starts with labels. Black boy. Problem child. Statistics. Risk factor. Aggressive. Non-compliant.

By the time I was ten, teachers talked about me like I was weather damage. Something to survive instead of nurture. Suspended for fighting back. Written up for "tone." Watched closer than the white kid who actually threw the first punch.

That's the first prison — perception.

When people decide who you are before you open your mouth, they build bars around your potential. You start moving inside the shape they expect. Shrinking. Adapting. Surviving. And survival ain't freedom.

When I caught my case, the headlines didn't say "Father of two makes mistake." They said "Repeat offender." They said "Threat to the community." They showed my mugshot like it was a prophecy fulfilled.

Systematic racism ain't always loud. Sometimes it's paperwork. Longer sentences. Harsher bonds. Public defenders juggling 200 cases like they're at a circus.

You sit in court watching your future get negotiated like a used car, and you realize something heavy: The system doesn't just punish crime. It manages bodies. And some bodies are more manageable behind walls.

The first week inside, I called home. No answer. Second week, voicemail. Third week, my daughter finally picked up. She sounded older. "Daddy, when are you coming back?" That question don't hit your ears. It hits your lungs.

I told her soon. I lied.

Prison don't just lock you up. It tests your relevance. Every missed birthday, every school play you don't attend, every bill your partner figures out without you — your absence becomes normal. And that's the real sentence. Being forgotten slowly.

Friends disappear first. Then cousins. Then people who swore they loved you forever. Your name turns into a story people tell in past tense — and you're still alive.

But here's what nobody tells you: Some men feel freer in prison than they ever did outside. Because outside, they were prisoners of expectations. Prisoner of the job that drained them. Prisoner of the street reputation they had to maintain. Prisoner of providing without rest. Prisoner of proving masculinity every damn day.

Out there, you wear masks. In here, you wear numbers. Strangely enough, numbers don't lie to you.

My celly, Marcus, told me something on month four. "They can cage your body, but if they get your mind? You're done."

Marcus had been down ten years. Law library every day. Read philosophy like it was oxygen. He said prison was a university if you let it be — or a graveyard if you didn't.

I watched men choose their fate daily. Some lifted weights and plotted revenge. Some gambled away commissary and hope. Some read. Some prayed. Some rotted.

The difference wasn't intelligence. It was belief.

If you believe you're only what they say you are, you'll decorate your cell like it's permanent. But if you believe you're more than the mistake — the cage becomes temporary.

Still.

Let's not romanticize it.

Prison is violence humming under fluorescent lights. It's tension in the chow line. It's racial politics you can't opt out of. It's knowing one wrong look can cost you teeth. It's lockdowns for fights you didn't start. It's guards who see you as paperwork.

Systematic racism don't disappear inside. It just changes uniforms.

The majority of faces behind those bars? Brown and Black. The majority of people deciding their fate? Not. That imbalance speaks louder than any protest. And it plants a seed in your mind: Maybe freedom was never fully offered.

But prison ain't just concrete.

I met men who were incarcerated by addiction long before cuffs touched their wrists. Prisoner to cocaine. Prisoner to pride. Prisoner to trauma passed down like inheritance.

One man told me he felt more trapped by his father's expectations than by the state.

"My pops said real men don't cry. So I stopped crying. Then I stopped feeling. Then I started hurting people."

That's a prison too. Emotional incarceration.

We teach boys to swallow pain, then act shocked when it explodes.

And what about the prison of work?

Before I got locked up, I was doing 60-hour weeks for a job that called me replaceable in polite language. I was exhausted. Angry. Invisible. But I stayed. Because society said a man without money is a man without worth.

That belief is a cage.

Some people clock in every morning to a sentence that never ends. Punch in. Punch out. Repeat until retirement or death. No bars. No chains. Still trapped.

Then there's the prison of relationships.

I loved hard. Too hard. Stayed loyal to people who treated me like a convenience. Stayed in arguments just to avoid loneliness. Stayed in dynamics that shrank me because being alone felt like solitary confinement.

We don't talk about that enough.

How sometimes love is just another cell. Jealousy becomes surveillance. Insecurity becomes interrogation. Control becomes routine.

You call it passion. It's probation.

In year two, something shifted.

I stopped waiting for letters that weren't coming. Stopped measuring love by visits. Stopped telling myself I was nothing without the outside world.

I started writing. Not excuses. Not blame. Truth.

Truth about how I participated in my own captivity. Truth about ego. Truth about chasing validation. Truth about letting rage guide my choices because rage felt powerful.

Accountability is the hardest freedom to earn.

When you stop blaming the system long enough to examine yourself, something dangerous happens. You grow. And growth in prison feels illegal.

I began mentoring younger inmates. Twenty-year-olds doing fifteen-year bids. Eyes still wide. Anger still fresh. They thought toughness was currency. I told them discipline was. They thought violence earned respect. I told them consistency did. They thought freedom meant getting out. I told them freedom meant mastering their mind before the gates ever opened.

Because I've seen men walk out physically and remain inmates mentally. Still reacting. Still defensive. Still suspicious. Still limited.

Prison walls follow you if you don't dismantle them internally.

Society loves simple narratives. Bad guy goes to prison. Serves time. Comes out redeemed or ruined.

But reality is layered.

Some men come out sharper. Some come out broken. Some come out institutionalized — more comfortable with rules than choices.

And society doesn't make reentry easy.

Felon on applications. Doors closing quietly. People pretending they're progressive until your record shows up. You become a prisoner of your past. Punished twice.

The day I was released, the sun felt disrespectful. Too bright. Too free.

My daughter hugged me like she wasn't sure I was solid. My partner looked at me like she was measuring the damage.

And I realized something else.

They had been imprisoned too. Single motherhood. Financial strain. Emotional exhaustion. Explaining my absence over and over.

When one man goes to prison, a family does time with him.

We don't calculate that cost in statistics. But it's real.

Freedom wasn't fireworks. It was awkward.

I had to relearn how to move without permission. How to shop without counting seconds. How to sleep without noise. I had to unlearn survival posture.

And I had to confront a hard truth: If I didn't rebuild my mind, I'd recreate the cage. Different address. Same confinement.

So I built differently.

Read daily. Worked with intention. Spoke to my kids with honesty about my mistakes instead of hiding them. Took accountability without drowning in shame.

I refused to let prison be my identity. It was a chapter. Not the title. But the bigger realization? Most people are incarcerated somewhere. Prisoner of debt. Prisoner of image. Prisoner of comparison through screens. Prisoner of generational trauma. Prisoner of racial hierarchies built centuries ago and still breathing today.

We mock inmates while scrolling from cubicles we hate. We judge felons while trapped in marriages that suffocate us. We call them criminals while corporations commit legal theft daily.

Bars just make it obvious. Other prisons are quieter. The most dangerous prison is the one you defend. The mindset that says: "This is just how life is." "This is as good as it gets." "People like me don't get more." That's a life sentence. And no judge signs that order but you.

I don't glamorize prison. It stole years. It strained relationships. It branded my record. But it forced confrontation. With the system. With society. With myself. And if I'm honest? The moment I stopped seeing myself as only a victim of injustice and started seeing myself as responsible for my next move — that's when the bars cracked.

Systematic racism is real. Mass incarceration is real. Bias in sentencing is real. But mental surrender? Optional. And that's not victim-blaming. That's survival strategy. Because if they can convince you your mind belongs to them too — then you never leave.

I tell my son this now: "They can lock your body. They can monitor your movements. They can track your record. But your mind is sacred territory. Guard it."

Read. Question. Heal. Build. Break generational cages. Refuse inherited limitations. Understand the system without becoming it.

Prison taught me something brutal and beautiful at the same time: Freedom is internal before it's external. If you are a prisoner to rage, you are confined. If you are a prisoner to ego, you are confined. If you are a prisoner to money, image, approval, trauma — you are confined. Bars are just steel metaphors. The real cell is fear. The real warden is doubt. The real sentence is believing you can't become more.

I walked out of prison years ago. But I still meet men who've never been locked up — and they're incarcerated by every invisible thing around them.

I recognize the posture. Shoulders tight. Eyes guarded. Dreams rationed.

They laugh at the idea of freedom because they've never tasted it.

And I want to shake them.

You are more than the label. More than the paycheck. More than the record. More than the stereotype.

But until you believe that — you're serving time.

I was a prisoner. Of the state. Of expectation. Of ego. Of fear.

Now?

I'm a man who understands cages.

And once you understand them, you stop decorating them. You dismantle them. Brick by brick. Thought by thought. Choice by choice.

Because the greatest rebellion in a system built to confine you—

Is becoming free anyway.

14

Love in Crossfire

The first time I touched her hand, I knew somebody was going to bleed over this love. Maybe him. Maybe me. Maybe both.

Her fingers were cold like she'd been living in fear for too long. Before she even smiled she looked around, like happiness itself was dangerous. That was when she told me the truth. She wasn't just married — she was trapped. Years back, young and desperate for stability, she signed contracts she didn't understand. Joint debt disguised as love. Property control hidden behind promises. Legal chains dressed up as a future. By the time she realized, her husband owned everything. If she left, she'd lose money, housing, and any life she tried to build. He had lawyers on payroll. She had bruises under makeup.

The ungrateful bastard didn't marry her. He sentenced her. He controlled her phone, her movements, her finances, and her silence. He whispered threats instead of yelling. And men who whisper always do worse.

Then she met me.

Late-night conversations turned into stolen touches. Touches turned into fire. Every moment together felt like stealing oxygen from the world. But every kiss came with paranoia. We met in abandoned lots, back roads, cheap motels that smelled like bleach and secrets. She trembled every time she stepped out the car — not from excitement, from fear. But she still came. Because love makes you brave and stupid at the same time.

She showed me bruises. Texts threatening to ruin her if she ever left. Bank statements proving he drained accounts to keep her dependent. Then one night she whispered something that froze my blood.

"He has life insurance on me." Seven figures. Accidental death coverage. Even domestic incidents. That's when I understood. She wasn't just trapped. She was worth more dead than alive.

We planned an escape quietly. Burner phones. Cash. A bag hidden in my trunk. But every move felt watched. Cars followed me. Unknown numbers called then hung up. Once her husband stood outside my apartment smiling without knocking. Just stared. Then left.

A warning.

The day we finally tried to run, a van screeched in front of us. Men jumped out. I swung but they grabbed her first. She screamed my name as they shoved her inside. I jumped onto the door as it sped off. A crowbar cracked against my ribs and the world went black.

When I woke, she was gone.

I drove straight to his house, blood soaking my shirt, kicked the door in and fought through security like a man already dead. When I got to him, he sat calm.

"She chose me," he said. "You're entertainment." I put a gun in his mouth. "Where is she."

He laughed. "Breach of contract. She owes me everything now. And if she dies trying to leave...I get rich."

That's when I knew this wasn't control anymore.

It was a planned execution.

I tracked the van to an abandoned warehouse by the river. Went alone. No cops. No backup. Inside smelled like oil and rust. She was tied to a chair crying. Gunfire exploded before I could reach her. I dove, fought, stabbed one man, shot another, took a knife in my shoulder from the third but kept moving.

I untied her and ran.

Outside, her husband was waiting.

"This is where the love story ends."

Shots flew. One grazed my arm. One burned my side. I fired back and he dropped. Not dead — but done.

Sirens screamed in the distance.

We escaped into the trees bleeding, shaking, alive.

After that, I tried to walk away. Tried to tell myself love shouldn't feel like war. But I couldn't leave her. Not the woman who ran to me despite fear. Not the woman who finally whispered by the river, "I don't love him anymore. I love you."

That was the moment I realized I'd die for her love without hesitation.

But prison didn't end him.

Threats kept coming. Photos of us. Notes on the car. Someone fired shots into our apartment one night. We moved cities, changed names, but danger followed. A man sat beside me in a diner once and said, "You should've let her go," then vanished.

She told me the truth.

Before the kidnapping, her husband offered her comfort and safety if she cut me off. She chose me instead. That's when he ordered the hit. Love had become war. So we stopped running. We fought back together.

She remembered his habits, his businesses, the places he hid money. We followed leads, recorded threats, filmed illegal deals. One slip from one of his men led us to warehouses filled with cash and weapons. An old accountant we tracked down exposed offshore accounts, bribes, and corruption.

We took it all to federal authorities. The empire collapsed fast. Raids everywhere. His people arrested. Money seized. Protection gone. In prison he tried one last threat through a crooked guard. That guard went down too. Then came the trial. They played recordings. Showed videos. Brought witnesses. Proof stacked high like a grave. Guilty on all counts. Life sentence. No parole.

When the judge spoke those words, I felt her hand shaking in mine. It was over. The sun outside the courthouse felt different. Like the world finally breathed again. We moved somewhere quiet by the water. The nightmares faded slowly. Scars healed. Laughter returned.

Sometimes she'd sit beside me watching the sunset and say, "You saved my life." I'd tell her, "We saved each other." Because love didn't just survive hell. It conquered it.

Some love stories are flowers and promises. Ours was blood and courage. Some people love safe. We loved fearless. I would've died for her without question. But I'm grateful I get to live with her instead. Because some prisons are worse than death. And some people are worth breaking the gates of hell to save. Even after the cousin was taken down, peace still felt fragile. Like glass. One hard hit away from shattering.

Freedom was new to us. We didn't know how to trust it yet.

Every time a car slowed near the house, her shoulders tightened. Every knock made my pulse jump. Trauma had trained our bodies to react before our minds could.

But little by little, normal started winning.

We learned how to sit in silence without waiting for something bad to happen. Learned how to laugh without feeling guilty. Learned how to plan tomorrow without fear being part of the equation.

She started therapy, something she never had control over before. The stories she came back with broke my heart. How abusers slowly isolate you. How contracts and finances are common traps. How fear rewires the brain to accept cages as safety. Hearing it made me understand how deep his control went. It wasn't just physical. He owned years of her thoughts.

But every session made her stronger. More confident. More free. And watching that transformation was beautiful.

One afternoon while cleaning out an old box she'd kept hidden all these years, she found letters. Letters he'd written early in their relationship. Back when he still pretended. Promises about forever. About protection. About love.

The handwriting was soft. Almost kind. It messed with her head. "How does someone go from this to what he became?" she asked. I didn't have an answer.

Sometimes monsters are born. Sometimes they're built. But I knew one thing.

Love doesn't cage. Love doesn't threaten. Love doesn't need contracts.

We burned the letters that night. Watched them curl into ash. It felt like closing a chapter of her life that should've never been written.

But closure doesn't always mean the past is quiet. One evening while I was closing the shop, a man approached me. Mid forties. Plain clothes. Nervous eyes. "You don't know me," he said softly, "but I used to work for him." My body went stiff. "What do you want?" He swallowed hard.

"I'm not here to hurt you. I'm here to warn you."

He told me some of the empire's money was never found. That a few loyal people still believed the husband would somehow get out one day. That some thought hurting us would earn them favor.

"They're not organized anymore," he said. "But desperation makes people reckless."

That night we tightened security again. Not out of panic. Out of preparation.

But days turned into weeks. Weeks into months. Nothing happened. The danger seemed to finally fade. Then came the anniversary of the trial.

The day everything changed. We were out celebrating quietly at a restaurant by the water. Laughing. Holding hands. Feeling normal. That's when I noticed a reflection in the window.

A man sitting at the bar staring at us. Not casually. Studying. When I turned my head, he looked away. My instincts screamed. I paid the bill fast. We left. Halfway home, headlights appeared behind us. Too close. Matching every turn. I told her to stay calm. Took random streets. The car stayed glued. I hit the gas. They hit it too. The chase ripped through quiet neighborhoods. Tires screaming. Heart pounding. I called the feds while driving. Gave location. Description.

The car tried to ram us. Clipped the bumper. We spun but I fought the wheel. Regained control.

Suddenly sirens exploded from all directions. Unmarked cars boxed them in. The chase ended in seconds. Agents pulled the men out at gunpoint.

Two of them. Weapons in the car. Turns out they were former associates. Desperate. High on drugs. Believed killing us would earn them loyalty points from a man who'd never see freedom again.

That was the last attempt. After that, it truly stopped. The shadows finally lifted. The danger finally died. We went home that night shaking but relieved. She held my face and said, "It keeps trying to take us." I kissed her forehead. "It won't anymore." And I meant it.

From then on, life settled into something real. We bought a house by the water. Started hosting small gatherings. Making memories that weren't built on fear. She went back to school full time. Studied counseling. Said she wanted to help women like her. Turn pain into purpose.

I supported every step.

Watching her grow into herself was everything.

Some nights we'd sit outside under the stars and talk about how close it all came to ending differently. How one bad moment could've taken us out. How love pushed us into hell but also dragged us back out.

"Do you ever regret it?" she asked once. "Everything we went through?" I looked at her. At the woman who fought for her life. For her freedom. For us. "Never," I said. "Because if I had walked away, you might not be here." She smiled softly.

"And if you hadn't stayed, I would've given up."

That's what love really is. Not butterflies. Not easy days. It's choosing someone when it's hardest. Choosing them when it's dangerous. Choosing them when walking away would be safer.

Our love wasn't safe. But it was real. It was strong. And it won.

We weren't just survivors. We were proof that even the darkest control can be broken. That prisons built on fear can be torn down. That love, when it's true, is stronger than contracts, money, violence, and evil.

We found peace. Not the quiet kind that comes from running. The earned kind. The kind you fight for. The kind nobody can take away.

As life slowed into something peaceful, we started noticing the little things most people take for granted. Sleeping through the night without jumping at every noise. Leaving the house without scanning every corner. Laughing in public without fear that eyes were watching. Freedom wasn't loud. It was quiet. And that quiet felt strange at first.

She started keeping a journal, writing down everything she went through — the contracts, the control, the fear, the escape, the chase, the trial. Some days she cried while writing. Some days she smiled. She said it helped her take power back over the story that once owned her.

Sometimes she'd read parts to me.

Stories about how he'd make her repeat lies until she believed them. How he'd convince her nobody else would love her. How he'd use money like a leash. How he'd turn small mistakes into proof she was worthless.

Hearing it made my blood boil all over again. But it also showed me how strong she was. How she survived what could've destroyed her.

We started meeting other survivors through support groups. Women who escaped abusive marriages. Men who lost everything trying to protect people they loved. Every story was different but pain spoke the same language. It made us realize we weren't alone. And that made healing easier.

One evening after a group meeting, a young woman approached her with tears in her eyes.

"You gave me hope," she said. "I thought there was no way out."

That moment changed her. She looked at me later and said, "I want to do this for real. I want to help people escape like I did."

That's when she committed fully to counseling school. And she crushed it.

Watching her grow confident, speak boldly, laugh freely — it was like watching someone come back to life.

Meanwhile my business started taking off. We poured ourselves into building something solid. A future not built on fear but effort.

We traveled. Not far at first. Just little trips. But every mile away from that old life felt like victory.

One night in a small beach town we walked barefoot in the sand. The moon lit the water silver. She stopped suddenly and turned to me. "You know what I realized?" she said.

"What?"

"For the first time in years, I'm not scared of tomorrow."

That hit me hard. Because tomorrow used to be something we survived. Now it was something we looked forward to.

Years passed. The scars faded but never disappeared completely. Sometimes loud noises still made her jump. Sometimes I still checked mirrors when driving. But fear no longer ran our lives. It was just a reminder of how far we'd come.

The evil that once controlled everything was now nothing but a memory and a prison number. The empire was gone. The threats gone. The prison contract shattered. Love had outlasted it all.

We built a home full of light. Photos on the walls. Music playing on weekends. Friends laughing around the table. Life. Real life.

Sometimes at night she'd lay on my chest and say softly, "You really would've died for me."

I'd always answer the same. "Without hesitation." "But I'm glad I didn't have to." She'd smile and whisper, "Me too." Because loving someone shouldn't cost your life. But sometimes it costs your comfort, your safety, your peace for a while. And when it's real, it gives everything back plus more.

Our love didn't come easy. It came earned. Through fear. Through pain. Through blood and courage. And in the end, it came victorious.

We didn't just escape. We overcame. We didn't just survive. We thrived.

Some people read love stories about romance and sunsets. Ours had gunshots and courtrooms and scars. But it also had healing and laughter and dreams. And peace. Real peace. The kind that feels like breathing after being underwater too long. The kind that feels like freedom.

I'm carrying the story straight into a powerful, emotionally charged finale — where tension meets healing, conflict turns into growth, and love finally finds balance and peace without losing the raw realism. Same free-flowing document. Same cinematic tone. This is the closing stretch of the book.

As the months rolled forward, love settled into something quieter, but the quiet brought its own challenges. When life isn't chaos anymore, you finally have time to feel everything. And sometimes that hurt worse than running ever did.

There were moments she wanted to rush happiness. Talk about marriage. About forever. About building everything fast like she was scared peace might disappear.

And there were moments I pulled back without realizing it. Not because I didn't love her. Because part of me was still bracing for impact. Still waiting for the next explosion.

That difference started to create distance. Small at first. Then louder.

One night, she finally said it. "Why do you keep acting like this isn't real?" I looked at her confused. "Acting like what?" "Like we're temporary. Like something bad is coming. Like you're halfway out the door."

The words hit harder than any punch.

"I'm not going anywhere," I said.

"But you don't live like it," she replied. "You love me... but you don't trust peace."

She was right. I trusted chaos. It had been my normal for too long. Peace felt unfamiliar. Almost fake. Like it could be taken at any moment.

I admitted it. Told her I was scared to relax. Scared to dream. Scared to love without armor.

She cried. Not angry. Just tired.

"I fought my whole life to be free," she said. "I don't want to keep surviving with you. I want to live."

That night we didn't touch. Didn't yell. Just sat in opposite corners of the room thinking. It was the first time silence felt heavy.

The next morning she packed a small bag. Not leaving forever. Just space.

"I love you," she said softly. "But we both need to heal in our own ways too."

It broke me. Not because she was wrong. Because she was brave enough to ask for growth instead of comfort.

Those days apart forced me to look at myself. At how trauma shaped me. At how I used protection as an excuse to not fully commit to happiness.

I talked to a therapist for the first time in my life. Admitted my anger. My fear. My need for control. Learned that peace requires vulnerability. That love requires trust. That growth requires letting go of survival mode.

Meanwhile she worked on herself too. Learning boundaries. Learning not to carry guilt. Learning to love without fear of abandonment.

When we met again after a week, it felt like the first time all over. Nervous. Hopeful. Honest.

"I don't want a war partner anymore," she said. "I want a life partner." I nodded. "I'm ready to be that." From that moment on, everything shifted. We communicated better. Checked in emotionally. Stopped assuming. Started listening. The tension slowly turned into understanding. The growth turned into strength.

We built routines that weren't about safety but connection. Sunday breakfasts. Evening walks. Talking about dreams instead of danger.

We learned each other's triggers and softened around them. When she needed reassurance, I gave it. When I needed space, she respected it.

Balance formed naturally. Love became steady.

One night months later, sitting by the water where so much of our healing began, I finally said what I'd been scared to say.

"I want forever with you." She smiled through tears.

"I've always wanted that with you." I took her hands. No fear. No rushing. Just certainty.

"We survived hell," I said. "Now let's build heaven."

She laughed softly.

"Heaven doesn't have to be perfect. Just peaceful."

And she was right.

Our love wasn't a movie fantasy. It was real. Scarred. Strong. Earned.

We moved forward together not as survivors, but as partners. The past didn't own us anymore. It shaped us. Made us deeper. More patient. More grateful.

Love wasn't about risking death now. It was about choosing life. Choosing growth. Choosing peace. Every single day.

We didn't just defeat evil. We defeated the damage it tried to leave behind. And that was the true victory.

Because finding love is easy. Finding love after trauma takes courage. We had that courage. Together.

And in that balance of passion, healing, and peace...

We finally found home in each other.

I fell in love with a woman who belonged to another man. Not legally just married. Spiritually owned. The type of man who don't argue — he reacts. The type of man who don't cry when he hurt. He make people disappear. And I knew it.

But love don't give a fuck about logic.

Love had me sneaking through back doors like a criminal. Love had me parking blocks away. Love had me checking mirrors every five seconds. Love had my heart racing harder than fear ever did.

She'd text me: "He's asleep." And I'd risk my life like sleep stops bullets. I knew if he caught us it wouldn't be a fight. It would be a funeral. But every time she looked at me like I was her escape, I forgot about death.

She'd lay on my chest whispering how trapped she felt. How lonely she was in a house full of money and control. How he chose her, but never loved her. I became her breath of fresh air. But fresh air can get you killed in a locked room.

She told me she loved me. And I believed it because her eyes shook when she said it. But love in secret always comes with blood on the receipt.

Every argument they had made my phone vibrate. Every time he came home mad I felt it in my chest. I was sleeping with a married woman and beef I never signed up for.

One night she called crying. "He knows something's going on." My heart dropped like an elevator with cut cables. She said he didn't have proof. But he had instincts. And instincts in men like him are deadlier than evidence.

From that moment on, everything felt like a setup. Cars slowing down near me. Unknown numbers calling. People staring too long.

Love turned into survival.

I still kept seeing her though. Because when you love someone for real, fear becomes background noise.

She told me she was gonna leave him. Soon. Soon is the most dangerous word in situations like this. Soon is how people die waiting.

Weeks passed. Months passed. She was still there. Still married. Still texting me "I love you" while sleeping next to him.

I started realizing something ugly. I was risking my life for a woman who wasn't risking her comfort. I was ready to die for love. She was scared to be uncomfortable for it. And that hurt worse than any bullet could.

Then one night...

I saw his car parked across the street from my place. Lights off. Engine running. Just sitting there. Watching. I didn't go inside. I kept walking. Heart beating in my throat.

That was the moment it hit me. This love wasn't romantic. It was suicidal. I wasn't fighting for love. I was slowly volunteering for death.

I called her. Told her I couldn't do it anymore. Told her I loved her but I wasn't trying to die for feelings that live in hiding. She cried. Begged. Said she needed me. But needing me in secret wasn't enough anymore. I hung up. And that was the hardest shit I ever did.

Because walking away from someone you love is harder than dying for them. But sometimes love ain't meant to be lived. Some love is meant to be survived.

I realized real love doesn't put a gun to your head and call it passion. Real love don't make you look over your shoulder every day. Real love don't make you choose between your heart and your life.

I still love her. Probably always will. But I love breathing more. I love waking up more. I love living more.

Some people come into your life as lessons, not lifetimes. And some love stories aren't meant to have happy endings... They meant to teach you when to walk away before you end up in a coffin.

www.ingramcontent.com/pod-product-compliance
Ingram Content Group UK Ltd.
Pitfield, Milton Keynes, MK11 3LW, UK
UKHW021434280726
14060UKWH00001BA/72

9 798902 359906